The New Politics of Race

The New Politics of Race

Globalism, Difference, Justice

Howard Winant

University of Minnesota Press
Minneapolis
London

Published by the University of Minnesota Press
111 Third Avenue South, Suite 290
Minneapolis, MN 55401-2520
http://www.upress.umn.edu

Library of Congress Cataloging-in-Publication Data

Winant, Howard.
    The new politics of race : globalism, difference, justice / Howard Winant.
        p.   cm.
    Includes bibliographical references and index.
    ISBN 0-8166-4279-6 (alk. paper) — ISBN 0-8166-4280-X (pbk. : alk. paper)
    1. Race relations.   2. Race relations—Political aspects.   I. Title.
    HT1521.W586 2004
    305.8—dc22   2004006603

Printed in the United States of America on acid-free paper

The University of Minnesota is an equal-opportunity educator and employer.

18   17   16   15   14   13   10   9   8   7   6   5   4   3

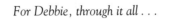

For Debbie, through it all . . .

Contents

Introduction

The Racial Present:
State, Society, Identity

Race is fundamental in modern politics. Race is situated at the crossroads of identity and social structure, where difference frames inequality, and where political processes operate with a comprehensiveness that ranges from the world historical to the intrapsychic. Always flexible and fungible, yet also always present since the inception of the "modern world-system" (c. 1500 CE), the system of racial classification has been invoked for half a millennium in the service both of domination and resistance.

Since the rise of Europe and the dawn of the capitalist era, there has been a continuous tendency, arguably a necessity, to organize and signify domination along the lines of corporeality/"phenotype." And since there is no domination without resistance, across half a millennium race has become a trope for the unfinished agendas of egalitarianism, democratization, and cultural pluralism. Not only was the concept of race born with modernity, not only was the meaning of race a preoccupation of the Enlightenment, but the racial practices of the modern age—slavery and imperial conquest, as well as abolitionism and anticolonialism—shaped all the social structures we take for granted today. The accumulation of capital, the organization of the labor process, the construction of the modern nation-state, the rise of movements for popular sovereignty, and our very understandings of cultural and personal identity were all fashioned in the global racial workshop that is modern history.

I should immediately set out what I mean by race. *Race is a concept that signifies and symbolizes sociopolitical conflicts and interests in reference to different types of human bodies.* Although the concept of race appeals to biologically based human characteristics (so-called phenotypes), selection of these particular human features for purposes of racial signification is always and necessarily a social and historical process.[1]

To grasp the political significance of race is obviously a formidable task. Race is a dimension of both state and civil society. It is manifestly relevant—in the modern world at least[2]—to all the familiar political "sites": the global system, the nation-state, social movements of all types, and political culture. At the same time it is a "social fact,"[3] shaping concepts of identity and "collective representation," and organizing social (as well as intrapsychic) experience quite comprehensively.

In this book I examine the politics of race broadly. I consider race to be a key organizational and ideological component of both state and civil society. Race shapes both public and personal life, historical and contemporary experience. To study so comprehensive a sociopolitical phenomenon is a fairly daunting task for a collection of essays, so I must apologize in advance for the unevenness of my attention and the unavoidable gaps and many repetitions that will be visible throughout the work. My objectives here may also be beyond my capacities: to reframe racial theory, to untangle the dynamics of a world racial system that has undergone a comprehensive crisis and reorganization over the past few decades, to understand U.S. racial politics in a global context, and to situate the racial "politics of experience" in the context of a new, and highly sophisticated, global racial hegemony.

My treatment of racial politics is a radical departure from standard analyses, which tend to hew far closer to mainstream approaches to politics.[4] To be sure, many of the standard themes retain their importance for me as well: inclusion/exclusion/citizenship, the political logic of racial stratification, and the vicissitudes of racially oriented social movements are simply so definitive of our experience and "life-chances" that they can never be ignored. But beyond these and similar issues lie problems that must be located in civil society and in the sphere of agency and consciousness: questions of identity, meaning, experience, and subjectivity.[5]

To synthesize these "state-centered" and "society-centered" approaches to racial politics is one of my key purposes here. This book contains three discrete but related sections. The first group of essays examines the contours of recent U.S. racial politics, occasionally venturing into historical background. Although I insist that all local and all national racial politics must constantly be examined from a comparative viewpoint as cases of a global pattern, I also consider it necessary to focus special attention on the United States because of its hegemonic position on the world scene. The essays in this section range over a variety of U.S. racial problems and developments: among the problems considered are the evolution of U.S. racial politics over the course of the twentieth century, the continuing significance of the Duboisian legacy in the United States, and the changing dynamics of U.S. racism in the century's later decades.[6] I have also included in this section an essay about whiteness and white identity; I strongly believe that both the continuing political and social significance of race and the indispensability of racism to modern forms of rule are problems that very directly confront white people, especially in the United States.

Another essay included here—perhaps somewhat awkwardly placed—deals with problems of teaching race and racism in the twenty-first century, the era of U.S. racial hegemony. This effort springs from my concern that "the higher learning in America"[7] is presently failing to come to grips with the continuing dynamics of racial formation: as an issue of teaching, of learning, and of experience, race must be approached more creatively in U.S. universities.

The second section, "Comparative Racial Studies," contains a series of essays about global racial politics. Here the central concern is the transition from racial domination to racial hegemony that occurred in the later half of the twentieth century. This racial "break" or "rupture" was a global political realignment of epochal proportions, a series of events that had few precedents in modern history. The aftereffects of that realignment have produced a confused pattern of racial politics, both in specific national contexts and on the world stage. "Postracialism"—taking such forms as "color blindness," multiculturalism, and racial "differentialism" (Taguieff 2001)—coexists with renewed biologistic racism and the effort to launch a new American imperialism.

Though primarily concerned with the post–World War II period, this section also includes essays on the comparative historical significance of slavery, and on imperialism, globalization, and racism in the twenty-first century. The Atlantic slave system was not only a key source of modern concepts of race and practices of racism; it also created many of the other, ostensibly nonracial social structures we take for granted today: economic, political, and cultural. Thus it is crucial to reflect rather continually on the continuing significance of slavery. The resurgence of U.S. imperial initiatives taking shape under the Bush II regime, with its orientation toward the global East, greatly complicates the picture. Supposedly a postcolonial orientation had become rather securely entrenched after the U.S. defeat in Vietnam and the end of the old imperial regimes in Africa and Asia. At least this was what many analysts (myself included) had presumed before the advent of the second Bush. The racial features of its new imperial policy have significant implications both on the global and national stages, and recall an epochal history in which the term *empire* looked outward from Europe toward both the global South and the global East, and in which the racial and ethnoreligious dimensions of global reach were far more closely intertwined than they have appeared in recent decades.

The final section, "Racial Theory," presents a series of essays designed to rethink the meaning of race and racism in the contemporary period. Our understanding of race, I suggest, has atrophied in recent decades. This too is a product of the contradictions and complexities of the post–World War II racial "break." Although long-standing patterns of racial stratification endure as global and local phenomena, many formerly oppositional viewpoints— rooted in the antiracist movements that burgeoned after World War II— have been incorporated into the new racial hegemony. Thus, to comprehend the present racial system, whether globally or locally, requires us to move beyond concepts of white supremacy that have their origins in a world of explicit colonialism and out-front segregation and apartheid. Of course I do not suggest that white supremacism has ended, that segregation is now a thing of the past, or even that the colonial era has definitively been surpassed; rather I think that these sociopolitical structures have been transformed and regrooved in ways that demand new understandings and analyses from racism's critics and opponents.

Of central importance to this rethinking is a reencounter with the problem of political agency, political action. In response to the political crisis that has overtaken democratic and emancipatory movements in the aftermath of the post–World War II racial "break," in the face of the incorporation of earlier challenges to racial and imperial dictatorship, and in opposition to a new racial hegemony that is reinventing white supremacy and even imperialism under the protective coloration of appeals to "color blindness" and "cultural pluralism," a new and insurgent racial theory is desperately needed. I cannot provide such a theory: no writer can. Only political practice—the creativity of action (Joas 1996), the experiments of many thousands of activists and movement participants—can generate these new understandings. But as an intellectual and an activist, I can throw out ideas in dialogue with other practitioners in the hope that these will shed a bit of light on the new racial conditions that confront us in our efforts to create democracy and social justice, at home and around the world.

After the Break

Starting after World War II and culminating in the 1960s, there was a global shift, a "break," in the worldwide racial system that had endured for centuries. The shift occurred because many challenges to the old forms of racial hierarchy converged after the war: anticolonialism, antiapartheid, worldwide revulsion at fascism, the U.S. civil rights movement, and U.S.-USSR competition in the world's South all called white supremacy into question to an extent unparalleled in modern history. These events and conflicts linked antiracism to democratic political development more strongly than ever before.

The rise of a worldwide, antiracist, democratizing tendency, from the late 1940s on, was but the first phase, the initiation of the shift or "break" in the old world racial system. A second phase was to come after several decades of fierce struggles: this was the incorporation and containment of the antiracist challenge, which had largely occurred by about 1970. Thus, despite all the political reforms and cultural transformations wrought by social movements and democratic politics around the world, despite the real amelioration of the most degrading features of the old world racial system, the centuries-old and deeply entrenched system of racial inequality and injustice was not eliminated. Rather, in a postwar social order faced with an unprecedented set of democratic and egalitarian demands, racism had to be *adapted*. Thus a new racial politics developed, a reformed variety that was able to concede much to racially based democratic and egalitarian movements, yet that could still maintain a strong continuity with the legacies of imperial rule, conquest, enslavement, and so on.

So, all around the world, a centuries-old pattern of white supremacy has been more fiercely contested, more thoroughly challenged *in our lifetimes* than has ever occurred before. As a result, for the first time in modern history, there is widespread, indeed worldwide, support for what had until recently been a "dream," Dr. King's dream, let us say, of racial equality.

But white supremacy is hardly dead. It has proven itself capable of absorbing and adapting much of the "dream," repackaging itself as "color-blind," nonracialist, and meritocratic. Paradoxically, in this reformed version racial inequality can live on, still battening on all sorts of stereotypes and fears, still resorting to exclusionism and scapegoating when politically necessary, still invoking the supposed superiority of "mainstream" (aka white) values, and cheerfully maintaining that equality has been largely achieved. It is rather ironic that this new, "color-blind" racial system may prove more effective in containing the challenges posed over the past few decades by movements for racial justice than any intransigent, overtly racist "backlash" could possibly have been.

Although the reformed and officially nonracial version of white supremacy has succeeded in curtailing progress toward the "dream" in many dubious battles—over immigration and citizenship, income redistribution and poverty, and in respect to the compensatory programs commonly called "affirmative action"—nonracialism has hardly won the day. It has certainly not eliminated the movement for racial justice that spawned it. Rather, the racial politics that results from this synthesis of challenge and incorporation, racial conflict and racial reform has proved neither stable nor certain. It is a strange brew, often appearing more inclusive, more pluralistic than ever before, yet also filled with threats: of "ethnic cleansing," of resurgent neofascism, and perhaps equally insidious, of renewed racial complacency.

The global racial situation, then, is fluid, contradictory, contentious. No longer unabashedly white supremacist, for the most part the world is, so to speak, abashedly white supremacist. The conflicts generated by the powerful movements for racial justice that succeeded World War II have been contained but not resolved. Thus no new world racial system has yet been created; instead the problems of the old system have come to a head, and the outlines of what will succeed it can at least be glimpsed, if not securely foreseen.

What does such a glimpse, however preliminary, reveal? Racial hegemony is developing in tense and contradictory ways. Its managers and mouthpieces seek in the metropolitan countries of the global North (or should I now say global West?) to adapt the post–World War II movement legacies to the exigencies of a new post–welfare state social policy. In a similar vein those at the apexes of the world's wealth and power centers (above all Washington and New York) endeavor to construct a new imperial system without succumbing to the fate of the old European empires, the old imperial system that was destroyed in those same decades.

Twenty-first-century anti-imperialist movements also have to confront new contradictions. At their core is the opposition, first demonstrated in Seattle in 1999, to transnational corporate control of the global economy and global politics. Although they are social justice movements with strong commitments to the global South, they have yet to demonstrate a strong antiracist awareness; they have yet to transcend fully their northern, white identities.

For their part, antiracist movements remain in disarray across the world, largely as a consequence of the adoption of reform policies and the rise of racial hegemony. At the global level, efforts to create transnational antiracist movements peaked with only limited success at the 2001 UN World Conference Against Racism held in Durban, South Africa. The meeting was both subverted by the United States (largely over the issue of reparations for slavery) and confounded by the twin problems of Israeli colonial occupation of the West Bank and Gaza on the one hand, and widespread anti-Semitism on the other. At the very promising World Social Forums held in Brazil since 2000, the issue of racism, though by no means entirely absent, has not been highly prominent. Nationally, governments that have enacted antidiscrimination laws (no matter that these are usually no match for the institutionalized racism they claim to redress, even in postapartheid South Africa, the most promising case), that have legalized large numbers of immigrants (no matter that millions more still risk their lives to migrate and remain relegated to extralegal status) are far more difficult targets for protest than were their intransigent predecessors. The demise of socialist ideals and the waning of the organizational resources of the Marxist left have also taken their toll on the capacities of antiracist movement.

While the power to prophesize has not been granted me, it does not require genius to recognize that over the coming period, both globally and locally, political systems will continue to be organized racially. Race will persist in playing its traditional role of stigmatizing signifier: the dangers and threats of disorder, criminality, and subversion will be regularly located by politicians and pundits as emanating from the U.S. ghettos and barrios, the Parisian *banlieues*, and (the disparagingly named) "casbahs" of Frankfurt and Düsseldorf. But at the same time the route to "success" and "participation" will be held open for those whose docility, or whose "moderate" and tempered criticism, reinforces the system, which after all continues to need both racially "different" workers to do its dirty work, and racially "different" administrators and politicians who maintain some credibility at a mass level. Thus passeth the racial system of the global North and West.

In the global South and East a similar triage will operate: the favelas and *ciudades perdidas*, the slums and shantytowns that shape urban life (and that are often if not always racially distinctive zones) are not going away. Here too the westernized and liberal leaderships and middle classes, the emergent class of southern trading partners and the "developing" social strata, will be welcomed into the circuits of capital and "international organization"—so long as they do not flout the disciplinary regime dictated by the northern (and western) powers. After all, labor at the periphery still counts, and no longer only to produce natural resources and cheap agricultural goods as in days gone by: today the *maquila* and sweatshop archipelago of the global South keeps the world clothed and shod; it provides the world's silicon circuits and kitchen appliances, and it even processes the world's air travel tickets and staffs its computer hotlines and help desks. For those unable or unwilling to join this superexploited army hundreds of millions strong, for those relegated to the landless and homeless sectors of the global South (and global East), for those in the slums who lack even a *maquiladora* or maid's job, what is the value of life on this earth? For them there are only the *madrassas* and the refugee camps; there is only peonage in the informal or criminal economies; there is the drug trade, the sex trade, the hunger and homelessness, the endless frustration and rage, and perhaps the glory of a martyr's death.

Globalism, Difference, Justice

How can we grasp the emergent racial politics of the twenty-first century? As the book's subtitle suggests, I am principally concerned with the three themes of *globalism, difference,* and *justice.*

I contrast the term *globalism* with the more common *globalization* to highlight two dimensions of the comparative historical dynamics of race: first, that there is a world racial system in which particular national/regional/ local/experiential patterns of racial signification and structure are immersed; and second, that these global racial patterns are not only the instrumentalities of domination and rule (*globalization*) but also a popular realm of contestation, resistance, and self-determination (*globalism*).

The recognition of the centrality of race to the evolution, continuity, and transformation of the modern world has been a long time coming. There are constant countertendencies: one is constantly adjured to view race as somehow peripheral, transitional, or epiphenomenal, to normalize one's own (or one's own national) racial milieu as paradigmatic, and to neglect the epochal and multiform interconnections among racially identified communities around the world.

From the earliest moments of confused and contradictory racial interpellation in the fifteenth century,[8] to our own confusions and contradictions at the dawn of the third Christian millennium, there have been racially demarcated diasporas. These were created by the travels of both the power wielders and the subjects of power. European identity (self-ascriptively white) gave rise to a certain collective self-recognition as a product of conquest and slavery; there is endless evidence of this. The conquered and enslaved were possessed of a great variety of well-established peoplehoods and cultures, but because these peoples were not white, their variety counted for nothing among the "lords of humankind" (Kiernan 1969; Pagden 1995). The natives and slaves were lumped together on racial grounds, subjected to an early and authoritarian version of what we would now call "panethnicity."

Because many groups, many African peoples, for example, were often trapped together in a common subordination, they necessarily formed ties of mutual interest and self-recognition (Thornton 1998). To be sure, both rulers and ruled sometimes fought among themselves; both sometimes betrayed their own and "crossed over" to the other side of the epochal battle line. There has always been internecine conflict and competition among both oppressors and oppressed, and globalism/diaspora has had an immense and complex genealogy. But the key point is that there *was* a battle; there has been a centuries-long conflict between the wretched of the earth and those who ruled and exploited them. Does anyone imagine that this situation has ended?

So let us dispense with the notion that our own racial experience is any more than an instance of a planetary pattern. With this recognition we join hands with a long tradition of resistance, and with some important currents of pan-Africanist thought, subalternity studies, critical race theory, and hegemony-oriented approaches (Kelley 2002; Walters 1993; Geiss 1974; Scott 1990; Brown 1995; Laclau 1996; Delgado and Stefancic 2001; Valdes, Culp, and Harris 2002).

The idea that racial formation occurs on a global scale is certainly not new, but it is unusual to think of global racial patterns as being shaped "from below." As with other accounts of the global (what I refer to here as "globalization" approaches), the tendency is to see things from the standpoint of domination, from the "top down." Yes, conquest and slavery, and in our own day such phenomena as transnational corporate reach, domination of the means of communication, and the power of hegemonic states combine to project an image of the planet as fused, and largely administered as well, from a few imperial centers: Washington, New York, and Los Angeles most centrally, but also (still) London, Paris, Frankfurt, Tokyo, and perhaps Beijing.

This is far from wrong, of course, but it is nevertheless exclusive and incomplete. In an alternative, more race-conscious account, globalism would be seen not only as the domain of corporations and imperial states but also as a popular domain. Cultural "survivals" would be recognized as the main materials of culture itself. Movements for democracy and freedom, for inclusion and social justice would be seen as both synthetic and syncretic: opposition movements have always inspired and taught each other; think of abolitionism, anticolonialism, socialism, feminism. Despite the overwhelming wave of national chauvinism that is pouring across the United States as I write (in California, in May 2003), exclusivist concepts of citizenship are over. Interdependence can be a source of strength. Diasporic globality can replace ethnonationality.

Racial *difference* is being rethought as well. The concept of race as a social construct has been hammered upon so long that it has become pretty flat. Let us recognize the historical dimension of this insight: that the meaning of race is constantly being remade by human beings over historical time. So race is a socio*historical* construct.

Race refers to the human body (it is not fully cultural), but even those references are constructed and thus vague. Racial identity cannot be reduced to an appurtenance of the body. Consider the immense vicissitudes of "mixed-race" identities, for example, with their spectrum of meanings that runs from the transgressive (miscegenation, etc.) to the normalized (*mestizaje* in Latin America, for example). So the body still counts but more as a signifier of something else. Blood still counts, but "blood quantum" seems hopelessly reductive. No racial identity can evade ascription (even uncertain ones attain a special, "problematic" status),[9] but social practices and action are not "given" by racial identity either. Whites can be "wiggers" or "go native." Blacks can "act white." Latinos can "blanquearse" (whiten themselves). And on and on. So to be racialized is both to differentiate oneself (and to be differentiated) from "others," and also to incorporate differences within oneself. Du Bois's concept of "double consciousness" or racial dualism best allows us to think about these issues. In the twenty-first century, though, even the "twoness" of this incorporative model may seem too narrow: "multiple consciousness" might now be a better version.

It is no accident that concepts of race have become so much more variegated, or that racial politics have grown so much more complicated, in the aftermath of the mid-twentieth-century racial "break." These are logical outcomes of the development of racial hegemony over the decades leading down to now.

Contemporary racial hegemony fosters the widespread claim—articulated at both the "highbrow" and "grassroots" cultural levels—that the world has entered a stage of "postracialism" after all the conflicts and reforms of recent years. As if to say, "At last! At last! We have progressed beyond those backward and benighted notions of race!" Postracialism takes such familiar forms as "color blindness" in the United States, "racial differential-ism" in France, "nonracialism" in South Africa, and "racial democracy" in Brazil.[10] It is important to recognize the highly variable provenance and uses of such accounts. At distinct moments, at different times and places, for example, the advocacy of color blindness has fueled demands for racial equality and racial justice. At other moments such claims have contributed to policies of neglect, whether malign or benign. Like all ideological con-structs, all interpellations, the ideas of color blindness, racial differentialism (Taguieff 2001), or racial democracy can be rearticulated: these racial meanings can be detached from the political contexts and practices that created them, and linked to quite different and sometimes opposing organi-zations and structures. Note the audacious and duplicitous seizure by U.S. neoconservatives, already decades ago, of Dr. King's "I Have a Dream" speech (Steele 1990; Thernstrom and Thernstrom 1997), or the Bush II regime's hijacking of the Children's Defense Fund's slogan "Leave No Child Behind." Color blindness has also at times been linked not only to "neoconservatism" and "neoliberalism" on the right but also to class reductionism on the left (Gitlin 1995; Reed 2000; Goldfield 1997).

A useful way to grasp post-"break" (post–civil rights, postapartheid, etc.) theories of racial difference is to remember that they are *incorporative* in the hegemonic sense of the term. In other words their apparent rejection of antinomic and conflictual models of racial difference is itself a product of the break in which they are historically embedded. Because antiracist and anticolonial movements produced the break, the reforms of state racial poli-cies undertaken in response to those movement challenges had necessarily to be inclusive and egalitarian, at least to some degree.[11]

From this shift emerges the discourse of postracialism. Somewhat para-doxically, incorporative concepts of racial difference tend to validate the very identities they purport to question, and to reinforce the racialized social structures (comprehensive racial stratification, discrimination, xenophobia, etc.) they so loudly repudiate. In other words, a "moderate" reformism that bevels off the jagged edges of racial dictatorship but leaves the underlying social structure of racial exclusion and injustice largely untouched is in a poor position to claim that it has "transcended" race. In many if not all respects it has reinforced the very system it claims to have surpassed. Race is here to stay, baby. Go home and tell your momma.

The historical abyss from which we have climbed has been largely devoid of racial justice. To an extent that is infrequently realized, the concept of justice in a political sense is deeply bound up with the history and current dynamics of race, once again both globally and locally. From the exploitation and oppression of non-Europeans was created the wealth, power, and cultural identity of the West (or should I say the North?). To organize, manage, and justify this process, then and now, has required an enormous amount and variety of injustice. Utilizing the concept of racial justice, we can think about the politics of race and the limitations of democracy that still obtain throughout the world despite centuries of fruitful struggle for justice.

In these essays the achievement of racial justice is viewed as a political process. It is inherently contradictory. On the one hand, it is accomplished through familiar measures: greater inclusion and enhanced equality for those groups that have experienced racial oppression; the termination or at least reduction of those unjust conditions. On the other hand, these accomplishments always have a cost: their very achievement demobilizes the democratic and popular movements whose political action impelled them, and marginalizes (or even eliminates) the more radical tendencies within them. The perpetuation of racial injustice around the world (modified and updated to be sure), and the unfulfilled promise of racial democracy (local and global) that is left over from the battles of the mid- to late twentieth century are paradoxical results of the partial victories of the movements of that period.

Because the movement victories of the post–World War II racial break were also in some measure movement defeats, because a new racial hegemony developed all around the world over the last decades of the twentieth century, racial justice in general—economic, political, and cultural—is now becoming less available. "Power concedes nothing without a demand," and whence cometh that demand in the twenty-first century? While not entirely demobilized, the global movement for racial justice is certainly more debilitated and divided today than it was a few decades ago.

Under these circumstances racially hegemonic regimes (both global and local) can afford to be less incorporative and more coercive. The old North-South divide and now the resurgent West-East divide are both racially demarcated. The international division of labor, the flow of commodities and capital in trade, and the global movement of people are organized racially. Military force is exercised, local systems of stratification and punishment are reproduced, and human groups are afforded or denied their "voice" (Hirschmann 1970) and rights in civil society, according to racial boundaries. We have to reinvent racial politics.

Part I
U.S. Racial Politics

One Hundred Years of Racial Politics

Race is above all a matter of politics. The assignment and acceptance of racial identity, the configuration of racially demarcated groups, the "logic of collective action" as practiced by members of these groups, and the stratification (imposed and opposed) of society along racial lines are but some of the main dimensions of racial politics. The state is a central player in racial matters: the modern state carries out racial classification, surveillance, and punishment of the population; it distributes resources along racial lines; it simultaneously facilitates and obstructs racial discrimination; and it is both structured and challenged by political mobilization along racial lines.

To make sense of the huge conundrum of racial politics is obviously not easy. To do so on a worldwide scale, taking into account the immense transformations that have occurred over the past century or so, is a daunting task indeed. Yet there is no escaping this work, for these epochal shifts have in many ways shaped us: nation and society, culture and individual, world system and psyche, all bear the mark of racial politics.

In this essay I proceed as follows. Initially I present an overview, necessarily schematic, of world racial politics a century ago. In 1903 the imperial system was at its height, racial slavery was very much a living memory (and indeed a continuing reality in some places), and the world's racial hierarchy was taken for granted, at least by the "lords of humankind" (Kiernan 1969), the rulers of the system. But from other standpoints this structure was entirely

3

unacceptable: exploitative, tyrannical, and boundlessly brutal. Because racial rule, white supremacy, had provided a structure of domination since its origins in the fifteenth and sixteenth centuries, it had also (always) drawn resistance. Born out of the independent and self-reliant cultures of the subordinated, resistance is an aspect of human autonomy that can never be fully abdicated, no matter how imprisoned or subjugated the resister.[1]

For many years, for centuries, racial resistance was effectively located outside the state. The racially subordinate were not even recognized as human beings in many cases much less as citizens.[2] But at the turn of the twentieth century that resistance was becoming more organized, more articulate. The tumultuous struggles to put an end to slavery had largely ceased by then, but the experience of abolitionism—the world's first transnational social movement (Keck and Sikkink 1998)—had provided invaluable political experience. Advancing industrialism was imposing new and more varied demands for labor, and the changing nature of the world economy was reshaping the parameters of empire. These developments created opportunities for participation and for political opposition that had hardly existed earlier. New subaltern elites were making their voices heard and generating new organizations. New avenues for racial politics were beginning to appear.

Next I survey racial politics in the interwar years. World War I deeply transformed the world racial system, mobilizing millions of soldiers and workers, prompting reassessment of the imperial system, touching off revolution in Russia and fear of communism everywhere, and elevating the United States to secure status among the world powers. The upheavals that followed the war cast a pall on the imperial system; indeed they foreshadowed its doom after World War II. The crises of the Depression and the rise of fascism had powerful racial undertones. The weakened position of the dominant nations during the 1930s made empire (and transnational spheres of influence) harder to maintain. The rise of fascism created new difficulties for the imperialist powers; fascism also revealed some discomfiting affinities with the traditional systems of empire. While it was particularly racist in its German form, it was not free of racial dimensions in either its Italian or Japanese versions. Fascism was an imperial project in its own right: an effort to replace the obsolescent empires with new ones. Mussolini's quest for an African empire, the "Greater East Asia Co-prosperity Sphere" (the Japanese imperial scheme), and Hitler's drive for Lebensraum were all justified in explicitly racial terms, much as the empires of "old" Europe had been.

The following section deals with the racial "break." World War II reshuffled the political deck again, far more comprehensively than the "war to end all wars" had ever done. World War II was an antifascist war, an anti-imperial war in part, an antiracist war in part. By fostering resistance to the Japanese in Asia and the Germans and Italians in Africa, World War II unwittingly lent support to anti-imperialist movements. By casting themselves (with some truth) as the champions of democracy, the Allies touched off a new phase of civil rights and human rights activities all over the world, including in their home countries. The breakup of the Grand Alliance and the onset of the cold war made the global South (soon to be the "third world" and the "nonaligned" world) a vast battleground, with the forces of empire on one side, and those of communism and nationalism on the other. All these developments were fundamentally structured by race. Furthermore, World War II occasioned vast population shifts. It drove labor recruitment efforts, military conscription and subsequent demobilization, and northward migrations by millions both during and after the hostilities. These processes vastly transformed the colonies and hinterlands of the entire world. As the population structures, residential patterns, and labor dynamics of many countries were altered, so too were their political systems. Thus did anti-imperial and civil rights movements arise; thus did these movements combine to impel a global "break" in racial politics that began during and continued after World War II.

Next I consider racial politics at century's end. After the movements, after the revolutions, after the empires' official retreats, there was reform. State-based racial reform took various forms. Passage of civil rights laws and adoption of more inclusive immigration policies, extension of citizenship and citizenship rights, repatriation of abandoned colonials like the "pieds noirs" from Algeria, and widespread official professions of commitment to racial equality were some of the chief lines of racial reform. With the fall of the apartheid regime in South Africa in 1994—an event halfway between racial reform and revolution—the post–World War II break reached its limits. Well before the collapse of apartheid (which was a late event in the cycle) the construction of a new racial hegemony was already well advanced, particularly in the United States. The United States had attained the status of leading superpower and culturally hegemonic society. Yet it was also a complex combination of the old and new racial systems. By undertaking "moderate" racial reforms in response to movement demands, the United States was able to derail the more radical potential of the domestic antiracist movements that formed a leading edge of the break and acquired huge (indeed worldwide) political influence. Yet while it touted "color blindness" and claimed largely to have achieved racial equality, the U.S. racial state had hardly transformed the fundamental social structures of race and racism. It was simply managing white supremacy in a significantly updated and revised fashion.

A concluding section muses theoretically on racial politics today. Here I offer some brief reflections on the tasks intellectuals and activists committed to racial justice face at the threshold of the twentieth-first century. We must reassess our understandings of the meaning of race and the dynamics of racism in the aftermath of the triumphs and tragedies our movements have experienced since the onset of the racial break during and after World War II. We face a new set of tasks at present. Racial hegemony has developed in an era when outright racial domination has been anathematized.

Was that all we antiracist activists accomplished? Is it likely that all the blood, sweat, and tears of the postwar movements, the labors undertaken in the service of revolution, "regime change," social justice, and racial reform can be absorbed and contained by modest adjustments in racial policy and rhetoric? Can a series of ineffectual efforts at the redistribution of economic resources and political power—so ineffectual that they have often been characterized as "token" or symbolic—put paid to the bill for half a millennium of coercion, decimation, and theft? I hardly think so.

World Racial Politics a Century Ago

One hundred years ago W. E. B. Du Bois published *The Souls of Black Folk*. The book was recently described by Du Bois's preeminent biographer David Levering Lewis as "an electrifying manifesto" and "a work of transcendent intellectual passion and numinous prose." For those readers who were prepared to receive it and digest it, *Souls* offered an entirely new, and in many ways prophetic, interpretation of racial politics. Largely focusing his attention on the United States, but at pains to set his native land in a global context,[3] Du Bois exhorted his long-oppressed people to mobilize and reconquer their rights and their place in history, to take new pride in their heritage and culture, and to understand their lives as situated in the vast historical drama of the human quest for freedom and dignity. *Souls* possessed an unparalleled emotional power and beauty: it was politics, history, and poetry all at once; it treated black religion, psychology, education, and music as variegated branches of a unified African American experience. It drank deeply from the well of Enlightenment rationality and European letters, yet gloried as well in the enormous contributions, the unique "gifts," the treasure-house of African American (and of African) culture. The book recollected the sweep of black history: the uprooting from Africa, slavery's unrequited labor and loss of millions of lives, the horrific bloodletting and suffering of the Civil War and the dashed hopes of inclusion and justice that followed ("Of the Dawn of Freedom"). Yet Du Bois did not despair. Instead he rejected the accommodationism that dominated black politics at the turn of the twentieth century ("Of Mr. Booker T. Washington and Others") and set forth the key principles of a political program for black enfranchisement and empowerment. He explored black life in city and country, looked closely at black families and black religion, and situated his own experience within the odyssey of his people. All this history, practice, and theory he synthesized in an account practical enough and resilient enough to endure for the rest of the century and beyond.

Let us consider the global racial environment of one century ago, the 1903 sky into which *Souls* was launched like a great illuminating flare. We begin with the United States, to which the book devoted its primary attention, and then look more broadly at the racial world of a century ago.

In the 1903 United States the great majority of black people still resided in the South, where Jim Crow was at its height. Most black people were peasants; debt peonage ("sharecropping") remained the chief form of labor and was often the only way to survive. The southern peasantry was not exclusively black by any means, but the ubiquity of Jim Crow continuously reinforced the near-total disempowerment of blacks, thus shoring up status differences between them and the often equally impoverished white "croppers" with whom they shared a landlord. Enforced by lynching and night-riding mobs of hooded white terrorists, southern racial "etiquette" required blacks to remove their hats in the presence of whites, to step off the sidewalk (where one existed) into the muddy street at the passage of a white, and to wait in such shops as would serve blacks until all whites had been served, no matter who had arrived first. A thousand other rules of this type were in place, most of them subject to the wildest interpretative variations imaginable. The institutionalized manifestations of Jim Crow were ubiquitous: separate schools (where there were schools for blacks at all), separate transportation, separate accommodation in respect to food service and lodging, separate everything. These systems all had the sanction and force of law; to violate them was to break the law and subject oneself to the tender mercies of the police, courts, chain gangs, and jails of the South; that is, if one was lucky enough to avoid the retribution of informal enforcers active in the KKK (McMillen 1989; Litwack 1980). Jim Crow reigned well beyond the old Confederacy: "up South" in the old Union states discrimination was rampant as well. In the Southwest racial segregation and lynch law ran together: they were applied in Texas and elsewhere to Mexican Americans as well as blacks. In California elaborate racial hierarchies secured cheap labor from immigrants and Mexicans.[4] Meanwhile anti-Asian nativism, though based in California, had become a nationwide movement with secure roots in the white working class. Anti-Chinese riots and constant agitation soon combined with restrictive immigration policies toward Asians; in contrast to this Pacific policy, Atlantic immigration was fostered until 1924 (Perlman 1950, 52; Saxton 1996; Almaguer 1994).

That was the domestic racial panorama in 1903. But the United States was also a racial power outside its own borders. The United States had always had *internal* colonies; it was after all a settler nation. It had slaughtered and evicted those indigenous peoples whose presence had been established in its territories for tens of thousands of years. Those who survived this holocaust it confined to native reserves (Stannard 1992).

But at the turn of the twentieth century the United States had entered the imperial world, despite a significant anti-imperialist movement at home, with the so-called Spanish-American War of 1898. Now firmly in possession of Puerto Rico and regent of Cuba after the passage of the Platt Amendment (1902), the United States had also secured possession of the Philippines with its brutal suppression of that country's independence movement and 1903 capture of nationalist leader Emilio Aguinaldo. This was a campaign that involved 125,000 U.S. troops and took something like 200,000 Filipino lives (Linn 2000; Stanley 1974).

Wherever the United States went, it took with it a racial system that had been honed in the post-Reconstruction South: in Cuba and Puerto Rico it sought to impose racial segregation; in the Philippines it assumed the white man's burden, as well as a certain Christian evangelism, no small matter in a country with a significant Muslim minority;[5] vis-a-vis China, Japan, and the Philippines it alternatively trolled for superexploitable labor and erected barriers against the "yellow peril"; and in Latin America it embarked on a series of interventions on behalf of various corporate predators.[6]

Let us look now at the 1903 world from a wider angle. By the turn of the twentieth century European imperialism had completed its transition to a new form of colonial rule. Not only the African slave trade but slavery internal to the continent was on the wane: the Belgian genocide had been a vast alchemical effort to forge gold (or in this case, rubber) directly out of human flesh. Peonage and even industrial labor was replacing slavery.[7] As export-oriented agriculture and mining became the key imperial activities in Africa, railroads and ports had to be built, and urban centers developed. Having carved up the continent at the Congress of Berlin (1885), the imperial powers had fallen into discord by the century's turn, as later arrivals at the African table tried to secure a heaping plate of spoils for themselves.[8]

Imperialism in Africa around 1900 was a very different system than it had been just half a century earlier. It was no longer expansive; it was now developmentalist. Drained of administrative and tutelary zeal (especially after the economic downturns of the 1870s and 1890s), the empires now relied more on indirect rule and native elites than they had in the past.[9] They maneuvered to maintain their comparative advantages vis-a-vis each other and sought stability rather than total control in the colonies. As the century turned, though, their imperial subjects began to stir in new ways. Schooled by abolitionism and generations of enterprising missionaries, trained by their own colonial masters to administer the empire locally—the British principle of indirect rule was the best example of this—the natives began to grow restless, to mobilize politically. Elites questioned colonial rule in the language and style of their colonial rulers. Subversion and noncompliance— always present as resistance tactics—became more widespread among the masses of imperial subjects (Scott 1986; Bhabha 1994). In particular the pan-African call began to echo across the imperial world: the first of five important pan-African congresses was held in England in 1900. Throughout the colonial world there were strikes and labor union activity (Cooper 1987; Wallerstein 1976; Chatterjee 1993). There were religiously based movements, sometimes millenarian (Fields 1985; Ranger 1967); there were the stirrings of nationalism.

Latin America had undergone most of its anticolonial upsurge over the course of the nineteenth century, yet the Americas were hardly free of North American and European domination. This was a relationship that remained quite racially inflected. The United States had declared the Americas its sphere of influence in 1832 and had intervened thereafter in pursuit of a series of goals: to defend slavery in the first half of the century, to dominate sea-lanes, where possible to shape terms of trade, and to "manifest destiny." The mid-nineteenth century had seen war with Mexico and a series of pro-slavery interventions in Central America. By the time of the "Spanish-American" war and the construction of the Panama Canal, the Caribbean was perceived in Washington as a North American lake, to the dismay of nationalists throughout Central and South America.

Still, for much of the nineteenth century the United States could not do more than impede European influence: Europe still constituted the major export market and provided Latin American elites with their key cultural reference points. By the turn of the century, though, the United States was far more interventive. At the same time, nationalism was sweeping Latin America, and the continent was entering a crisis of identity that was highly racial. On the one hand the "whitening ideal" remained in force; on the other the national character (typically mestizo) was being venerated: in *Os Sertoes*, the epic account of a millenarian rebellion in the backlands of Brazil (Cunha 1995; Levine 1992), in the efforts of Cuban revolutionary José Marti to define an America independent of the big bully to the north, and most comprehensively in the revolution that convulsed Mexico after 1910, a new Latin American nationalist politics was being defined. Though contradictory and uncertain, Latin American political insurgencies of this period were uniformly concerned to distinguish their societies' racial practices from those on view in North America.[10] These differences would acquire greater definition and significance as the twentieth century progressed.

In Asia anti-imperialism was also on the increase. I have already mentioned the Philippines. In China the Boxer Rebellion of 1900—an explicitly nationalist, anticolonial campaign that targeted foreigners and demanded the cessation of the Qing concessions to the imperial powers of "spheres of influence" in Shanghai and elsewhere—reached such a level of influence that an expeditionary force of 19,000 soldiers—2,500 U.S. marines among them—had to be dispatched to China to suppress it. China was forced to indemnify the colonial powers for the losses they had suffered in the rebellion. These events laid the groundwork for the 1911 overthrow of the Qings and the establishment of the republic, as well as reinforcing the nationalism that was to bring forth the May 4th Movement after World War I and the Communist Party a few years later (Preston 2001).

In India opposition to British rule also began to crystallize anew around the turn of the century. The legacy of the 1857 rebellion and its fierce repression by the British had now receded somewhat, and political organization was taking place through the Congress. Gandhi's arrival from South Africa during World War I is usually taken as the starting point for a new wave of anticolonial mobilization, but it is obvious to all that Gandhi and his associates did not invent that movement, however much they were to lead it in new directions. After the war the independence movement would take off in earnest, employing protest tactics of an entirely new type (L. James 1998).[11]

Racial Politics in the Interwar Years

In the carnage and aftermath of World War I the world racial system was deeply transformed. The war placed millions under arms for the first time: not only Europeans and white Americans, but Africans, African Americans, South Asians, and Caribbeans as well. Although it was not the fully cataclysmic, truly global confrontation that World War II would prove to be—the Pacific basin, for example, was largely though not totally untouched by World War I—the war still shattered the former world order of the "long 19th century." In a memorable 1915 essay Du Bois located the source of the war in the contradictions and instabilities of imperial and racial rule, in the insatiable greed of the "advanced" nations:

> Whence comes this new wealth and on what does its accumulation depend? It comes primarily from the darker nations of the world—Asia and Africa, South and Central America, the West Indies and the islands of the South Seas. There are still, we may believe, many parts of white countries like Russia and North America, not to mention Europe itself, where the older exploitation still holds. But the knell has sounded faint and far, even there. In the lands of the darker folk, however, no knell has sounded. Chinese, East Indians, Negroes, and South American Indians, are by common consent for governance by white folk and economic subjection to them. To the furtherance of this highly profitable economic dictum has been brought every available resource of science and religion. Thus arises the astonishing doctrine of the natural inferiority of most men to the few, and the interpretation of "Christian brotherhood" as meaning anything that one of the "brothers" may at any time want it to mean. (Du Bois 1915, 645)

For a moment consider this analysis as an artifact of its time. Step beyond the marvels of Du Bois's expressive skills, beyond his critique of empire, which reveals as much about the present world in the throes of "globalization" (fully ninety years after this essay's appearance) as it does about the world of 1915. Note that the mere handing up of this indictment indicated how much race consciousness had already changed in the early twentieth century from what it had been a few decades earlier. Granted, Du Bois was a genius, with vastly greater cultural capital at his disposal than had most of his contemporary brothers and sisters "behind the veil." Yet his insights and critique cannot properly be seen as the product of his own labors and genius alone. Rather, they issued from a deeper well: the fierce struggles of his people for human rights and dignity. He drew from that deep well and cultivated the territory on which it stood (to his great credit). It nurtured him as well as his people.

So Russia fell to the first successful socialist revolution in history. Russia withdrew from the war and made peace at Brest-Litovsk. At Versailles the imperial powers could not fully grasp the "consequences of the peace";[12] they contented themselves with ratifying the prewar global order as far as possible: extracting punitive reparations from their defeated foes; taking control of the former German colonies in Africa; sharing out the booty of the Ottoman world—Syria, Egypt, the newly created Iraq—among other territories; and creating "mandates" for the victors where outright territorial appropriation might be too embarrassing.

In the face of socialist revolution in Russia the Allies were far less complacent. They invaded in support of the Whites in the ensuing civil war, and deployed the Wilsonian doctrine of "national self-determination" in the vain hope of derailing the updated communist call for anticolonial revolution.[13] In the wake of the Russian events and as a fairly direct consequence of the war, millions of colonial subjects gravitated toward communism.

In the United States wartime conscription and augmented economic demand had spurred the first "great migrations" of blacks northward from the South: now Chicago, Philadelphia, Cleveland, Pittsburgh, and Detroit were much darker than they had been. The "making of the ghetto" began in earnest. Blacks "up South" in these cities and others began to make demands: they wanted to vote and work for wages, to join unions, and end lynchings. They resonated to the mass appeal of Marcus M. Garvey and his United Negro Improvement Association, which brought a pan-Africanist and to some degree anticolonialist message to the streets of the ghetto for the first time.

So, far from producing greater racial equality as many had hoped, the war brought greater racial conflict. Black soldiers had distinguished themselves in the Ardennes and elsewhere, distressing their white American officers and winning the admiration of the French. Their return home brought both parades (down Fifth Avenue from Harlem) and four years of white assaults ("race riots") on black communities across the country. Demobilized black soldiers of radical leanings formed the African Black Brotherhood (Solomon 1998) to resist white marauders, in some places successfully. More often, however, armed whites acted with the support of police and military units to destroy entire neighborhoods, as in the case of the Tulsa "riot" of 1921, which razed the previously prosperous black area of Greenwood, killing hundreds in "death squad" style and burning and looting indiscriminately (Madigan 2001).

Meanwhile, back on the plantation, fear of communism and racism were beginning to blend as mass deportations took place in the early 1920s,[14] new immigration restrictions were imposed in 1924,[15] and eugenics was endorsed by the Supreme Court as a constitutional social policy.[16]

Just as World War I elevated the United States to secure status among the world powers, it also confronted the country—as much as the "old European" empires—with the political instability inherent in racial rule. Although it did not have an old-fashioned empire to police in the manner of the British in India or the French in the Maghreb, the United States had developed abundant imperial inclinations as the century dawned. By the end of World War I there were interventions underway in Mexico, Haiti, Nicaragua, Cuba, Panama, Honduras, and the Dominican Republic. Those "little brown men," as McKinley might have said, also wanted to eat and vote and run their own countries, it seemed. Speaking of McKinley, during the years between the wars the Philippines, his great imperial conquest, remained a U.S. regency, under the suzerainty of two U.S. generals, the MacArthurs, father and son.

Indeed the upheavals that followed the war threatened the imperial system, anticipating the break that would demolish it after World War II. The attraction of communism, especially during the Depression, and the elective affinity between the communist movement and the anti-imperialist and antiracist ones, confronted the imperial "mother countries" with enormous dilemmas. The rise of pan-Africanism, both in the socialist version (which was associated with Du Bois, Padmore, and many others), and in the Garveyite version (which achieved a tremendous level of mass support and was rooted in the legacy of Booker T. Washington), was also troubling to imperial elites in the United States, the Caribbean, the United Kingdom, and Africa itself.

The rise of fascism further complicated the picture. Here was a racist and imperialist political movement, equipped with power in several industrialized nations, and endowed as well with widespread popular support. German fascism was particularly racist, but fascism as an Italian and even Japanese phenomenon was not free of racial dimensions. Fascism was an imperial project as well: it sought to revive the old empires (Mussolini claimed to be reawakening the greatness of Rome) as well as to create new ones. Mussolini's quest for an African empire, the "Greater East Asia Co-prosperity Sphere" (the Japanese imperial scheme), and Hitler's drive for Lebensraum were all justified in explicitly racial terms, much as the empires of "old" Europe had been.

In the face of this challenge, the imperial democracies wobbled: they all had supporters of fascism within their own ranks, and their policies over-lapped more than a bit with those of the fascist powers, especially where race was concerned. On the one hand the United Kingdom, France, and the United States were democracies, flawed to be sure, but not authoritar-ian police states (at least not at home, at least not systematically). Yet to their dark-skinned subjects trapped in rural debt peonage, confined to native reserves, or crammed into urban slums, democracy seemed in short supply as well. Is it a mere accident, for example, that during the twentieth century the term *ghetto* came to characterize black slums in U.S. cities? There was indeed an uncomfortable resemblance between the fascism that Whitehall, the White House, and the Élysée deplored and denounced, and those same "democratic" countries' racial practices in Mississippi, Malaya, and Madagascar.

In short the crises of the Depression and the rise of fascism, themselves both direct "consequences of the peace," had powerful racial undertones. During the 1930s, as Andre Gunder Frank (1969) has famously suggested in respect to Latin America, the weakened position of the dominant nations made empire (and transnational spheres of influence) harder to maintain. Frank argued that national economic autonomy grew in Latin America dur-ing the 1930s because the international imperialist regime lost a measure of its power: as it was wracked by economic crisis at home and confronted by the rise of new and hostile powers, both communist and fascist, the U.S. big daddy could devote less attention to managing the little Latino kids down south. From the perspective I am advancing here, it appears that antiracist and anticolonialist activity also benefited during this same period from the crisis of the ruling regimes.

Few today would question the claim that the interwar years were a par-ticularly difficult period for the big powers: the nations that had triumphed in World War I now experienced new crises, new instabilities, a new popu-lar disillusionment and bitterness. Their recent victory was turned inside out as bread grew scarce and the rivals they had so recently humiliated rose up in terrifying strength to challenge them once again. But in all the con-sensus that permeates this account of the interwar years, has the theme of racial rule and racial insurgency received the attention it deserves? Have race and racism, continuing colonial rule and white supremacy been recognized as pivotal elements and central contradictions in the run-up to World War II? I think not.

The Racial "Break"

World War II reshuffled the global political deck once again, far more comprehensively than the "war to end all wars" had ever done. During and after the war the world underwent a profound shift in the global logic of race, a crisis of world *racial formation*. This racial metamorphosis, perhaps the most comprehensive to have occurred since the rise of the "modern world-system" (Wallerstein 1974–89), is what I am calling the racial "break"; it was a complex of sociopolitical conflicts and adjustments that both modified and preserved the world racial system in our own era.

The racial break was the most significant challenge to white supremacy that had been mounted since the rise of Europe a half-millennium earlier. Yet, world-shaking as it was, it could not dislodge, but only somewhat weaken, the tenacious traditions of white racist world domination. I have written at length about the break elsewhere (Winant 2001). Here I can only begin to suggest the forces that contributed to the new situation.

Above all, the break was an accretion of innumerable conflicts and experiences, which flowed together and accumulated in a politically overdetermined pattern during the post–World War II decades. Some of the main elements of this conjuncture, this buildup of political confrontations, were the following:

The upsurge of anticolonial and antiracist movements. The mass mobilizations that the war drove forward resulted, in its aftermath, in the presence around the world of millions of demobilized fighters. Armed and trained to fight against fascism and imperialism, well-schooled in the ideologies of democracy and self-determination, many veterans made a seamless transition between fighting a world war and fighting an anticolonial war. Many who had experienced the trenches and wartime factories of the Allies (especially in the United States) did not look kindly upon the segregation and second-class citizenship to which they were told to return at the war's end. Of course, not only demobilized soldiers found themselves opposed to attempts to restore the old colonial and white supremacist system; soldiers have families, communities, friends as well. Many colonial subjects and racially identified "others" had not fought in the war but had weathered "the war at home." They had found new jobs, moved to the cities, and so on. Such experiences made return to antebellum conditions quite unthinkable. These patterns, themselves redolent of the end of World War I and indeed of the defeat of Reconstruction, deeply shaped postwar social movements both in the United States and on a global level.

The consolidation of the cold war. Competition between the super-powers developed quickly after World War II's end. As a neocolonial power, the United States engaged in numerous wars with insurgent national liberation movements, which almost always identified themselves as communists as well as nationalists. Although these conflicts were generally more anti-imperialist than cold war–based, in the United States they were inevitably interpreted as great-power confrontations; opponents were branded as surrogates for the USSR. The United States generally took a direct hand in these wars— though not always; it had surrogates as well such as France, Portugal, Pakistan, and Israel. In contrast the USSR never directly entered into armed conflict with the United States.[17] The conflict between the superpowers was largely fought out in the global South, where colonialism and white supremacy were (correctly) perceived as U.S. policies. The very persistence in the United States proper of racial segregation, lynching, disenfranchisement, and racist practices of every type thus quickly became an international issue of the first order. The accruing international political disadvantage of this sit-uation, combined with increasingly effective domestic movements for civil and human rights, contributed to the momentum of racial reform initiatives at home (Dudziak 2000).

Worldwide demographic transition. World War II brought about huge population shifts both during and after hostilities. The war made vast labor recruitment efforts necessary; it also involved military conscription and subsequent demobilization on an unprecedented scale. The northward migration of millions resulted both from labor demand (for both military production and reconstruction) and from the hunger of the "wretched of the earth" for a better life in the post-war years. The old empires "struck back" as former colonial subjects— East and West Indians, Caribeños, Maghrebines and sub-Saharans,

Filipinos and Moluccans, Koreans and Chinese—set off in unprecedented numbers for the northern metropoles. Migration not only
meant movement from South to North on a global scale; it also
meant population shifts from countryside to city within virtually
every nation. Rural people—typically poor, less educated, and
dark-skinned—made their way to urban shantytowns and ghettos
in Rabat and Rome, São Paulo and San Francisco, Dakar and
Düsseldorf, Capetown and Cleveland. After a few years of this in
the United States, black people were no longer concentrated in the
South, no longer mainly rural. In Europe, former working-class
suburbs had now sprouted mosques and halal butcher shops. In
Africa and Latin America, in the Philippines and the Arab countries,
the shantytowns on the urban periphery became hotbeds of despair,
criminality, and political opposition. All this migration meant that
an enormous cultural mixing was underway: Europe's "others"—its
former wogs, niggers, noirs, coolies, and kaffirs—were now inside the
"motherland" to a far greater extent than previously. The United
States became a far browner and yellower country than it had ever
been before. Yet proximity did not in general lead to assimilation,
"melting," or miscegenation (although of course it did increase these
phenomena as well), so much as it advanced diasporic consciousness,
ethnonationalism, and antiracist politics.

These processes vastly transformed the colonies and hinterlands of the
entire world. As the population structures, residential patterns, and labor
dynamics of many countries were altered, so too were their political systems.
Thus did anti-imperialist and civil rights movements arise; thus did these
movements combine to impel a global break in racial politics that began
during World War II and continued after its end for decades.

World War II had been an antifascist war, an anti-imperial war (in part),
an antiracist war (in part). It had schooled resistance to the Japanese in
Asia and the Germans and Italians in Africa, and thus advanced the causes
of anti-imperialism and antiracism. Much of this was unwitting or at least
unavoidable. The Allies had cast themselves during the war (with some
truth) as the champions of democracy. In a kind of "blowback," then, they
set in motion a new phase of civil rights and human rights activity all over
the world, including in their home countries. At home they were compelled
to undertake racial reforms and engage in more inclusive practices—economic, political, and cultural—than ever before.

The onset of the cold war made the old imperial domains (or the "third world," or the "nonaligned nations") a vast battleground, with the forces of empire on one side, and those of communism and nationalism on the other. In short order, the old empires began to collapse. The Dutch left Indonesia, after a brutal but hopeless colonial war, in 1948. The British abandoned Malaya in 1950; the French were defeated at Dien Bien Phu in 1954. Africa was cleared of the Union Jack by the 1960s, and in 1962 the French admitted defeat in their long and bloody campaign to hold on to Algeria. Of course, the imperial death throes were more prolonged than that. The Portuguese empire did not fall until 1975, and it took a military revolt within the colonial army to accomplish that feat. The world had by then moved into a neocolonial stage (Nkrumah 1965). The waning of the old European empires left a power vacuum that the United States rushed to fill, most notably in Vietnam but also in Congo, Iran, and Indonesia, as well as in its traditional backyard: Latin America and the Caribbean.

All these developments were fundamentally affected by racial dynamics. All echoed past global tensions and conflicts over race, such as those that occurred after Versailles. All this contributed to the worldwide racial break.

Racial Politics at Century's End

After the movements, after the revolutions, after the empires' official retreats, there was reform. State-based racial reform took various patterns: passage of civil rights laws and adoption of more inclusionist immigration policies, extension of citizenship and citizenship rights, repatriation of abandoned colonials, like the "pieds noirs" from Algeria, and widespread official professions of commitment to racial equality were some of the chief lines of racial reform. With the fall of the apartheid regime in South Africa in 1994—an event halfway between racial reform and revolution—the post–World War II break reached its limits. Well before the collapse of apartheid (which was a late event in the cycle) the construction of a new racial hegemony was already well advanced, particularly in the United States.

In part as a consequence of the transformed conditions that succeeded the break, a new world economic system came into being: postimperial, postcolonial, but subject to a multilateral discipline as onerous as any that had preceded it. Ushered in by the oil shocks and the explosion of "third world" debt during the 1980s, the economic unraveling of much of the global South meant an end to dreams of "development." By the 1990s a new postcolonial regime was in place, one of spiraling indebtedness and seemingly eternal discipline at the hands of avaricious creditors. This was the world economic order, administered in the main by the International Monetary Fund (IMF). It was a system controlled from the global North and fully dedicated to indirect rule of the global South on the behalf of transnational capital. Its institutions and policies went by various names: the World Trade Organization (WTO), the General Agreement on Tariffs and Trade (GATT), "structural adjustment policies," as well as the more general term "globalization" and the old imperial chestnut "free trade." Something had certainly changed since the heyday of the "old Europe's" imperial era. The United States was the new boss, for one thing. The names and acronyms were certainly different: what had once been colonial territories and then "Less Developed Countries" (LDCs) were now "Highly Indebted Poor Countries" (HIPCs).

So the imperial system continued, transformed to be sure from the pre–World War II modality of direct rule by the various "mother countries," transformed even from the cold war setup of competing power blocs and a certain intermediate, "nonaligned" group of countries. Yet something remained the same at the turn of the twenty-first century. The North-South system was still, so to speak, color-coded. It still operated a worldwide racial division of labor. It still relied on a (updated to be sure) means of racially organized exploitation: global debt peonage.

Just as in the days of African slavery, when dark-skinned workers labored in chains to subsidize their white "owners" and "masters," so now in the twenty-first century Africans labored in the chains of transnational debt peonage to subsidize the great banks, securities markets, and "developed" nations that were their creditors, or perhaps one should say their modern slave masters. Latin Americans ravaged their forests and abandoned subsistence crops for cash-crop, export-oriented cultivation. Marooned in the shantytowns and slums of hundreds of hungry cities, Asians now toiled in sweatshops, making apparel, televisions, circuit boards, and suitcases. Laboring under an unimaginable weight of indebtedness, the "independent" countries in Africa, Asia, and Latin America danced to the tune played by their northern lenders. Unable to represent the interests of their peoples, the "independent" governments of these countries instead secured the discipline of their subjects by means of coercion and corruption. Thus much of the world's population was governed (indirectly, to be sure) on behalf of the world's northern rulers. This "indirect rule" was a great improvement (in the eyes of those who benefited from it, anyway), on nineteenth-century imperial practices that went by the same name.

By 1998 African debt/annual GDP ratios had reached the obscene level of 125 percent, and debt service in many southern countries amounted to more than 50 percent of state revenues per year. By way of contrast, consider that in 1953 the victorious Allies *cancelled* 80 percent of defeated Germany's war debt, and only insisted on a repayment rate on the remaining 20 percent of 3 to 5 percent of annual export earnings. The IMF and other big lenders have imposed similar lenient terms on central Europe debtors after the fall of communism. So why was Africa expected to pay the rich countries at as much as fifteen times the interest rates charged to European debtor countries (Sassen 2001; Stiglitz 2002; Bello 2001; Chua 2002)?

The global "debt trap" now engulfs not only impoverished nations but fairly developed ones like Argentina, Mexico, and South Korea. Assaults on the world's poor via the global financial system—notably the debt and its policing by the IMF through "structural adjustment policies"—result in the deaths of millions every year (Benería 1999; Weissman 2000). All this can readily be understood in terms of racism: the world's poor are largely peasants and superexploited workers; they are dark-skinned sharecroppers and peons of a global corporate plantation, owned and run by white men in business suits.

To be sure, a new transnational movement has emerged against this state of affairs and has even scored some successes, notably the string of mass demonstrations that have been mounted over the past few years in Seattle, Washington, Genoa, Quebec, New York, and Cancún at the annual meetings of the World Trade Organization, the IMF/World Bank, the Free Trade Association of the Americas, and similar conclaves of world economic managers. The World Social Forum, which has met in Porto Alegre, Brazil, since 2001, has launched a series of initiatives aimed at creating a transnational agenda for "globalism from below"; numerous progressive organizations and activists—political, religious, indigenous, workers', and community groups— have signed on. There is a movement out there.

Turning to U.S. racial politics after the break: during the post–World War II decades the United States has grown used to its role as leading superpower and culturally hegemonic society. Yet it also remains a complex combination of the old and new racial systems. By acceding to certain "moderate" movement demands, by revisioning and reinterpreting long-standing racial policies in order to incorporate their more digestible features, by co-opting movement leaders and adopting movement rhetoric, the United

States was not only able to defuse and marginalize the radical potential of the antiracist movements that confronted it in the post–World War II period. It was also able to manage racial inequality and racial divisions far more effectively than it could have done using the old-style, intransigent means. Yet while it sang the siren song of democracy and civil rights, the U.S. racial state did not transform essential social structures of race and racism; that would have required far more thoroughgoing reforms. Such measures would have been undesirable to established elites, of course, and the mass constituency for such radical reforms was unavailable after moderate ones had been enacted.

So after the antiracist movement's rising phase, which began during the war itself and gradually consolidated as a mass movement over the 1950s and 1960s, there was a second phase of containment that took effect over several decades of fierce struggles. This was the accommodationist or reformist moment—the last phase of the break in the United States—which was largely completed by about 1970. Although profoundly changed in the upheavals of the post–World War II period, the centuries-old and deeply entrenched system of racial inequality and injustice was hardly eliminated. Rather the postwar racial order, faced with an unprecedented set of democratic and egalitarian demands, was adapted over the course of a decades-long political struggle. Through an extended interplay of conflict and compromise, a multileveled and nuanced encounter between that which was dying and that which was struggling to be born, the racial state incorporated its opposition. A new racial politics developed in the United States; racial hegemony replaced racial domination.

From the standpoint of the racial state, the contentious politics (McAdam, Tarrow, and Tilly 2001) of the break were resolved by a brokered or "pacted" racial peace. This consisted of a combination of significant concessions to antiracist movements on the one hand, with the utter repudiation of the movements' more radical demands on the other. Thus civil rights legislation, as well as administrative and judicial intervention on its behalf, made no effort to achieve income and wealth redistribution along racial lines, to enhance political participation in any substantial way on the part of racially defined minorities, or to foster widespread cultural reorientation with respect to race and racism.

From the standpoint of the antiracist movements, official white supremacy and de jure segregation were defeated, and a modicum of access to the mainstream institutions of the country—economic, political, and cultural—

was achieved, at least for minority middle-classes.[18] But this came at the price of having to abandon larger hopes for more radical reforms and social restructuring. It required the repudiation of those activists and organizations who sought such broader social transformations, and the abandonment of the hopes of millions of immiserated ghetto and barrio dwellers, now labeled the "underclass."

Plus ça change, plus c'est la même chose. The epoch of the postwar racial break ended in the United States with the onset of a new racial regime, one that could defuse the ferocious conflicts that had developed since the war, yet that could still maintain a substantial continuity with the legacies of past white supremacism. Yes, white supremacy had been wounded, but not mortally. It had again proven itself quite capable of metamorphosis: absorbing and adapting much of the "dream," and repackaging itself as "colorblind," pluralist, nonracialist, and meritocratic.

Racial Politics Today

The racial politics that results from this synthesis of challenge and incorporation, racial conflict and racial reform, has proved neither stable nor satisfying. Both globally and locally it is a strange brew, often appearing more inclusive, more pluralistic than ever before, yet also filled with threats of "ethnic cleansing," resurgent neofascism, and perhaps equally insidious, renewed racial complacency. What conclusions, theoretical and political, can we draw from all this about twenty-first-century racial dynamics?

First, to understand the changing significance of race at the end of the twentieth century, the century whose central malady was diagnosed by Du Bois as "the problem of the color-line," requires us to acknowledge the possibility that racial inequality and injustice no longer operate so clearly through a color-line at all. This is not to deny the continuing significance of race and color; it is merely to recognize the augmented flexibility, the fungibility, of racial meanings and racialized social structures after the complex realignments of the post–World War II racial break.[19]

If the meaning of race and the logic of racism have changed, our understandings and practices of antiracism must change too. The inheritors of the postwar antiracist movements, from the African National Congress in South Africa and the Movimento Negro Unificado in Brazil, to SOS Racisme in France and a wide variety of antiracist groups in the United States, must recognize the obsolescence of their own concepts, at least in the following ways:

They (we) must realize that it is dangerous to assign to the state the task of safeguarding racial justice. Seeking redress for grievances of racial discrimination, hate crimes, or institutionalized racism tends to underestimate the extent to which the state is already itself racialized. The exercise of racial hegemony, the incorporation of antiracist opposition, has demonstrated yet again that the state is a thoroughly racial institution, just as much as it was in the days of de jure segregation, apartheid, or colonialism. As such it is incapable of intervening effectively in racial conflicts from an outside and putatively "neutral" position, incapable of more than palliative antiracist action. While it may still be desirable to place such demands on the state—for example, by seeking extension of civil rights laws or judicial intervention against discriminatory practices—this cannot substitute for direct political mobilization: confrontational, negotiated, or even electoral. Indeed, casting the state in the role of resolving racial conflict tends to discredit and delegitimate autonomous (civil society–based) mobilization on racial grounds.

They (we) must reexamine our time-honored reliance on egalitarianism. As the New Right and neoconservatives in the United States, and neofascists like the Front Nationale in France and the FPÖ in Austria have demonstrated,[20] after the racial break it is has become possible to uphold the principle of racial equality while simultaneously steadfastly opposing such practical antiracist policies as income and wealth redistribution or positive antidiscrimination (for example, affirmative action, reparations for slavery, and cancellation of international debt).[21]

Both these points draw on critical race theory (CRT) and its understanding of the limits of rights-based politics (Delgado and Stefancic 2001; Valdes, Culp, and Harris 2002). I do not wish to imply, though, (and I don't think CRT people do either) that rights politics and egalitarian demands are entirely wrong or impractical; rather they are inadequate in the face of racial hegemony, and largely incapable of effectively countering their rearticulation by the political right in the aftermath of the racial break.

Amid all this analysis of racially grounded social structures, we should look more closely at the microsocial dynamics of race: the way racial practices operate on the experiential level. Here the whole legacy of sociological pragmatism comes into play:[22] a crucial "micro-" legacy of the racial break is the recognition that a whole lot of everyday life is racially interpreted, experienced in a way inflected by race, and therefore at least potentially subject to a deep set of democratic impulses and motivations.

Finally, we really must jettison our tendency to see racial matters as belonging to domestic political and policy spheres. In this essay I have attempted to address more seriously the international dimensions of racial injustice and racial politics. As social movements, including antiracist ones, become ever more transnational in their orientation, it becomes possible to see the local and national features of racism more clearly and comparatively. Indeed racial dynamics can be more effectively grasped when they are understood not as deviations from supposedly central democratic and egalitarian ideals (of the nation, the Enlightenment, modernity, etc.), but as historically and sociologically constitutive of nation, economy, polity, culture, and personal experience.[23]

One hundred years after the publication of *The Souls of Black Folk*, a century after Du Bois's announcement of the "problem of the color-line" and presentation of the first radical democratic theory of racism, half a century after the onset of the racial break and the prolonged invention of racial hegemony, where do racial politics stand? In this essay I have traced, undoubtedly in all too schematic and cursory fashion, the vast trajectory of racial conflict over the course of the twentieth century. This vertiginous history of triumph and tragedy has left us, on the threshold of the twenty-first century, still far short of the racially inclusive democracy we seek. Despite real gains achieved by enormous effort and sacrifice, racial justice still remains in short supply all across the planet. The stigmata of race are still highly visible.

The struggle continues.

Dialectics of the Veil

W. E. B. Du Bois's concept of "the veil," first fully articulated in *The Souls of Black Folk* (1903b), contains the most nuanced and powerful theory of race and racism ever developed. Du Bois understands the veil dialectically. This philosophical term *dialectic* refers to a relationship that simultaneously embodies both antagonism and interdependence, that develops over historical time, and that links the small-scale and large-scale (or "micro" and "macro") dimensions of social life. The concept represented by Du Bois as the veil operates, in other words, both at the level of the personal or intrapsychic and at the institutional or structural level of social interaction. It evolves over historical time. And it expresses both the conflict, exclusion, and alienation inherent in the dynamics of race and racism, and the interdependence, knowledge of "the other," and thwarted desires that characterize these phenomena.

Souls, of course, is about race and racism in the United States. Although elsewhere in Du Bois's lifework the concept of the veil is applied more broadly, he first theorized it—drawing on a wide range of philosophical sources of both European and African American provenance—in order to interpret and transform the black-white racial dynamic that had been historically and socially dominant in the United States since the onset of African slavery.

The most famous point Du Bois makes in presenting his concept of the veil is his idea of "double consciousness" or racial dualism. He argues that "double consciousness" both afflicts and transfigures the black soul: dividing its experience and self-awareness, "introjecting" racism into the racially oppressed self,[1] and also affording that self some means of defense against racial oppression. Here at the individual and experiential level we already have a fully fledged dialectic. Yet Du Bois is at pains to show how the veil's operation at this "microsocial" level is but an instance, albeit a vital one, of a far broader and deeper phenomenon. The veil not only divides the individual self; it also fissures the community, nation, and society as a whole (and, ultimately, world society in its entirety). The veil's antagonisms, however, are also thoroughgoing interrelationships, such that it not only splits self and world along the "color-line," but simultaneously founds the self and produces the social world.

I first read *The Souls of Black Folk* in the mid-1960s. I was a teenage antiracist activist then, and I was particularly struck by the concept: it seemed a symbol for the irrationality of racism. For quite a few years after that, I thought of the veil only as an obstacle to racial justice and equality. It all seemed so simple: any barrier dividing human beings along racial grounds, I thought in my movement zeal, needed to be removed. I wanted the veil to be immediately lifted, so that we could "just be" with one another: equal, free at last, undifferentiated by race.

Today—many years later—I see Du Bois's concept of the veil somewhat differently. I still understand the veil as a metaphor for the racial barrier of the "color-line," Du Bois's "problem of the twentieth century." Du Bois surely meant it that way, but that was not all he meant. He did not only seek to lift the veil, the act I naively thought would achieve the straightforward restoration of the common humanity that had been so cruelly and illogically deformed by racism. He was also searching for a means to transform the veil, a way to preserve the differences it demarcated but not the status distinctions it reified.

For Du Bois, the veil is a complex metaphor for the dynamics of race. It represents both barrier and connection between white and black. Imagine it as a filmy fabric, a soft and semitransparent border marker, that both keeps the races apart and mediates between them. On the one hand Du Bois harbored the faith—especially in his younger days—that once the country, once white America in particular, came to understand more fully the injustice of racism, it would move to overcome it, perhaps invoking its Lincolnian "better angels." In some time to come, then, when whites would at last evince a willingness fully to share American life and society with blacks, when whites' and blacks' acceptance of each other (and even love for each other, absurd as that might initially sound) could finally be acknowledged and made manifest, then the veil would no longer be needed, or wanted, or accepted.

Du Bois was certainly a committed antiracist, but as his lifework and political trajectory advanced, he came to doubt that the United States could ever achieve true racial equality, that it could ever abolish the "color-line," that it could ever lift the veil.

If this had been the ideal of his early days, by his middle career he was struggling with the racial transformations that accompanied World War I: the contradictions of Wilsonian doctrine, the disappointments of Versailles, the horrors of the "red summer" of 1919, and the racial meaning of the Russian Revolution. From the 1930s on he embraced a more radical perspective, one that drew strongly on Marxism and on a militant and anti-colonialist nationalism. So by the appearance of *Dusk of Dawn* (1940) the veil had acquired a great deal more solidity. Du Bois depicts it there not as a thin film but as a thick glass barrier. It is still transparent, but it is also impenetrable. It cuts off all sound and communication. It renders black experience unintelligible—but also cruelly amusing—to whites who bother to look through it. And for blacks looking out at their tormentors from within the glass cage, there can be little more than rage and despair.

During the last years of his life, when the postwar civil rights movement had already burst upon the scene, and when (during the cold war) he had been meretriciously attacked and abused, Du Bois expressed deep skepticism about the possibility of a reform-oriented, integrationist racial politics. Increasingly he argued that the veil not only confined and excluded black people, but that it also protected them from at least some forms of white violence and domination.

Is racism indeed so fundamental to U.S. culture and social structure, so deeply interwoven into white character structure, that it occludes all transracial empathy? Does it pose such a systematic barrier not only to black progress and mobility but also to black self-awareness? Du Bois wrestled with these issues throughout his life. But no matter how disillusioned he became, he never succumbed to unremitting gloom and despair. Just as he retained his dual commitment to black peoplehood and American equality, just as he upheld his dual commitment to black peoplehood and socialism, he always recognized the ambiguities and contradictions, the political flexibility of the veil. He was ever its dialectician.

At the end of his life he saw that the veil was being transformed again. His last years were the cold war years, the time of the downfall of the old imperialisms and the onset of the civil rights era. In the 1950s and early 1960s (Du Bois died in 1963 at the age of ninety-five) he was still saying that the veil could not be lifted: this would only serve to expose black folk to the full force of racial subjugation, which by the mid-twentieth century would not have meant renewed slavery but might have portended something almost worse, if that is possible: the "bleaching" of the black soul, the compulsory abandonment of blackness and black identity (Du Bois 1960).

So what is the veil then? Is it a barrier or a defense, a curse or a blessing? Is it a flimsy and rent fabric or a rigid, imprisoning cage? Is it a mark we wear or a role we play? Is it the demands we make for our freedom or the restriction of our freedom brought about by state racial policy? Is it a cleavage within our racialized society or indeed a schism inside every racialized self? It is, I want to argue here, all of these, and more.

The Veil as Racial Dialectic

The philosophical term *dialectic* refers to a logical method, a style of reasoning, that proceeds through the posing and resolution of contradictions. Although dialectical thinking has its origins in Greek philosophy, its deepest modern association is with the Enlightenment-based philosophies of Hegel and Marx, who applied it to social theory and the philosophy of history. For them, all social relationships simultaneously contained both antagonistic and interdependent elements; they developed over historical time through the framing and resolution of contradiction; and they inexorably linked the experiential and the structural dimensions of social existence (Marcuse 1963).

Du Bois's concept of the veil was certainly rooted in the Hegelian tradition. The whole framework of double consciousness draws on this legacy: it describes a subjectivity both sundered and fused, an identity divided by forces originating both within and outside the self. The concept of the veil also recognizes the black soul's striving for wholeness, for synthesis and integration: after all, its "dogged strength alone keeps it from being torn asunder." Besides this, Du Bois drew on the various currents of German nationalist thought—themselves Hegelian—to which he had been exposed during his studies in that country. The concept also contained images of racial collectivity, destiny, and mission that he had absorbed at Fisk: the abolitionist legacy, Ethiopianism, racial uplift, the legacy of the Jubilee singers, the influences of Crummell and Blyden. Du Bois also infused his theory of the veil with the developing pragmatist philosophy of Pierce and James that he had absorbed at Harvard. This was a body of thought that had great affinities with dialectical reasoning.[2] Finally, there were his historical studies, which bore fruit in his dissertation on the suppression of the African slave trade (Du Bois 1896). Here was the early macrohistory of the veil, which lay in the world historical conflict between the Atlantic slave system and nascent capitalism's developing interest in "free" (that is, rented, not owned) labor. The ongoing historical dialectic of the veil plays a central role in *Souls*—notably in the chapter "Of the Dawn of Freedom" and the treatment of Booker T. Washington—and then reaches its climax in Du Bois's masterpiece *Black Reconstruction* (1935).

Because race and racism are more or less omnipresent in U.S. society, the veil—which is their metaphor—does not need documentation. What I aim to do here is to demonstrate the flexibility of the veil and its quintessentially political character. In a general way I adopt an "overdetermination" approach to the problem of the dialectic of the veil. In other words, I argue that the concept of the veil is effective in analyzing the depth and breadth of race and racism because it so seamlessly links the numerous sites where they are present in U.S. society (and ultimately on a global scale, though that is not my main subject here). Certainly the veil divides the human psyche and figures the human body; yet it also fissures soul and body, nation, collectivity, polity, history, and culture. Since every U.S. institution as well as every identity is partitioned by race and racism, fractured by the veil, and since at the same time the entire society owes its existence to the workings of race and racism[3]—to the presence of the veil—the concept necessarily takes on an accretive quality. The veil signifies a profound social structure that has been built up for centuries, accumulating among the infinite contradictions of race and racism as they have shaped our identities and social organization.

This great weight of accrued indignity and injustice, privilege and exclusion, at times seems to pinion the social system under an immovable burden, to constitute a deadening inertia made of a racial injustice that seemingly can never be budged. Yet the veil is always unstable and contradictory: the weight of racial oppression is bound up with the implacable will to resist. Thus, at key moments, more rare perhaps but still crucially important, the sheer weight of the veil—qua social structure—becomes insupportable. The built-up rage and inequity, the irrationality and inutility, and the explosive force of dreams denied have sometimes been mobilized politically in

ways that can only be termed quasi-revolutionary. When racially based challenges have occurred at this level, they have brought about "breaks" in the
system: if not revolutions, at least serious social transformations. Such ruptural moments are rare and necessarily conjunctural: they arise only when
large-scale social crises occur, crises that both enable such seismic political
ruptures and are themselves produced by them. Hence "breaks" or ruptures
in the veil may be said to be *overdetermined*.[4] In U.S. racial history we may
discern two such breaks, two moments when the fabric of the veil was torn,
if not dissolved: during and after the Civil War, and during and after World
War II.

Such shifts are primarily political events, phenomena of crisis. They occur
when the instability of the old racial system becomes too great and opposition
acquires too much disruptive power to be successfully ignored or repressed.
When the dialectic of the veil means in practical terms that the white
supremacist system depends too comprehensively and openly on the racially
oppressed—as occurred during the Civil War and during the post–World
War II period—then the logic of racial rule, the very fabric of the veil,
threatens to burst apart.[5] Du Bois's lifelong emphasis on the primacy of
racial politics—visible most clearly in his controversies with Washington
and with Garvey, both of whom refused engagement with the U.S. political
system—can best be understood in terms of this larger or macrosocial understanding of the veil.

At such ruptural moments both identity and social structure undergo
profound alteration. Racial identity is fundamental in the United States;
when slavery was abolished (if not entirely superseded) after the Civil War,
when a century later the system of official segregation was outlawed (if not
entirely abolished), these developments profoundly altered U.S. racial identities and social practices. At the same time, obviously enough, such racial
breaks deeply transformed the larger social structure. They overturned established patterns of economic, political, and cultural life. They fostered widespread conflict and new modes of social organization and collective
action (from the reaction of the Klan, to the rise of new forms of black
nationalism). And they engendered new efforts to explain and theorize the
meaning of race. Du Bois's own development and indeed his theory of the
veil were themselves products of his particular national and historical location; this fact is repeatedly emphasized in *Souls*. Indeed the book's entire
structure is predicated on the interaction between the transformative experience undergone by all of Afro-America in the post–Civil War period on
the one hand, and the author's own developing awareness of race, his bur-

geoning encounter with the "peculiar sensation" of "double consciousness," on the other.

Thus, we can understand the veil as operating simultaneously at the "micro" level of identity, experience, the divisions and struggles within the racialized self, and at the "macro" level of the social whole, the collectivity, the state, history, the nation. It furnishes a conceptual tool, an "anatomy" of racial formation, whose significance derives precisely from the various levels (or the various "instances," to speak structuralese for a moment) at which it shapes society. Such is the dialectic of the veil.

The Twentieth-Century History of the Veil

The past century was the one whose "problem," Du Bois famously predicted, was to be "the color-line." And it was. But now that century is over; its "problem" is certainly not.

During the first half of the twentieth century, from the moment when *Souls* appeared until the onset of World War II, the taken-for-granted rule of the system of white supremacy remained in place. That is to say, although faced with increasing opposition and perhaps unraveling incrementally, the fabric of the veil was not ruptured. Numerous conflicts and tensions accumulated as black people left the South by the millions and established greater influence in the North and Midwest. Black migration, entrance into the industrial labor force, participation in the Great War, and above all political mobilization along various lines—reformist, nationalist/pan-Africanist, socialist/communist—all called the dynamics of race and racism into question.

The veil was being tugged and stretched from what Du Bois called "within"—from its black side. But it was also being reinforced from "without"—from the white side. The "Atlanta compromise" of Booker T. Washington had not pacified racial conflict very much, and had ameliorated racial oppression not at all; Washington's death in 1915 left a vacuum in the zone of racial collaboration. Returning soldiers were lynched, and black communities assaulted after World War I ended, and the red scares of the 1920s were black scares too. The Ku Klux Klan attained a formidable public presence in the 1920s, operating not only in the South but also in the midwestern heartland. In the 1930s the Democratic "solid South" adhered to the New Deal coalition, demanding (and receiving) in return the loyalty of Roosevelt: there was to be no federal sanction on lynching, no serious inclusion of black workers in the labor reforms of the 1930s, no intrusion on the

Dixiecrats' disenfranchisement of blacks, indeed no challenge to their exercise of a racial dictatorship in the American South, which was effectively an American internal colony. That the Democratic Party could remain so monolithically racist at the same time that black voters (those who were permitted to vote) were deserting the party of Lincoln in droves (see Weiss 1983) testifies both to the resilience of the veil and to its impending political crisis. Yes, there were small reforms, and there was Mrs. Roosevelt, the president's ambassador across the color-line, but her role was largely confined to the propitiatory and symbolic.

Only with the coming of World War II was national attention turned again to the black hand side: indeed the hands of black workers were needed; black soldiers and sailors were required again, as they had been during World War I. Once again blacks responded to the call, but this time they made more serious demands: for desegregation of war industries and for integration of the armed forces. Roosevelt defused A. Philip Randolph's threatened march on Washington in 1941 by acceding to the former demand (although wartime labor practices were only partially reformed). But military desegregation was delayed until 1947. The war years were riddled with racial conflict—sometimes armed confrontations and "riots"—on military bases and even on the battlefield (Kryder 2000; Peery 1995).

Still, for obvious reasons the black movement grew and deepened during the war, sparking the break that occurred in racial politics in the postwar decades. Racial reform followed hard upon the war's end: not only did military desegregation take place, but epic battles were fought for control of the trade unions and the Democratic Party in the 1940s. Anticommunism was the main tune being played, but very often the shrill notes of McCarthyism were grounded in a firm base (or "bass"?) of racism (N. Lichtenstein 1989).

The break represented by the rise of the civil rights movement—usually dated from the *Brown* decision of 1954 and the Montgomery events of 1955—was really but a continuous building up of the contradictions of the veil, an overdetermined outgrowth of the consequences of the war, combined with numerous other racial pressures: the long-simmering struggles of earlier decades, the greatly transformed world situation in which the United States was now the hegemonic power (Dudziak 2000), and above all the massive mobilization of black people on a scale not seen since the Civil War or perhaps the Garvey movement's heyday.

As a result of this conjuncture of pressures the veil was dramatically rewoven: the most loathsome forms of racial dictatorship were ameliorated as state racial policy abandoned its explicit support for Jim Crow. As noted, a shift in racial identity also occurred, generating greater pride among blacks and other racially defined minority groups in the United States, and also initiating a mild version of racial "double consciousness" among whites and "other others"; let us call it a "paler" version. This shift in racial politics took shape at both the micro- and macrosocial levels, prompted both by movement pressure and by various global influences. As a result of the enactment of civil rights reforms, political exclusion was replaced by a limited form of political participation. Blacks were finally enfranchised—though not without problems—a full century after the passage of the Fourteenth Amendment (July 25, 1868).

During the second half of the twentieth century, and in most respects down to now (2003), racial politics and race consciousness have been transformed again. The veil is being rewoven again.

The achievement of reforms in U.S. racial policy was a real victory. It was a limited one, however: only "moderate" black currents were deemed fit for representation in the American political mainstream, significant racial repression was maintained, and radical alternatives were isolated, discredited, and assaulted. Perhaps most damaging to the cause of freedom and racial justice, the egalitarian demands of the movement were incorporated in suitably neutered form into mainstream racial discourse and policy. Thus did the rhetoric of "color blindness" and "reverse racism" frame some familiar tropes in post–civil rights era America.

Today racially conscious political opposition and indeed antiracist movements in general have been divided by the successes of the very reforms they sought, even though those successes were never more than partial and incomplete. The movement is no longer what it was in the 1960s or 1970s. It has been a victim of its own victories; it has been incorporated. The racial state has proved relatively effective at reinterpreting (or "rearticulating") movement demands in conservative and individualist, though ostensibly egalitarian, terms. Because it has "learned a new racial language," so to speak, the state has actually been able to fortify the racially oppressive policy of "lockdown America" in the criminal (so-called) justice system, and to maintain the "savage inequalities" of the public education system, all the while claiming that it is now "beyond race." Again the veil has shifted: to promote black (or brown, or red, or yellow) race "consciousness" today is to invite criticism from whites—and from those few nonwhites who have adopted the "color-blind" stance—that one is a "reverse racist." Radicals and nationalists are told to "get over it." Those who sneer at antiracism evince little concern for redlining and racial steering in the housing market, employment discrimination, persistent and comprehensive school segregation, and ongoing violence and racial profiling by the police, the border patrol, the courts, the electoral system, and the media.

Indeed, the same people who today avow color blindness find themselves experiencing a new version of "double consciousness": *the white kind.* "I don't see color," many of my white students tell me. "You can be black, white, green, or purple. I treat everyone as an individual." Yet they also stick closely to their own segregated neighborhoods, listen to their own rock stations, and count on the benevolence of the police.[6] Of course, the veil is not only about separation; it is also about "crossing over." Many of these same (male) students wear their pants in the baggy "sag" fashion of the black B-boys who set popular styles in this country. White working-class girls show up in class with cornrows or dress in "ghetto fabulous" fashion. "Wiggers" abound: the desire for "otherness," so central to the veil, lives on among whites. They know they are supposed to reject racism, and indeed they consider themselves nonracist. But they also *need* racism: it protects their jobs, their property, their neighborhood schools, their "standard of living." Their psychic demand for "security" is still served by it; their feelings of vulnerability are still figured racially. Their racial privileges—and the contradictions inherent within them—are the lineaments of their social identities.

The Future of the Veil

What patterns of development can we expect to see in U.S. race and racism in the twenty-first century? What principal contradictions will inform and transform the dialectic of the veil in the years ahead? Of course both prediction and prescription are off-limits to us. But I still wish to consider these questions, perhaps rushing in where angels fear to tread.

Three general patterns, I think, will be woven into the fabric of the veil in the years ahead. These are the continuing depth and comprehensiveness of racial identity, the tenacity of racism as a system of social injustice and unfreedom, and the precarious state of racial democracy.

Racial identity remains. It is continually being undermined and reproduced at both the experiential and institutional levels of social life. The meaning of race is permanently in question, as is the content of any racialized group identity: consider not only whiteness and blackness in this context but also Asianness, *conciencia de la raza*, Indianness, the revived credibility of orientalism, and the resurgent Islamophobia of the present, just to pick some major contemporary examples.

The boundaries of the race concept are also problematic: to what extent is race somaticized, phenotypic, corporeal (to use but some of the familiar terms that link racial identity to the body), and to what extent is race performative, socialized, cultural?[7] This last question problematizes the border between the racial, which is supposedly inherent, ineluctable, and intrinsic, and the ethnonational, which can be learned (or unlearned).

These are extremely large issues that cannot be adequately managed in the space of a brief essay.[8] The boundary between the two categories of race and ethnicity is always contested. Race and ethnicity are social constructs, not objective phenomena. In practice racial and ethnonational ways of seeing the social world often compete for explanatory and mobilizational purchase. That is to say, they signify distinct but overlapping discourses, similar but far from congruent identities and practices.

Cultural differences matter, but at the same time any "ethnic" group can be racialized. Some examples: the Nazis effectively racialized the German Jews, although they could often not tell by mere visual cues who was Jewish; the British racialized the Irish, and the Bosnian Serbs racialized the Bosnian Muslims, although there were no categorical phenotypical differences between either pair. The Rwanda and Burundi Hutu and Tutsi racialized each other. In all these cases (and many others we could name) there had been substantial interbreeding, group mixing via migration and colonial rule, and significant if intermittent periods when racial distinctions were notably effaced.[9]

Why does racial identity remain significant in the face of its contemporary dismissal as a relic of a benighted past, an "illusion" that we must now "get beyond"? We return to the dialectic of the veil to answer this question. For all its fungibility and flexibility, race continues to code the social locations and identities of individuals and groups in terms of what Weber called status. It continues to offer an immediately available classificatory framework that is useful in establishing what Blumer (1958) labeled "group position" in respect to a great variety of issues: resource distribution, group demographic differences and territoriality, political power, cultural practices, and so on. Most significant in perpetuating racial distinctions, though, is the dualism that Du Bois suggested traversed and informed these differences. Dualism remains the essential meaning of the veil, the heart of its dialectic: racial identity establishes not only the norms of oppression and subordination but also those of self-assurance and autogestion or self-determination. The latter concept, whether understood in the familiar collective and nationalist sense ("imagined communities," etc.) or in terms of the "centering" of the self, is as much a component of racialization as group-based domination. Where there is domination, there is resistance; this is another fundamental dimension of the dialectics of the veil.

Thus racial identity is not merely an instrument of rule; it is also an arena and medium of social practice. It is an aspect of individual and collective selfhood. Racial identity, in other words, does all sorts of practical "work": it shapes privileged status for some and undermines the social standing of others. It appeals to varied political constituencies, inclusive and exclusive. It codes everyday life in an infinite number of ways. How foolish, then, to claim that race is merely an archaism, a concept left over from an unenlightened past![10] The idea of getting "beyond race" is as utopian—and ultimately as undesirable—as other homogenizing utopian objectives: a classless society, a world government, the abolition of gender distinctions, and so on.

Yet the permanence of race, the continuity of the veil, does not preclude movement toward greater justice and freedom. Other group distinctions, once seen as similarly intractable—such as religious difference—have been transmuted into far less invidious forms. Obviously I would not want to overstate that, for religious intolerance and oppression still abound. But I think the point is clear: pluralism matters; substantive (not merely formal) equality matters; freedom matters; democracy remains precarious.

Racism remains. Racism continues to operate as a system of social injustice and unfreedom, even in an era—after the post–World War II break— when nonracism has achieved some degree of official consensus as a universal norm. In this historical situation, when white supremacy has been delegitimized so extensively, what accounts for the continuity of racism?

The work of Joe R. Feagin is indispensable in answering this question in the U.S. context. Feagin and his coauthor Hernán Vera argue that most racist practices are relatively invisible. Whites in particular find it easy not to think about race, not to consider themselves prejudiced toward racially defined minorities, not to recognize the ways in which they

> ...have created a set of "sincere fictions"—personal mythologies that
> reproduce societal mythologies at the individual level. Whites generally
> use these fictions to define themselves as "not racist," as "good people,"
> even as they think and act in antiblack ways.... The sincere fictions
> embedded in white personalities and white society are about both the black
> other *and* the white self. (Feagin and Vera 1995, 14; emphasis in original)

In other words racism inheres in us as individuals not as some outworn relic, but because it performs valuable psychological work. This analysis of "sincere fictions" is deeply linked to Du Bois's account of white racial identity as producing a "psychological wage"—that is, a privileged social location—relative to blacks' social positioning in the United States. This model has some important consequences: because racism is a social structure in which all Americans are embedded—Feagin calls this "slavery refusing to die" (2000)—the fact that it is recognized or even criticized does not serve to dispel it. This is a peculiar situation for antiracists, even antiracist activists: we occupy and indeed have been socialized into the very terrain we are trying to transform. Here again we see the dialectic of the veil in operation.[11]

So racism remains because it has played a central role in creating American society (and the modern world) over the past half millennium or so, and because it continues unjustly to allocate the values that Americans (and the world's peoples in general) produce. Racism remains, in short, because it still "pays off" in substantial ways, even under the putatively antiracist consensus of the twenty-first century. So the veil has proved itself capable of adapting very well to antiracist reforms. This is true both at the microsocial level of the self, the individual who must interpret and "theorize" her own experience, and at the macrosocial level of our economic, political, and cultural institutions, where resources are distributed and our "collective representations" (a Durkheimian phrase) are produced, challenged, and changed.

Democracy remains precarious. Du Bois's intellectual and practical accomplishments continue to inspire. One hundred years after the appearance of *The Souls of Black Folk,* his analysis of race and racism, explored through the concept of the veil, retains its explanatory power. Why is this so? Because the idea of the veil helps explain the vast importance of racial identity, racial oppression and resistance, and racialized social structures in the creation and organization of the modern world. As a theoretical framework that addresses and links the "micro" and "macro" social meaning of race, that illuminates the continuity and transformation of racial conflict from the historic past to the unresolved racial present, and that illustrates the connections between the racial contradictions within the human soul and those of national (and global) society, the concept of the veil transcends all other attempts to thematize and analyze racial dynamics. I have argued here that this sort of conceptual range and depth is best understood by grasping the dialectical reasoning that informs and molds the concept of the veil.

The meaning of race has evolved tremendously over the one hundred years since *Souls.* Especially over the past decades, understandings of race and racism, and social structures and practices crucial to the contours of the veil, have changed dramatically. Yet in racial terms democracy remains precarious. Race-conscious democracy has never been realized. The dialectical synthesis of Duboisian racial dualism has yet to be achieved. Neither in the United States nor at a transnational level is it at all possible to synthesize recognition of racial difference with full-scale equality, social justice, and freedom for all.

To be sure, there has been real racial reform. But ironically this has imposed huge new dilemmas on those who strive for racial justice, both through political work and through cultural/intellectual work. Much of the current confusion, anxiety, and debate about the continuity and extent of racism, as well as about various issues of racial politics (affirmative action, debt peonage, immigration, welfare, etc.) can be explained in terms of this unprecedented situation. The dialectics of the veil still operate.

In this confused and tormented atmosphere, in which race and racism are simultaneously acknowledged and denied, the figure of the veil can prove useful once more. The deep dialectic of race and racism must be affirmed against those who consider these themes anachronistic or wish to "get over" them. The belief is commonplace, the idea is everywhere, from right to left, from integrationism to nationalism, and so on, that race is declining in significance, that it is an outmoded analytical concept, and that it plays no important part in the organization of the "new world order." This position must be challenged in different ways: by disputing it through historical analysis, by contrasting its variations among nations as they have emerged in recent years, and by exploring the interplay between global racial dynamics and national racial formations. But most centrally, the idea that we are somehow "beyond race" must be challenged in terms of theoretical and political analysis. Vital as it was to overcome the old systems of racial oppression, it is just as important to understand that today new antiracist battle lines have appeared. The concept of the veil, the dialectics of the veil, still provide our most effective tool in the struggle to achieve racial justice and democracy.

Racism Today:
Continuity and Change in the
Post–Civil Rights United States

In the complex crosscurrents of the post–civil rights era, what is racism? Is it the same old thing, or has it changed in response to the changing dynamics of race itself in the post–civil rights era? To answer such questions, to understand the meaning of racism today, to take an informed and politically effective stand in such complex crosscurrents is no easy matter.

Before we even tackle the matter of racism, we must first develop a working understanding of what we mean by race. This is not so easy either. Today we recognize that the concept of race is problematic, that the meaning of race is socially constructed and politically contested. This is a hard-won recognition, one that has obtained fairly generally only since World War II (Omi and Winant 1994).

But obviously problematizing race is not enough. We must steer between the Scylla of thinking that race is a mere illusion, mere ideology (in the sense of false consciousness), on the one hand, and the Charybdis of thinking that race is something objective and fixed. Both of these positions have their temptations, and by no means only for those who would deny the significance of race. The former position ("race as illusory") is upheld today not only by neoconservatives (such as Shelby Steele or Jim Sleeper) but also by more radical theorists of race (such as Anthony Appiah and Barbara Fields). In the work of these scholars, whatever its other merits, there is little recognition of the autonomy and depth of racialization in the United

States. The latter view ("race as objective") is accepted not only by biological determinists and scientific racists but also by many social scientists (some of them quite progressive), for example, William Julius Wilson, Milton Gordon, and Michael Banton. In the work of these analysts, whatever its other merits, there is little recognition of the socially constructed, politically contested meaning of racial categories, of racial identity, of racialized experience.

In contrast to these approaches, Michael Omi and I have proposed a theory of racial formation, which looks at race not only as the subject of struggle and contest at the level of social structure but also as a contested theme at the level of social signification, of the production of meanings. By the former we mean such issues as the racial dimensions of social stratification and distribution, of institutional arrangements, political systems, laws, and so on. By the latter we mean the ways in which race is culturally figured and represented, the manner in which race comes to be meaningful as a descriptor of group or individual identity, social issues, and experience.

We have sought to theorize racial formation as a permanent process in which historically situated projects interact: in the clash and conflict, as well as the accommodation and overlap of these projects, human bodies and consciousness, as well as social institutions and structures, are represented and organized. We argue that in any given historical context, racial signification and racial structuration are ineluctably linked. To represent, interpret, or signify upon race, then, to assign meaning to it, is at least implicitly and often explicitly to locate it in social structural terms.

The linkage between culture and structure, which is at the core of the racial formation process, gives racial projects their coherence and unity. Thus, once it is argued that the United States is inherently a "white man's country" (as in certain far right racial discourses), or that race is a spurious anachronism beneath the notice of the state (as in neoconservative positions), or that racial difference is a matter of "self-determination" (as in certain radical racial discourses), the appropriate political orientations, economic and social programs, and so on follow rather quickly.

The reverse is also true: when organizations, institutions, or state agencies advocate or resist a certain racial policy or practice, when they mobilize politically along racial lines, they necessarily engage in racial signification, at least implicitly and usually explicitly. Thus, when the Supreme Court rules that individualism and meritocracy are the only legitimate criteria for employment decisions or university admissions, it inevitably and simultaneously represents race as illusory and spurious. Let me give some other examples.

Consider the implications when spokespersons for the Aryan Nations or the Church of the Creator (two U.S. fascist groups) propose setting aside areas of the country for "whites only": in this structural initiative they simultaneously represent race as a natural, invariant, biological difference. On the polar opposite end of the political spectrum, consider what happens when radical democratic organizations, such as the Highlander Center or UNITE—the needle trades union—engage in community or labor organizing that seeks both to build multiracial organizations and to recognize the relevance of distinct racialized experiences among their constituents. Here too, in this effort to mobilize politically, to change the social structure, they necessarily represent race in terms of decenteredness, flexibility, and the relative permanence of difference, embracing the Duboisian synthesis of full democracy and racial "conservation" (Du Bois 1897).

Keep this idea of racial formation via racial projects on hold while the discussion is refocused on racism; I shall return to the dynamics of racial formation presently. In what follows I shall first discuss the transformations that have affected the concept of racism since the ambiguous triumph of the civil rights "revolution" in the mid-1960s. Next, I shall offer an account of contemporary racism that I believe more adequately addresses present conditions. Finally, in a brief conclusion, I shall offer some thoughts about the changing link between racial formation and racism in the twenty-first century.

Our Concept of Racism Has Deteriorated

The understanding we have of racism, an understanding that was forged in the 1960s, is now severely deficient. A quarter century of sociopolitical struggle has rendered it inadequate to the demands of the present. At the same time, I would hardly wish to argue (in the manner of neoconservatives) that racism itself has been largely eliminated in the post–civil rights era. But although we are quite sure that racism continues to exist, indeed flourish, we are less than certain about what it means today.

In fact, since the ambiguous triumph of the civil rights movement in the mid-1960s, clarity about what racism means has been slipping away. The concept entered the lexicon of "common sense" only in the 1960s. Before that, although the term had surfaced occasionally, the problem of racial injustice and inequality was generally understood in a more limited fashion, as a matter of prejudiced attitudes or bigotry on the one hand, and of discriminatory actions on the other.

Solutions, it was believed, would therefore involve two elements: first, the overcoming of prejudiced attitudes through the achievement of toler-ance, the acceptance of "brotherhood," and so on; and second, the passage of laws that prohibited discrimination with respect to access to public accom-modations, jobs, education, and so on. Social scientific work tended to focus on the origins of prejudiced attitudes (Adorno et al. 1950; Allport 1954), on the interests served by discrimination (Rose 1948; Becker 1957; Thurow 1969), and on the ways in which prejudice and discrimination combined or conflicted with each other (Merton 1949).

The early civil rights movement explicitly reflected such views. In its espousal of integration and its quest for a "beloved community," it sought to overcome racial prejudice. In its litigation activities and agitation for civil rights legislation, it sought to challenge discriminatory practices.

The later 1960s, however, signaled a sharp break with this vision. The emergence of the slogan "black power" (and, soon after, "brown power," "red power," and "yellow power"), the wave of riots that swept the urban ghettos from 1964 to 1968, and the founding of radical movement organizations of nationalist and Marxist orientation, all coincided with the recognition that racial inequality and injustice had much deeper roots. They were not simply the product of prejudice, nor was discrimination only a matter of intention-ally informed action. Rather, prejudice was an almost unavoidable outcome of patterns of socialization that were "bred in the bone," affecting not only whites but even minorities themselves. Discrimination, far from manifesting itself only (or even principally) through individual actions or conscious policies, was a structural feature of U.S. society, a product of centuries of sys-tematic exclusion, exploitation, and also cultural assaults of various types upon racially defined minorities. Although patterns of structural inequality might change and ideas about race might be flexible (or even "socially con-structed"), their elementality and continuity, their importance in providing fundamental order within U.S. society, were never in doubt.

It was this combination of relationships, prejudice, discrimination, and structural inequality (aka "institutional racism") that defined the concept of racism at the end of the 1960s (Carmichael and Hamilton 1967). Without a doubt, such a synthesis was an advance over previous conceptions. Its very comprehensiveness was better suited to the rising tide of movement activity and critique of white supremacy. Notably, its emphasis on the struc-tural dimensions of racism allowed it to address the intransigence that racial injustice and inequality continued to exhibit, even after discrimination had supposedly been outlawed and bigoted expression stigmatized.

But such an approach also had clear limitations. As Robert Miles has argued (1989), it tended to "inflate" the concept of racism to a point at which it lost precision. If the "institutional" component of racism were so pervasive and deeply rooted, it became difficult to recognize what accomplishments the movement had achieved or what progress civil rights reforms represented. How, under these conditions, could one validate the premises of political action aimed at racial justice and greater substantive social equality? If institutional racism were indeed so ubiquitous, it became difficult to affirm the existence of any democracy at all where race was concerned. The result was a leveling critique that denied any distinction between the Jim Crow era (or even the whole *longue durée* of racism beginning with European conquest and leading through racial slavery and Jim Crow) and the present. Similarly, if the prejudice component of racism were so deeply inbred, it became difficult to account for the apparent racial hybridity and cultural interpenetration that characterizes civil society in the United States, as evidenced not only by the shaping of popular mores, values, language, and style, for example, but also by the millions of people, white and black (and neither white nor black) who occupied interstitial and ambiguous racial positions. The result of the "inflation" of the concept of racism was thus a deep pessimism about any efforts to overcome racial barriers—in the workplace, the community, or any other sphere of lived experience. An overly comprehensive view of racism, then, potentially served as a self-fulfilling prophecy.

Yet the alternative view, which surfaced with a vengeance in the 1970s and urged a return to the conception of racism held before the movement's "radical turn," was equally inadequate. This was the neoconservative project, which deliberately restricted its attention to injury done to the individual as opposed to the group, and to advocacy of a "color-blind" racial policy. Such an approach reduced race to ethnicity and almost entirely neglected the continuing organization of social inequality and oppression along racial lines. Worse yet, it tended to rationalize racial injustice as a supposedly natural outcome of group attributes in competition (Sowell 1983).

Thus have we arrived at today's dilemmas. In the post–civil rights era, U.S. society has undergone a substantial modification of the previously far more rigid lines of exclusion and segregation, permitting real mobility for more favored sectors (that is, certain class-based segments) of racially defined minority groups. This period has also witnessed the substantial diversification of the North American population, in the aftermath of the 1965 reform of immigration laws. Panethnic phenomena have increased among Asians,

Latinos, and Native Americans, reconstituting the U.S. racial panorama in a multipolar (as opposed to the old bipolar) direction. Racial identity has been problematized (at least somewhat) for whites—a fact that has its dangers but also reflects progress—and the movements to which the black struggle gave initial impetus, notably feminism and gay liberation in their many forms, have developed to the point where a whole range of crosscutting subjectivities and tensions (as well as new alliances) have been framed.

But the post–civil rights era has also witnessed a significant racial reaction. The racial reaction has rearticulated the demands for equality and justice made by the black movement and its allies in a conservative discourse of individualism, competition, and laissez-faire. We must recognize that it is this "New Right" discourse that is hegemonic today, and that in these terms racism is rendered invisible and marginalized. It is treated as largely an artifact of the past.

Racism Today

Today, then, the absence of a clear "commonsense" understanding of what racism means has become a significant obstacle to efforts aimed at challenging it. As usual there are different interpretations—different racial projects—in conflict with one another over the very meaning and structure of racism. It is common to find the view, especially among whites (but also among nonwhites), that we must somehow get "beyond" race in order to overcome racism. For example, I often hear in my classes comments such as, "I don't care if someone is black, white, green, or purple; a person's just a person to me . . . ," and so on. This implies that racism is equivalent to color consciousness, and consequently nonracism must be a lack of color consciousness. We should recognize that this type of idea, however naive, is a true product of the civil rights era, notably the movement's early, "liberal" years.

On the other hand, I hear from other students (from my black and brown students particularly but by no means only from them) that racism "equals prejudice plus power." This idea implies that only whites have power, and thus only they can be racists. We should also recognize the origins of this idea, which exhibits a different but no less dangerous naïveté—for it is highly problematic to assert that racially defined minorities are powerless in the contemporary United States—in the radicalized later years of the civil rights era.[1]

Without question, whites occupy the vast majority of the power-wielding positions in the United States—in government and the corporate world most centrally. Beyond that, whiteness is still "normalized" and rendered relatively transparent on a social structural level (as the "institutional racism" analysis stresses), hierarchizing power in such a way that whites are, shall we say, relatively warmed by it, while nonwhites are relatively distanced from it, or "frozen out." Thus there is a certain justness in my students' assessment. Yet at the same time the mobility of racially defined minorities (especially those of the middle class), the greater significance of their voting, the partial integration of some (though by no means all) institutions, and the heightened racial pluralism of public culture, all occurring in the post–civil rights era, point to a more differentiated and less monolithically racial system of power than existed earlier. Finally, the self-attribution of "powerlessness" is extremely debilitating politically.

Given this crisis of meaning, and in the absence of any "commonsense" understanding, does the concept of racism retain any validity? If so, what view of racism should we adopt? Is a more coherent theoretical approach possible? I believe it is.

Recall my discussion of racial formation theory at this point. Let us recognize that, like race, racism has changed over time. It is obvious that the attitudes, practices, and institutions of the epochs of slavery, say, or of Jim Crow, no longer exist today. Employing a similar logic, it is reasonable to question whether concepts of racism that were developed in the early days of the post–civil rights era, when the limitations of both moderate reform and militant racial radicalism of various types had not yet been encountered, could possibly remain adequate to explain circumstances and conflicts a quarter century later.

Racial formation theory also allows us to differentiate between race and racism. The two concepts should not be used interchangeably. I have argued that race has no fixed meaning but is constructed and transformed sociohistorically through competing political projects, through the necessary and ineluctable link between the structural and cultural dimensions of race in the United States This emphasis on projects allows us to refocus our understanding of racism as well, for racism can now be seen as characterizing some, but not all, racial projects.

Today, a racial project can be defined as racist *if it creates or reproduces hierarchical social structures based on essentialized racial categories*. This approach recognizes the importance of locating racism within a fluid and contested

history of racially based social structures and discourses. It allows us to recognize that there can be no timeless and absolute standard for what constitutes racism, because social structures undergo reform (and reaction), and
discourses are always subject to rearticulation. This definition, therefore, does
not invest the concept of racism with any permanent content but instead
sees racism as a property of certain political projects that link the representation and organization of race—that engage in the "work" of racial formation. Such an approach focuses on the "work" essentialism does for domination, and the "need" domination displays to essentialize the subordinated.[2]

It is also important to distinguish racial awareness from racial essentialism. Attribution of merits or faults, allocation of values or resources, and/or
representations of individuals or groups on the basis of racial categories
should not be considered racist in and of themselves. Such projects may in
fact be quite benign. Of course, any of these projects may be considered racist,
but only if they meet the criteria I have just outlined; in other words, essen-
tialization and subordination (which are always linked) must be present.

Consider the following examples. First, a discursive one: the statement
"Today, many Asian Americans are highly entrepreneurial." Second, a structural one: the organization of an association of, say, black accountants. The
first racial project signifies or represents a racial category ("Asian Americans") and locates that representation within the social structure of the
contemporary United States (in regard to business, class issues, socialization, etc.). It does not, however, essentialize; it is qualified in time ("today")
and in respect to overgeneralization ("many"). The second racial project is
organizational or social structural and therefore must engage in racial
signification. Black accountants, the organizers might maintain, have certain common experiences and characteristics, can offer each other certain
support, and so on. The effort to organize such a group is not in and of itself
antagonistic to other groups; it does not aim at others' subordination but
only at members' well-being and uplift.

Neither of these racial projects, then, can fairly be labeled racist. Of
course, racial representations may be biased or misinterpret their subjects,
just as racially based organizational efforts may be unfair or unjustifiably
exclusive. If such were the case, if, for instance, in our first example the statement in question read, "Asian Americans are naturally entrepreneurial,"
this would by my criterion be racist. Similarly, if the effort to organize black
accountants had as its rationale the raiding of clients from nonblack accountants, it would by my criterion be racist as well.

Proceeding with this standard, to allocate values or resources—let us say, academic scholarships to racially defined minority students—is not racist, since no essentializing/subordinating standard is at work here. Scholarships are awarded to Rotarians, children of insurance company employees, and residents of the Pittsburgh metropolitan area. Why, then, should they not also be offered, in particular cases, to blacks or Chicanos or Native Americans? The latter categories are no more suspect than the former ones.

What if scholarships were offered only to whites? Such action would be suspect not on the grounds of essentialism but on those of domination and subordination, since the logic of such a racial project would be to reproduce an existing racial hierarchy.

Let us take an example that is much on our minds today: the effort to invalidate affirmative action programs on the grounds that these constitute "reverse discrimination." This project would, I think, be vulnerable to criticism under the criterion of racism I am developing here. This is because, as we have learned in the post–civil rights era, it is possible to reproduce racial categories even while ostensibly repudiating them. The preservation of racial hierarchy may operate through an essentializing logic that dissembles or operates subtextually:

> The scenario . . . reads as follows: when science apologizes and says there is no such thing, all talk of "race" must cease. Hence "race," as a recently emergent, unifying, and forceful sign of difference in the service of the "Other," is held up to scientific ridicule as, ironically, "unscientific." A proudly emergent sense of ethnic diversity *in the service* of the new world arrangements is disparaged by white male science as the most foolish sort of anachronism. (Baker 1986, 385; emphasis in original)

The familiar "code word" phenomenon, that is, the subtextual signification of race, has much the same effect. Thus the claim, first made in 1896 and recently elevated to nearly hegemonic jurisprudential doctrine, that "our Constitution is color-blind," can in fact be understood in two ways. It can mean, as Justice Harlan evidently intended in his ringing dissent in the *Plessy* case, and as the early civil rights movement clearly understood it as well, that the power of the state should not be used to enforce invidious racial distinctions. But it can also mean that the power of the state should not be used to uproot those distinctions either. Based on the criteria I have advanced here, I suggest that despite its antiessentialist appearance, the "color-blind" denial of the significance of race is in fact an essentializing representation of race, an "erasure" of race, so to speak, which in the present-day United States is generally linked to the perpetuation of racial hierarchy. It is, then, a form of racism, a type of racial project (Gotanda 1995).

To identify a social project as racist using the criterion I have proposed here, one must demonstrate a link between essentializing representations of race and hierarchical social structures. Such a link might be revealed in efforts to protect dominant interests, framed in racial terms, from democratizing racial initiatives. For example, changing to at-large voting systems when minority voters threaten to achieve significant representation. But such a link might also consist of efforts simply to reverse the roles of racially dominant and racially subordinate. In melanin theories of racial superiority (Welsing 1991), for example, or in the racial ontology of the Nation of Islam with its mad scientist Dr. Yacub, we see racist projects that have a black provenance. Racism is not necessarily white, though in the nature of things, it is more often so. It inheres in those political projects that link racial essentialism and racial hierarchy, wherever and however that link is forged.

Racism and Racial Formation

Although we can conclude that racism is not invariably white, we must also recognize that today, as in the past, there is a hegemonic racial project—that of the "New Right"—which in general defends white racial privilege. It employs a particular interpretive schema, a particular logic of racial representation, to justify a hierarchical racial order in which, albeit more imperfectly than in the past, dark skin still correlates with subordination, and subordinate status often, though not always, is still represented in racial terms.

Furthermore, a key problem of racism, today as in the past, is its denial, or flattening, of difference within the categories it represents in essentialist fashion. Members of racially defined subordinate groups have for a long time faced practices of exclusion, discrimination, and even of outright extermination. Such groups are thus forced to band together in order to defend their interests (if not, in some instances, their very lives). Following the argument I am making here, such "strategic essentialism" cannot be equated with the essentialism practiced in service of hierarchical social structures. Nor would it prevent the interrogation of internal group differences, though these are sometimes overridden by the imperative for group "conservation," to use Du Bois's term.

Obviously, any abstract concept of racism is severely put to the test by the untidy world of reality. Yet I believe that it is imperative to meet that test at the level of theory, and indeed at the level of practice that ought to flow from theory, just as we must meet the test in our everyday lives.

Today we live in a situation in which "the old is dying and the new cannot be born," in which formerly unquestioned white supremacy is now questioned. It is a situation in which an antiracist countertradition in politics and culture has made significant gains. But despite all the changes wrought by this antiracist project, this radical democratic initiative that derives from the postwar black movement, it has not been possible to overthrow the deeply rooted belief that the United States is still, as the phrase goes, a "white man's country." It has not been possible fully to transform the social, political, economic, and cultural institutions that afford systematic privileges to whites. It has not been possible to alter the displacement of the burdens and problems of the society (such as unemployment, undereducation, poverty, and disease) onto the shoulders of nonwhites.

Thus, the racial dualism that Du Bois identified nearly one hundred years ago continues to operate. Recall his famous characterization of the black experience as a conflict between "two souls, two thoughts, two unreconciled strivings" (Du Bois 1903a). This now applies, albeit in very different ways, to everybody. The full exposition of this point is beyond the scope of this essay, but I have discussed it more fully elsewhere (Winant 1997, 1994a). Suffice it to say here that, as a society and as individuals, we both uphold and resist white supremacy. We experience both our particular privilege or subalternity, and to the extent we can, we resist it.

Confronting racism in such a situation is difficult. It is a moving target, a contested terrain. Inevitably, as a society, as political movements, and as individuals, we have to make lots of mistakes; we have to see our action and our thought, our praxis, in pragmatic terms. Because racism changes and develops, because it is simultaneously a vast phenomenon framed by epochal historical developments, and a moment-to-moment experiential reality, we can never expect fully to capture it theoretically. Nor can we expect that it will ever be fully overcome. That does not mean, however, that we are free to desist from trying.

Behind Blue Eyes:
Contemporary White Racial Politics

In a quiet office at a Washington think tank, a tract is composed on the bio-logically determined intellectual inferiority of blacks. On a Brooklyn street, as black demonstrators march through a segregated white enclave, white residents yell racist epithets. At an urban college campus in California, Latinos and Asians, whites and blacks, sit side by side in the overcrowded classroom, and in their own separate groups in the cafeteria. As they drive home to their segregated neighborhoods, they pump the same high-volume hip-hop sounds through their car speakers. A few miles up the interstate, neo-Nazis train at a private ranch. A few miles the other way, an organizing drive is going on for UNITE, the needle trades union; a majority of the workers in the bargaining unit are Asians and Latinos, but there are some whites. Among the organizers, one of the most effective is a young white woman who speaks good Spanish.

This essay examines racial politics and culture as they shape the status of whites. Clearly, there are many varieties of "whiteness." I begin from the premise that it is no longer possible to assume a "normalized" whiteness, whose invisibility and relatively monolithic character signify immunity from political or cultural challenge. An alternative perspective is demanded, one that begins from a recognition of *white racial dualism*. My discussion of this theme is an extension to whites of a Duboisian idea about racism: that the "color-line" fractures not only society but the self, that it imposes a sort of schizophrenia on the bearers of racialized identities, which forces them to see themselves simultaneously from within and without. Du Bois of course intended this analysis to explain problems of black politics and culture at the turn of the twentieth century; it was a time when few publicly questioned the normalization of whiteness. Here I want to extrapolate his idea to the white "politics of identity" at the end of the twentieth century.

The temporal context matters: only in the aftermath of the partial and ambiguous successes of the 1960s social movements could such an analysis make sense. Here I argue that since the enactment of civil rights reforms, contemporary racial discourse has been unable to function only as a logic of racial superiority and justified exclusion. The racial conflicts of the post–civil rights period have fissured white supremacy and fractured the old racial "common sense" of the United States, although they have hardly destroyed it. An unprecedented period of racial anxiety and opportunity has resulted, in which competing racial projects struggle to reinterpret the meaning of race and to redefine racial identity. A crucial theme in these struggles has turned out to be the identity of whites, and the meaning of whiteness.

Whiteness in the Post–Civil Rights Era

That white identity has been problematized in the years since 1960 is really not so surprising. The downfall of official racial segregation brought about significant gains for racially defined minorities, yet the preservation of substantive racial inequality—in income, education, housing, and other spheres—quickly demonstrated the limits of the civil rights "revolution." The Immigration Act of 1965—an important civil rights era reform in its own right—led to a growing population of "other others," mainly Latinos and Asians. The rapid growth of these racially defined groups over the past few decades has replaced the old black-white racial polarity with a multifaceted racial order in which whiteness is no longer the negation of nonwhiteness but merely another form of racial "difference." Meanwhile white ethnicity has declined in significance, resulting in a "postethnic" Euro-American identity whose bearers are far more open to political alliances with WASP elite (and generally Republican) groups than their parents would have been.

Other factors too have worked to refigure whiteness. Shortly after the enactment of racial reform legislation in the 1960s, working-class incomes stagnated or declined in real terms as profits soared; this provoked growing resentments that were often articulated racially, in line with venerable U.S. traditions of racially based class formation. Assaults on unions and plant closings were seen in terms of the transfer of jobs to largely nonwhite workers in the South, the Southwest, and the underdeveloped world. Democratic Party support for civil rights and affirmative action led many white workers to vote Republican. As one respondent told Stanley Greenberg, the "average American white guy" gets a "raw deal" from the government because "blacks get advantages, Hispanics get advantages, Orientals get advantages. Everybody but the white male race gets advantages now" (Greenberg 1985, 70). Attacks on the welfare state and renewed paroxysms about the supposed parasitism of the poor followed naturally from this perspective. Politicians of the right trumpeted the charge that the taxes paid by "productive citizens" who "play by the rules" and "go to work each day" were going to subsidize unproductive and indolent and promiscuous "welfare queens" and "career criminals" who "don't want to work." The racial subtext of this discourse hardly needs elaboration.

Thus, from the late 1960s on, white identity has been reinterpreted, rearticulated in a dualistic fashion: on the one hand, egalitarian, on the other hand, privileged; on the one hand, individualistic and "color-blind," on the other hand, "normalized" and besieged. Nowhere is this new framework of the white "politics of difference" more clearly on display than in the reaction to affirmative action policies of all sorts (in hiring, university admissions, federal contracting, etc.). Assaults on these policies, which have been developing since their introduction as tentative and quite limited efforts at racial redistribution, have sometimes reached hysterical levels. These attacks are clearly designed to effect ideological shifts rather than to shift resources in any meaningful way. They represent whiteness as disadvantage, something that has few precedents in U.S. racial history (Gallagher 1995). This imaginary white disadvantage—for which there is almost no evidence at the empirical level—has achieved widespread popular credence and provides the cultural and political "glue" that holds together a wide variety of reactionary racial politics.

White Racial Projects

Thus, in the post–civil rights era we are witnessing the fragmentation of earlier concepts of white racial identity and of white supremacy more generally. In their place, a variety of concepts of the meaning of whiteness have emerged. How can we analyze and evaluate in systematic fashion this range of white racial projects?

As I have argued elsewhere (Omi and Winant 1994; Winant 1994a), the concept of racial projects is crucial to understanding the dynamics of contemporary racial formation. The link between meaning and structure, discourse and institution, signification and organization is concretized in the notion of the racial project. To interpret the meaning of race in a particular way at a given time is at least implicitly, but more often explicitly, to propose or defend a certain social policy, a particular racialized social structure, a racial order. The reverse is also true: in a highly racialized society, to put in place a particular social policy, or to mobilize for social or political action, is at least implicitly, but more often explicitly, to articulate a particular set of racial meanings, to signify race in certain ways. The discord and conflict among various racial projects construct the racial order visible at any given moment; over time they produce a deeply racialized society, as preexisting themes are reworked and social institutions reformed time and again.

To analyze the struggle over the meaning of whiteness today, we must classify racial projects along a political continuum, according to the meaning each project attaches to "whiteness." Such a classification will necessarily be somewhat schematic. Nevertheless, I think it would be beneficial to sort out alternative conceptions of whiteness, along with the politics that both flow from and inform these conceptions. This is what I attempt here, focusing on five key racial projects, which I term far right, new right, neoconservative, liberal, and new abolitionist.

The Far Right Racial Project

On the far right the cornerstone of white identity is belief in an ineluctable, unalterable racialized difference between whites and nonwhites. Traditionally, this belief has been biologically grounded, and in many respects it remains so today. But a distinct modernizing tendency exists on the far right as well. It is thus necessary to distinguish between explicitly fascist and "neofascist" currents within the far right racial project.

Explicitly fascist elements on the far right can be identified by two features: their frank belief in the biological superiority of whites over nonwhites (and Jews), and their insurrectionary posture vis-a-vis the state. Although their accounts of the nature and sources of racial difference vary, often relying on religious doctrine (as in the case of the so-called Christian Identity movement, which identifies blacks and Jews as "mud people" whose origins are different from those of "Aryans"), a biologistic element is always present. Explicitly fascist groups on the far right openly admire Nazi race thinking, fantasize about racial genocide, and dream of establishing an all-white North American nation, or, failing that, seceding from the United States to establish such a nation, possibly in the Northwest (Ridgeway 1990; Diamond 1995; Novick 1995). While acts of racial and anti-Semitic terror continue and even increase, significant modernizing currents have appeared on the far right, so that the "neofascist" dimension of the far right's racial project has gained considerable ground. These tendencies occupy an intermediate position between the explicit fascism I have discussed and the more mainstream new right racial project that I address in the following section.

Neofascists generally have an ultraright provenance—a history of association with the KKK or Nazi groups—but they now actively seek to renovate the far right's traditions of white racial nationalism (Walters 1987) and open advocacy of white supremacy. Largely as a result of the challenges posed by the 1960s, the far right, no less than other U.S. political currents, has been forced to rearticulate racial meanings, to reinterpret the content of "whiteness" and the politics that flows from it.

Neofascism's response has been political mobilization on racial grounds: if blacks have their organizations and movements, why shouldn't whites? The various activities of David Duke exemplify the new trend: his electoral campaigns, his attempts at student organization (for example, his effort to create white student unions on college campuses), and his emblematic National Association for the Advancement of White People. Neofascists believe that open avowal of white supremacy, or explicit defense of white racial privilege, will be counterproductive today. They differ from the explicitly fascist currents on the far right because they are willing to engage in mainstream politics; they are not, at least officially, insurrectionary.

While the far right is not at present a real political threat, its advocacy and practice of racial terrorism should generate far more concern than has been evidenced so far. Assaults on minority and Jewish institutions and individuals, and the targeting and threatening of prominent antiracist activists and organizations continue a long-standing U.S. tradition of white violence and intimidation. The openly insurrectionary stance of a range of far right groups, their possession of substantial quantities of arms, their determination to recruit disaffected and anomic white youth, their widespread circles of adherents in police agencies and the military, their growing international coordination, and their adoption of far more sophisticated techniques of organization (so-called leaderless cell structures, for example) are all disturbing in their own right.

In the far right's view, the state has been captured by "race mixers" and will have to be recaptured by white racial nationalists in order to end the betrayal of "traditional values" that a racially egalitarian and pluralistic national politics and culture would portend. Whether this reactionary objective could happen by peaceful means, or whether an armed insurrection would be required to achieve it remains a matter of dispute. Whether a rhetoric of absolute racial difference (à la the explicitly fascist currents on the far right) will be most effective in accomplishing this, or whether a rhetoric of white victimization and white rights (à la the renovated neo-fascist currents on the far right) will work better in the post–civil rights era is also in question. But on one objective both currents of the far right project are united: the United States must remain a white man's country.

The New Right Racial Project

The contemporary new right has its origins in resistance to the black movement of the 1950s and 1960s; with the Wallace presidential campaign of 1968, this resistance crystallized as a national, electorally oriented, reactionary social movement. Wallace's right-wing populism recognized the deep threat that substantive racial equality posed to fundamental ideas about the kind of society and the kind of nation-state the United States was supposed to be (Edsall 1992). In effect, Wallace and his minions understood the same thing that black radicals and their allies had understood about the United States in the 1960s, although of course they were on opposite sides of the conflict. Through whatever optics they employed—anticommunism, racism, southern chauvinism, states' rights doctrines going back to Calhoun, agrarian populism, nativism, America First isolationism—they grasped a deep truth: that white supremacy was not an excrescence on the basically egalitarian and democratic "American creed" but a fundamental component of U.S. society. To destroy it meant reinventing the country, the social order, the government.

Indeed, for the United States to come to terms in the mid-twentieth century with its own history of conquest and enslavement would have involved a deep national reckoning. It would have severely threatened the foundations of the nation-state. The consequences of this agonizing self-appraisal would necessarily have included massive economic redistribution and the kind of atonement for white supremacy that was later to be associated with demands for compensatory programs such as affirmative action—or more properly, reparations. Thus, the threat posed by the black movement—material, political, and psychic—to the key institutions of the Pax Americana, not to mention the majority of the U.S. population, the white majority, was profound.

In opposition to this threat, building on the foundation laid down by Wallace, the new right developed a political orientation that was nationalist, populist, and authoritarian. This position, of course, has numerous precedents in earlier historical moments. It seeks by covert means to legitimate the "psychological wage" that Du Bois argued was an essential benefit allocated to whites by white supremacy (Du Bois 1935). It continues the racist legacy of southern populism, which in the past bred the likes of Ben Tillman and Theodore Bilbo (Woodward 1973). It revives the anti-immigration hysteria that earlier nativist movements had directed most notably against southern Europeans and Asians, this time targeting Latinos in the Southwest most directly (although anti-Asian sentiment is also on the rise). Finally, new right populism associates whiteness with a range of capitalist virtues: productivity, thrift, obedience to law, self-denial, and sexual repression. This in turn permits the crucial articulation of corporate and white working-class interests—the cross-class racial alliance—that endows new right positions with such strategic advantage today.

Like the far right, the new right seeks to present itself as the tribune of disenfranchised whites. But the new right is distinguished—if not always sharply—from the far right by several factors. First, rather than espouse racism and white supremacy, it prefers to present these themes subtextually: the familiar "code word" phenomenon. Second, it wholeheartedly embraces mainstream political activity, rather than abjuring it or looking at it suspiciously. Third, it can accept a measure of nonwhite social and political participation, and even membership,[1] so long as this is pursued on a "color-blind" basis and adheres to the rest of the authoritarian formula. For the far right in general, "color blindness" is race mixing and therefore verboten. For the new right, suitably authoritarian versions of "color blindness" are fine.

The new right diverges from neoconservatism (discussed below) in its willingness to practice racial politics subtextually, through coding, manipulation of racial fears, and so on. De facto, it recognizes the persistence of racial difference in U.S. society. The new right understands perfectly well that its mass base is white, and that its political success depends on its ability to interpret white identity in positive political terms. The demagoguery employed by George Bush in the 1988 Willie Horton campaign ads, and by Pete Wilson, Phil Gramm, Peter Brimelow, and numerous others in their attacks on immigrants and affirmative action, shows this strategy is far from exhausted. Neoconservatism has not, and could not, deliver such tangible political benefits, and in fact lacks an equivalent mass political base.

At present, the new right racial project is poised to achieve—or perhaps has already achieved—political hegemony. If this is consolidated, it will follow the formula of "color blindness" plus repression. In this approach, U.S. society is conceived as nonracial, "color-blind," and democratic above a certain socioeconomic line, and acutely race-conscious and coercive below that line. The range of repressive policy options being seriously considered for the ghettos and barrios includes forced sterilization, widespread stop-and-frisk policies, coerced menial labor, and further increases in overall levels of repression, or (if you prefer this term) occupation.

Such draconian racial policies are justified on the basis of the "dysfunctionality" and "parasitism" of the ghetto poor. But beyond the suffering they ratchet up to ever higher levels, these initiatives contain significant contradictions in their efforts to mobilize and reaffirm the whiteness that serves as their base. Repressive racial policies share with the entire complex of new right politics and provenance the objective of consolidating whiteness, which is conceptualized as all that the "underclass" is supposedly not: productive, law-abiding, sexually "under control," and so on. But in the post–civil rights era, the tensions of racial dualism can be seen even in these repressive tendencies. If "tough love" is to be applied only to the ghetto and barrio poor, on what grounds does it exempt the white poor? Is it, in the final analysis, a complex of racially oriented measures? But if it is fundamentally racist, to what extent can the substantial racially defined minority middle classes escape its implications? Even the new right, it seems, cannot do without at least a fig leaf of ostensible antiracism in its campaign to rearticulate and relegitimize white supremacy.

The Neoconservative Racial Project

Neoconservative discourse seeks to preserve white advantages through denial of racial difference. For neoconservatism, racial difference is something to be overcome, a blight on the core United States values—both politically and culturally speaking—of universalism and individualism.

Unfortunately, it is easier to declare these values to be operative in U.S. politics and culture—and to read them back into earlier stages of U.S. history—than it is to demonstrate that they apply to race. Without question, the Enlightenment doctrine of natural rights was partly constitutive of the U.S. sociopolitical order. But it is equally true that countervailing principles existed—notably, doctrines of European superiority—that justified

the conquest and enslavement of supposedly lesser peoples. Indeed the Enlightenment principle itself was troubled by various idealisms that persisted
within it: its assertion of the existence of a detached and impartial Reason,
for example. Supposed possession of this faculty provided a warrant for
domination of the natural world, and a principle for classification of human
subjects (and human bodies) according to attributions about their closeness
to or distance from this ideal (Young 1990; Horkheimer and Adorno 1972).
Europeans attributed to non-Europeans a lack of access to this faculty (or a
lesser, "lower" grasp of it), thus justifying their arrogation of power and privilege (Jefferson 1787).

The doctrine of natural rights frames the liberal view of citizenship that
in turn informs the neoconservative vision of race. It is visible in the dissent
of Justice Harlan from the *Plessy* decision in 1896. It is visible in "the American creed" that Myrdal (1944) claimed was a universalizing and individu-
ating tendency that would ultimately sweep away irrational race prejudice
and bigotry in the United States. It is visible in the founding documents of
U.S. neoconservatism, such as Nathan Glazer's essay (1978) on "the American ethnic pattern." And it is visible in the basic anti-statism and laissez-
faire attitude of neoconservatives, particularly in regard to racial matters
(Murray 1984; Sowell 1983).

Besides its fundamental suspicion of racial difference, the neoconservative project has cast doubt on the tractability of issues of racial equality,
tending to argue that the state cannot ameliorate poverty through social
policy but in fact only exacerbates it (W. Williams 1982). These positions
indicate the substantial distance the neoconservative project has traveled
from the liberal statism, and indeed the racial pluralism, with which its
chief spokespeople once identified, for example, in Glazer and Moynihan's
1970 book *Beyond the Melting Pot* (Steinberg 1995).

The appeal to universalism—in social policy or critical educational or
literary standards—is more subtle than open or coded appeals to white racial
fears, since it has far greater capacity to represent race in apparently egalitarian and democratic terms. Indeed the very hallmark of the neoconservative argument has been that beyond the proscription of explicit racial discrimination, every invocation of racial significance manifests "race thinking,"
and is thus suspect. Yet a refusal to engage in "race thinking" amounts to a
defense of the racial status quo, in which systematic racial inequality and,
yes, discrimination as well, are omnipresent.

To the extent that it serves as an argument against policies aimed at increasing substantive racial equality, it is not difficult to explain the wholesale

conversion of "moderate" whites, as well as many upwardly mobile minority professionals, politicians, and intellectuals, to neoconservative racial politics in the post–civil rights era. Especially after 1980, neoconservative racial ideology—with its commitment to formal racial equality and its professions of "color blindness"—proved particularly useful: it served to organize and rationalize both white working-class and minority middle-class resentments. In the former case, the objectionable element was declining living standards ostensibly brought on by "reverse discrimination." In the latter case the complaint was the "racial lumping" minority elites perceived in affirmative action policies: to challenge racial discrimination was to demean their achievements; it was to insult them by suggesting that they needed special treatment to attain upward mobility (Carter 1999; Loury 1995). This complaint also extended to "other others" (notably Asian Americans, but also some Latinos), whom neoconservatives sought to label as "model minorities," in other words, groups whose achievements and "values" distinguished them from the (implicitly black) underclass (Takagi 1992). The neoconservative approach to these groups thus sought to identify them as aspiring whites—much as Italians, Greeks, and Jews had been categorized a century earlier—and simultaneously to exempt them from the logic of affirmative action.

The neoconservative project now extends beyond strictly racial issues to a quasi-imperial defense of the political and cultural canons of Western culture tout court (D'Souza 1995). It not only argues for a "color-blind" racial politics but rearticulates formerly antiracist perspectives in a discourse denying any validity to perceptions of racial difference.

Thus, the neoconservative perspective on race is not as inclusionary as it superficially appears. Indeed, neoconservatism suffers from bad faith. It may serve for some as a rationalizing formula, a lament about the complexities of a social world in which the traditional verities, and indeed the traditional speakers, writers, and political actors, have come under challenge from a host of "others," but as soon as it advances beyond critique to proposals for action, its pious professions of universality and liberality are quickly replaced by advocacy of laissez-faire social policies, and hence of the status quo.

The Liberal Racial Project

Liberal discourse seeks to limit white advantages through denial of racial difference. The overlap with neoconservatism is, of course, hardly accidental. Yet there are significant differences in political orientation between the two projects.

Liberalism recognizes the crosscutting and competitive dynamics of race- and class-based forms of subordination in the postindustrial, post–civil rights era. It seeks systematically to narrow the differences that divide working- and middle-class people as a strategy for improving the "life chances" of minorities, who are disproportionately poor. It thus attempts to appeal to whites with arguments about the medium- and long-term consequences for their living standards of downward mobility and greater impoverishment of nonwhites. The liberal racial project can thus be described as social demo- cratic, focused on social structure (as opposed to cultural representation à la the various right-wing racial projects), and somewhat class reductionist in its approach to race.

The most effective, as well as controversial, spokesperson for the liberal racial project has undoubtedly been William Julius Wilson, the preeminent black social scientist in the United States today. In a series of prominent scholarly works and political interventions, Wilson has argued for the use of class-based criteria (and, consequently, against the use of racial logics) in for- mulating social policy aimed at achieving greater substantive racial equality. He has contended that this reorientation of social policy priorities is both better suited to the contemporary dynamics of capitalist development, and is politically strategic in ways that explicit racially oriented policies are not.

While Wilson does not dismiss the effects of historical racial discrimina- tion, he argues that since the civil rights era, capital has been "color-blind," and that consequently the large-scale demographic, economic, and political changes that have negatively affected the ghettos and barrios do not have their origins in racial discrimination. Therefore, "group-specific" policies such as affirmative action in all its incarnations cannot improve the situa- tion experienced by the African American "underclass." Wilson thus calls for "universal programs," rather than group-targeted ones, to halt the deteri- oration of inner-city communities, arguing that such measures will dispro- portionately help the minority poor:

> The hidden agenda is to improve the life chances of groups such as the
> ghetto underclass by emphasizing programs to which the more advantaged
> groups of all races can positively relate. (Wilson 1987, 120)

This "hidden agenda," of course, is designed to woo white middle-class voters. Their needs—for more and better jobs, access to education and health care, and reductions in drug trafficking and crime—can be linked to those of the minority poor if the "wedge issue" of race can be blunted. To this end Wilson has urged political actors (notably President Clinton, whom he served as an advisor) to create "biracial coalitions" by promoting programs that unite, as opposed to divide, racial minorities (particularly blacks) and whites:

> [I]f the message emphasizes issues and programs that concern the families of all racial and ethnic groups, whites will see their mutual interests and join in a coalition with minorities to elect a progressive candidate. (Wilson 1992, A15)

A similar argument has been proposed by Michael Lind, who argues that "the American elites that subsidize and staff both the Republican and the Democratic parties have steadfastly waged a generation-long class war against the middle and working classes" (Lind 1995a, 35), using race, as well as other divisions, to achieve unprecedented levels of power and concentrated wealth. Affirmative action and other race-based initiatives aimed at achieving greater substantive social equality only contribute, according to Lind, to the effectiveness of the "overclass's" divide-and-conquer strategy:

> [T]he overclass shores up its defense against genuinely representative democracy (i.e., a popular coalition uniting middle-class and working-class Americans of all races and regions) by adopting a strategy of divide and rule expressed in the language of multiculturalism. . . . Unified along the lines of economic interest, the wealthy American minority hold the fragmented majority at bay by pitting blacks against whites in zero-sum struggles for government patronage and by bribing potential black and Hispanic leaders, who might otherwise propose something other than rhetorical rebellion, with the gifts of affirmative action. (Lind 1995a, 44)

Both Wilson and Lind call for a nationalism of the Left, a populist alliance of the have-nots, regardless of race, against the haves. Lind's version is perhaps more radical and certainly more explicitly nationalist: he proposes specific measures to tax corporate flight, restrict immigration, and establish a "common high-wage trading bloc." Like Wilson, he argues against affirmative action, which he would replace with a

> transracial America . . . , [where] a color-blind, gender neutral regime of individual rights would be combined with government activism promoting a high degree of substantive social and economic equality. (Lind 1995b, 15)

Wilson's proposals, though more circumspect, conform in all their essentials to this perspective. He too identifies deindustrialization and the continuing influx of new migrants to the depressed cities as key sources of ghetto and barrio poverty; he too calls for government activism in support of a high-wage economy and a tight labor market, as the recipe for achieving substantive, transracial social justice.

Todd Gitlin's book *The Twilight of Common Dreams: Why America Is Wracked by Culture Wars* (1995), is the latest entry in the liberal lists. Gitlin's explanation for the "wracking" is that separatism (particularly racial separatism) and identity politics (particularly racial identity politics) have devoured the universalism that was previously a hallmark of the Left. This "minoritarian thinking," antipragmatic and in a certain sense antipolitical, has lost sight of the genuine goal of political struggle, that of equality.

In contrast to Wilson's and Lind's analyses, Gitlin's book is more centrally an ex–new leftist's cri de coeur than a serious appraisal of racial politics. Gitlin's exhortation to "build bridges" is certainly right and places him squarely in the liberal camp, but he offers little detail about how this is to be done. His book has an odd and contradictory texture. Perhaps this is because he simultaneously recognizes the reality of racism and argues against "separatist" group organization to combat it. This position locates Gitlin in a long tradition of white radicals—socialists, communists, and new leftists alike—who have argued that minorities should see their problems in terms of the "universal contradiction" of class rather than the "secondary" problem of race.[2]

The liberal project in all its variants actively promotes an expedient vision of greater substantive equality, linking class and race, and arguing for the necessity of transracial coalition politics. These themes seem worthy of support, and receive more discussion in this essay's concluding section.

Yet, powerful as some of Wilson's, Lind's, and Gitlin's arguments are, they do not succeed in demonstrating the demise of racism or white privilege. They largely fail to recognize the ongoing racial dualism that prevails in the contemporary period. They perceive post–civil rights era conflicts between whites and racially defined minorities merely as strategic problems and pay less attention to the deep-seated structural racial conflicts endemic to U.S. society.

The weakness of the liberal project, then, is that it does not challenge whites either to renounce the real wage subsidies, the artificially low unemployment rates, or the host of other material benefits they receive in virtue of their whiteness (Lipsitz 1995), or to disavow the "psychological wage"—their privileged status in the eyes of authority: police, welfare workers, teachers, retail clerks, and so on—which amounts to a tangible benefit acquired at the expense of nonwhites (Du Bois 1935; Roediger 1991; Harris 1993). Nevertheless, the liberal project does undertake a crucial task: the construction of a transracial political agenda, and the articulation of white and minority interests in a viable strategic perspective. This is something that has been missing from the U.S. political scene since the enactment of civil rights legislation thirty years ago.

The New Abolitionist Racial Project

The new abolitionist project stresses the "invention of whiteness" as a pivotal development in the rise of U.S. capitalism. Advocates of this view, notably radical historians and critical legal theorists, have begun a process of historical reinterpretation that aims to set race—or more properly, the gestation and evolution of white supremacy—at the center of U.S. politics and culture. Thus far, they have focused attention on a series of formative events and processes: the precedent of British colonial treatment of the Irish; the early, multiracial resistance to indentured servitude and quasi-slavery, which culminated in the defeat of Bacon's Rebellion in late-seventeenth-century Virginia; the self-identification of "free" workers as white in the antebellum North; and the construction of a "white republic" in the late nineteenth century (T. W. Allen 1994; Roediger 1991; Ignatiev 1995; Saxton 1990).

These studies, in some cases quite prodigious intellectual efforts, have had a significant impact on how we understand not only racial formation but also class formation and the developing forms of popular culture in U.S. history. What they reveal above all is how crucial the construction of whiteness was, and remains, for the development and maintenance of capitalist class rule in the United States. Furthermore, these studies also show how the meaning of whiteness, like that of race in general, has time and again proved flexible enough to adapt to shifts in the capitalist division of labor, to reform initiatives that extended democratic rights, and to changes in ideology and cultural representation.

The core message of the new abolitionist project is the imperative of repudiation of white identity and white privilege, the requirement that "the lie of whiteness" be exposed. This rejection of whiteness on the part of those who benefit from it, this "new abolitionism," it is argued, is a precondition for the establishment of substantive racial equality and social justice—or more properly, socialism—in the United States. Whites must become "race traitors," as the journal of the new abolitionist project calls itself. Its motto: "Treason to whiteness is loyalty to humanity."

How is this rejection of whiteness to be accomplished? Both intellectual and practical measures are envisioned. On the intellectual level, the new abolitionist project invites us to contemplate the emptiness, indeed vacuity, of the white category:

> It is not merely that whiteness is oppressive and false; it is that whiteness is *nothing but* oppressive and false. . . . It is the empty and terrifying attempt to build an identity based on what one isn't and on whom one can hold back. (Roediger 1991, 13; emphasis in original)

In short, there is no white culture, no white politics, no whiteness, except in the sense of distancing and rejection of racially defined "otherness."

On the practical level, whites can become "race traitors" by rejecting their privilege, by refusing to collude with white supremacy. When you hear that racist joke, confront its teller. When you see the police harassing a nonwhite youth, try to intervene or at least bear witness. In short, recognize that white supremacy depends on the thousands of minute acts that reproduce it from moment to moment; it must "deliver" to whites a sense of their own security and superiority; it must make them feel that "I am different from those 'others.'" Single gestures of this sort, *Race Traitor*'s editors say,

> . . . would [not] in all likelihood be of much consequence. But if enough of those who looked white broke the rules of the club to make the cops doubt their ability to recognize a white person merely by looking at him or her, how would it affect the cops' behavior? ("Editorial," *Race Traitor* 1993, 4–5)

Thus, the goal is not that all whites recognize the lie of their privilege, but that enough whites do so, and act out their rejection of that lie to disrupt the "white club's" ability to enforce its supremacy.

It is easy to sympathize with this analysis, at least up to a point. The postwar black movement, which in the U.S. context at least served as the point of origin for all the "new social movements" and the much reviled "politics of identity," taught the valuable lesson that politics went "all the way down." That is, meaningful efforts to achieve greater social justice could not tolerate a public/private or a collective/individual distinction. Trying to change society meant trying to change one's own life. The formula "the personal is political," commonly associated with feminism, had its early origins among the militants of the civil rights movement.

Well and good. But is whiteness so flimsy that it can be repudiated by a mere act of political will, or even by widespread and repeated acts aimed at rejecting white privilege? I think not; whiteness may not be a legitimate cultural identity in the sense of having a discrete, "positive" content, but it is certainly an overdetermined political and cultural identity nevertheless, having to do with socioeconomic status, religious affiliation, ideologies of individualism, opportunity, and citizenship, nationalism, and so on. Like any other complex of beliefs and practices, "whiteness" is embedded in a highly articulated social structure and system of significations; rather than trying to repudiate it, we shall have to rearticulate it.

That sounds like a daunting task, and of course it is, but it is not nearly as impossible as erasing whiteness altogether, as the new abolitionist project seeks to do. Furthermore, because whiteness is a relational concept, unintelligible without reference to nonwhiteness—note how this is true even of Roediger's formulation about "build[ing] an identity based on what one isn't"—that rearticulation (or reinterpretation, or deconstruction) of whiteness can begin relatively easily, in the messy present, with the recognition that whiteness already contains substantial nonwhite elements. Of course, that recognition is only the beginning of a large and arduous process of political labor, to which I return in the concluding section of this essay.

Notwithstanding these criticisms of the new abolitionist project, many of its insights remain vital to the process of reformulating, or synthesizing, a progressive approach to whiteness. Its attention is directed toward precisely the place where the liberal racial project is weak: the point at which white identity constitutes a crucial support to white supremacy, and a central obstacle to the achievement of substantive social equality and racial justice.

The Future of Whiteness

In a situation of racial dualism, as Du Bois observed more than ninety years ago, race operates both to assign us and to deny us our identity. It both makes the social world intelligible and simultaneously renders it opaque and mysterious. Not only does it allocate resources, power, and privilege, it also provides means for challenging that allocation. The contradictory character of race provides the context in which racial dualism—or the "color-line," as Du Bois designated it—has developed as "the problem of the twentieth century."

So what's new? Only that as a result of incalculable human effort, suffering, and sacrifice, we now realize that these truths apply across the board. Whites and whiteness can no longer be exempted from the comprehensive racialization process that is the hallmark of U.S. history and social structure.

This is the present-day context for racial conflict and thus for U.S. politics in general, since race continues to play its designated role of crystallizing all the fundamental issues in U.S. society. As ever, we understand our anxieties in racial terms: wealth and poverty, crime and punishment, gender and sexuality, nationality and citizenship, culture and power are all articulated in the United States primarily through race.

So, once again, what's new? It's the problematic of whiteness that has emerged as a principal source of anxiety and conflict in the postwar United States. Although this situation was anticipated or prefigured at earlier moments in the nation's past—for example, in the eugenics movement (Kevles 1985; Barkan 1992; Gould 1981)—it is far more complicated now than ever before, largely due to the present unavailability of biologistic forms of racism as a convenient rationale for white supremacy.[3]

Whiteness—visible whiteness, resurgent whiteness, whiteness as a color, whiteness as difference—this is what's new, and newly problematic, in contemporary U.S. politics. Most centrally, the problem of the meaning of whiteness appears as a direct consequence of the movement challenge posed in the 1960s to white supremacy. The battles of that period have not been resolved; they have not been won or lost; however battered and bruised, the demand for substantive racial equality and general social justice still lives. And while it lives, the strength of white supremacy is in doubt.

The racial projects of the Right are clear efforts to resist the challenge to white supremacy posed by the movements of the 1960s and their contemporary inheritors. Each of these projects has a particular relationship to the white supremacist legacy, ranging from the far right's efforts to justify and solidify white entitlements, through the new right's attempts to utilize the white supremacist tradition for more immediate and expedient political ends, to the neoconservative project's quixotic quest to surgically separate the liberal democratic tradition from the racism that traditionally underwrote it. The biologistic racism of the far right, the expedient and subtextual racism of the new right, and the bad-faith antiracism of the neoconservatives have many differences from each other, but they have at least one thing in common. They all seek to maintain the long-standing associations between whiteness and U.S. political traditions, between whiteness and U.S. nationalism, between whiteness and universalism. They all seek in different ways to preserve white identity from the particularity, the difference, which the 1960s movement challenge assigned to it.

The racial projects of the Left are the movement's successors (as is neoconservatism, in a somewhat perverse sense). Both the liberal project and the new abolitionist project seek to fulfill the movement's thwarted dreams of a genuinely (i.e., substantively) egalitarian society, one in which significant redistribution of wealth and power has taken place, and race no longer serves as the most significant marker between winners and losers, haves and have nots, powerful and powerless. Although they diverge significantly—since the liberals seek to accomplish their ends through a conscious diminution of the significance of race, and the new abolitionists hope to achieve similar ends through a conscious reemphasizing of the importance of race—they also have one very important thing in common. They both seek to rupture the barrier between whites and racially defined minorities, the obstacle that prevents joint political action. They both seek to associate whites and non-whites, to reinterpret the meaning of whiteness in such a way that it no longer has the power to impede class alliances.

Although the differences and indeed the hostility—between the liberal and new abolitionist projects, between the reform-oriented and radical con-ceptions of whiteness—are quite severe, it is vital that adherents of these two progressive racial projects recognize that they each hold part of the key to challenging white supremacy in the contemporary United States, and that their counterpart project holds the other part. Liberals rightfully argue that a pragmatic approach to transracial politics is vital if the momentum of racial reaction is to be halted or reversed. New abolitionists properly empha-size challenging the ongoing commitment to white supremacy on the part of many whites.

Both of these positions need to draw on each other, not only in strategic terms but in theoretical ones as well. The recognition that racial identities—all racial identities, including whiteness—have become implacably dualis-tic could be far more liberating on the left than it has thus far been. For lib-erals, it could permit and indeed justify an acceptance of race consciousness and even nationalism among racially defined minorities as a necessary but partial response to disenfranchisement, disempowerment, and superexploita-tion. There is no inherent reason why such a political position could not coexist with a strategic awareness of the need for strong, class-conscious, transracial coalitions. We have seen many such examples in the past: in the antislavery movement, in the communist movement of the 1930s (Kelley 1994), and in the 1988 presidential bid of Jesse Jackson, to name but a few. This is not to say that all would be peace and harmony if such alliances could come more permanently into being. But there is no excuse for not attempting to find the political "common ground" necessary to create them.

New abolitionists could also benefit from a recognition that whites can ally with racially defined minorities without renouncing their whiteness. If they truly agree that race is a socially constructed concept, as they claim, new abolitionists should also be able to recognize that racial identities are not either-or matters, not closed concepts that must be upheld in a reactionary fashion or disavowed in a comprehensive act of renunciation. To use a postmodern language I dislike: racial identities are deeply "hybridized"; they are not "sutured" but remain open to rearticulation. "To be white in America is to be very black. If you don't know how black you are, you don't know how American you are" (Thompson 1995, 429).

Teaching Race and Racism in the Twenty-first Century

This is a crucial moment for those of us who teach about race and racism. People, we are experiencing a crisis of racial meaning. In the classic definition, a crisis is a situation in which "the old is dying and the new cannot be born." That is the situation in which racial pedagogy finds itself at the start of the twenty-first century.

More is at stake than just what we teach. What we teach is what people learn, and what they learn is what they know. A straightforward argument can made that higher education curricula, taken as a whole, embody what is known in a given society at a given time.[1] This certainly applies to curricula that deal with the complex subject of race: its history, theoretical and philosophical status, multiple manifestations in socioeconomic, political, and cultural relationships, embodiment in artistic production and in the toils of the human psyche, and so on. Race is a big topic. Sociopolitical confusion, uncertainty, and anxiety about such a complex theme will be reflected in curricula focused on it and will be fostered in the hearts and minds of those students who seek knowledge about it. Such is the present situation in the academic treatment of race.

It is no secret that much of what is taught about race is outmoded, that ethnic studies departments are often riven by fierce controversies and antagonisms, and that in mainstream disciplinary settings too (English, history, sociology) there is confusion: the post–civil rights era racial ethos has become "common sense"; decades of advocacy of "color blindness," diversity, and multiculturalism have taken their toll.

Space is not available here for a full assessment of the conflicts and uncertainties besetting racial studies today, but it is at least possible to provide a glancing overview of the crisis. In what follows I first discuss the changing meaning and political dynamics of race at the start of the twenty-first century. Next I take note of the centrality of racial studies in the curriculum. I conclude with some notes, necessarily preliminary and sketchy, toward a new racial studies.

The Changing Meaning and Political Dynamics of Race

In the post–civil rights period, after decades of political and cultural conflict over the meaning of race and the persistence of structural racism in the United States, the outlines of the country's twenty-first-century racial crisis are beginning to emerge. New racial formations have developed from the processes of confrontation and accommodation, of conflict and reform that swept across much of the world over the past few decades. Changing racial dynamics are in part the effects of antiracist movements and of the achievement of democratic reform in the latter half of the twentieth century. They are linked as well to new patterns of globalization, to the unsteady and unfulfilled postcolonial situation that obtains across the world's South, and to the tremendous international flows of people, capital, and information around the planet. Here, however, I propose a narrower "take" on the changing meaning of race, focused on what is to be taught and studied about race in the American university during the twenty-first century.

These changes, I argue here, have set off a crisis in racial pedagogy. Generally speaking, the crisis comes from two sources. The first of these proceeds from the politics of the post–civil rights era, from what I have called in other work "racial hegemony" (Omi and Winant 1994). As the United States underwent a transition from the fairly explicit white supremacism and racial domination of the pre–civil rights era to the reform-based and incorporative logic of "color blindness," diversity, and so on that had become the new racial "common sense" sometime in the 1970s, racial studies had also to confront the newly emergent, hegemonic situation. To be sure, the old issues that had spawned the movement still remained highly salient: discrimination and white privilege, structural and cultural racism, and so on. But because reform had occurred, because the incorporation of movement demands (and persons) had taken place, racial studies were beset with a host of new challenges: pedagogical, empirical, and theoretical. Just as fierce debates took place across the country about the supposed "declining significance of race," so too conflicts engulfed numerous academic departments, both mainstream discipline- and ethnic studies–based, over curricular content.

The second source of crisis is linked to globalization. It may be seen in terms of national versus transnational perspectives on race. This debate of course has a long history, stretching back to controversies over slavery, conquest, and colonialism, and touching upon such complex issues as pan-Africanism and other panethnic movements, nationalism, dependency, world systems theory, and migration. Here I can offer only the most schematic characterization of this complex question.

Briefly, the post–World War II world racial scene was shaped jointly by racial reform in the global North and decolonization in the global South, two processes that were themselves highly related. As this dual transition unfolded, racial politics became more global: a sustained period of nationalism linked antiracist struggles in the United States to anticolonial revolution, for example, and "internal colonialism" theories enjoyed a significant vogue. Later, while civil rights reforms marginalized racial radicals in the United States, postcolonial regimes also lost favor because they descended into corruption, dictatorship, brutal civil war, and new forms of dependency and neocolonial subordination.[2] Complicating this huge transition in the United States was burgeoning immigration to that country after its 1965 immigration reform—which was itself an important and often neglected piece of civil rights legislation. Finally, the ever-expanding quest by the United States for global economic power—embodied in NAFTA, the WTO, and other forms of interventionism—began to cast transnational political economic issues in a newly racialized mold. This process reached new heights at the 2001 UN World Conference Against Racism in Durban, South Africa, where the United States did its best to undermine and marginalize demands for global racial justice; new global racial politics have also influenced the second Bush administration's "war on terrorism" and its Iraq intervention in various ways.

Advancing globalization tends in general to internationalize the racial curriculum. For example, teaching about various racial diasporas—African, Chinese, Filipino, Dominican, and others—is heightened. Even Afrocentrism—which in my view is largely an inchoate and retro effort to revive the black cultural nationalism of the late 1960s—in some measure works to direct greater attention to diasporic issues. At the same time the internationalization of the racial curriculum disturbs and alienates more locally and nationally oriented scholars whose commitments to specific racially defined communities and to equality and justice are focused on domestic U.S. racial conditions.

This pattern of divergence and debate is not going away; it is driven by social structure itself. The United States increasingly throws its weight around in the big world: neoimperialism is the name of the game. And it does this at a historical moment when its own demographics are more non-white, more replete with recent immigrants from the global South, more "diasporic," in short, than ever before. At the same time domestic racial discontent is rising, as the United States tears up its residual commitments to the welfare state, jams its prisons with more and more people of color, and exports poverty and unemployment as much as possible to the ghettos, barrios, and reservations.

All these tensions and conflicts flow inevitably into the racial curriculum. Post–World War II racial transformations and upheavals, most centrally the reforms of the post–civil rights era and the onset of the racial ideology of "color blindness," have unmoored higher learning in America, racially speaking, leaving faculty, students, and administrators (even those specializing in this area) uncertain as to what should be taught and what is to be learned about race and racism. The significance of race ("declining" or increasing?), the interpretation of racial equality ("color-blind" or color-conscious?), the institutionalization of racial justice ("reverse discrimination" or affirmative action?), and the very categories—black, white, Latino/Hispanic, Asian American, and Native American—employed to classify racial groups have all been called into question over recent decades. The paradigmatic approaches to studying these issues—both in traditional academic disciplines (my main focus here is on the social sciences) and in the widespread interdisciplinary programs that may be grouped under the "ethnic studies" rubric—largely derive from sociopolitical and cultural conditions that have now been superseded, at least in part.

Exclusion of critical race-oriented problematics from the curriculum and the disciplinary canons has largely ended, reflecting the transformation of the university setting from an apparatus of racial domination to one of racial incorporation. By the 1980s, many universities and colleges had made watchwords of the terms *diversity* and *multiculturalism*, although the practical meaning of this was debatable: as "diversity" was being celebrated, affirmative action programs were coming under attack, and racially defined minority enrollments were decreasing. Did attention to racial and ethnic studies, whether proceeding from traditional disciplines or from the newer ethnic studies departments and programs, benefit from this new approbation, or was serious academic commitment to these areas of study being rendered symbolic in the newly dawning "post–civil rights," "color-blind" era?

More recently affirmative action has now found new defenders, not in the relatively debilitated organizations and thinkers (myself included) who see themselves as carrying forward the movement's legacy, but in such mainstream and often conservative sectors as large corporations and the military, whose spokespeople have argued that "diversity" and upward mobility for racially defined minorities are crucial to their organizations' efforts to maintain market share and loyalty in the ranks.

This situation, in which formerly radical democratic demands now serve to undergird elite power, at first seems highly ironic. It calls forth cynicism, and perhaps even mockery, of the movement's legacy. But hold on there, my friends. When we look more deeply, we can see that every successful social movement realizes its goals by embedding them in the heart of the establishment, the power structure. That is what success means: lodging the arrows of your movement's demands in the bosom of your antagonist, most often the state but sometimes corporations, cultural elites, or other power-wielding groups. These elites and state administrators generally come to understand that honey works better than vinegar: moderate reform/hegemony is strategically more effective in maintaining consensual rule than intransigence, repression, or domination could ever be (Gramsci 1971, 182; Winant 1994a).

At the same time, there is an implicit contradiction in the success that movements sometimes achieve. What Michael Omi and I characterized as the political "trajectory" of racially based movements sets in here (Omi and Winant 1994, 84–88). Achieving your goals as a movement involves becoming incorporated: again, within the state, the corporation, and so on. Success means that "moderate" versions of movement demands are accepted and institutionalized, while more radical versions (and voices) are marginalized, or worse. Winning counts; winning reforms can mean accomplishing great transformations in patterns of social injustice; it can mean bringing the light of democracy to places where only the darkness of dictatorship existed before. But winning is also losing; it means that not only the state and power structure have made concessions, but that the movements that previously opposed them have compromised as well.

In the aftermath of intense political conflict, when reforms have become institutionalized and movement opposition has waned, the political "trajectory" reenters a period of abeyance. But during this period, uncertainty, doubt, and anger simmer: in cultural forums, in political organizations, in the "hood," and in the academy as well. How much did we (or previous generations) accomplish with all our movement blood, sweat, and tears? How much has changed, and how much remains the same? What new issues confront us now, in the age of "color blindness" and multiculturalism?

The Centrality of Racial Studies in the Curriculum

Whatever one's answer to those questions, the evidence remains strong that *approaches to teaching race and ethnicity have hewed closely to the political and cultural climate of the times.* There has always—always!—been some version of "racial and ethnic studies" in operation on American campuses. At one time there was racial theology; Drs. Morton and Louis Agassiz were once prominent racial authorities; Herbert Spencer and E. A. Ross had their day. When racial segregation, quotas on Jews, and immigration restrictions were in place, the predominant view was white supremacist, restrictive, and given to eugenicism. For a long time—let us say until the aftermath of World War II—the study of race was almost entirely a conversation among whites. Only in a few places—notably the Historically Black Colleges and Universities (HBCUs)—were racially defined minorities even present in any significant number. In the mainstream and elite universities, only an occasional scholar, often beleaguered and derided, could make his voice (and it was almost inevitably a male voice) heard.

Only in the 1960s, when students brought pressure on the universities to make changes—impelled by shifting demographics, social movements, and political changes at the national and even international levels—did the institutions finally respond. Only then were ethnic studies programs created and some measure of affirmative action instituted in hiring, admissions, and so on. And often these changes came grudgingly and unevenly. Only in the 1970s, when ethnic studies programs were already in place and the problems of racial inequality and ethnic difference widely studied, did the histories, identities, and cultural varieties of the American "mosaic" even begin to be treated with any degree of respect across the curriculum.

What has happened in recent years? A notable stasis has developed: a gap may be opening up again, as has certainly occurred in the past. The teaching/learning strategies in place today at American institutions of higher learning developed in parallel with the racial and ethnic political and cultural milieux of the 1960s and 1970s. Now, more than three decades later, a new situation confronts this pedagogy, one for which it is unprepared. Such themes as hybridized identities, ethnically and racially based experience and "role-taking," generational shifts in specific groups and communities, global and national patterns of racial/ethnic stratification, ethnonationalism and ethnoglobality, race/gender/class "intersectionality," and overlap and antagonism between racially and ethnically based concepts of difference/identity/ stratification, a new attentiveness toward "whiteness," and a resurgent interest in genocide and "ethnic cleansing," to name just a few of the many issues that confront teaching and learning strategies in this area, seem to call for new investigation and new responses.

Ironically, these new challenges are emerging at a moment when movement activity has waned, when "diversity" commitments are under attack, and when new claims of meritocratism, postraciality, and "color blindness" are being advanced from numerous quarters (usually from the center-right but sometimes even from the left or from liberal quarters, and sometimes from interventive courts and legislatures). It is no accident that debates over race/ethnicity on campus, conflict over the legacy of the civil rights movement, and discord within ethnic studies departments have become disturbingly familiar phenomena.

Toward a New Racial Studies

These large themes have been the subjects of a great deal of recent work, including my own (Winant 2001). It is not my intention to address them all in the context of a single essay. Rather I offer a tentative list of emergent issues in racial studies. This is but a hint of some of the axes of promising new work being developed in "new racial studies." These are at least some of the issues given us by the new sociopolitical conditions we face in the twenty-first century.

Consider the following themes:

Diaspora/globality/migration as racialized processes. Here I am thinking of contested borders and citizenships; the racial continuity of the North-South divide, as expressed in debt peonage, unequal exchange, and so on.

Micro-macro racial linkages. Here I mean the zone where the whole comparative/historical approach to race (the "macro" stuff) meets the whole experience-based, identity/difference dimension of race (the "micro" stuff).

Means of communication/media as racial phenomena. Here I mean the acceleration of culture contact as both (1) a diasporic (or, if you prefer, "global") organizational phenomenon: hip-hop in São Paulo, "one nation under a groove," the globalization of reggae, and so on, as well as films, Internet connections, and so on; and (2) a means of cultural domination, "appropriation," delocalization, and thus disempowerment and suppression of people's expressive needs.

The legacies of conquest and slavery. These can be seen, for example, in labor processes and ideologies, concepts of "freedom," local/national/global divisions of labor, state form, mobilizational and political capacity, and notions of personal identity.

Race and revolution. This is an evident but underexplored connection visible, for example, in the historical legacy of the Haitian revolution, and in parallels between nineteenth-century decolonization in the Americas and twentieth-century decolonization in Africa and Asia.

Race and capitalism. Here I mean the need for rethinking the world system's development as a racially instituted process; even old Karl Marx denounced "the turning of Africa into a warren for the commercial hunting of black skins." C. L. R. James's (1938) account of the sugar industry as foundational to industrialism, Du Bois's (1935) analysis of the U.S. Civil War and Reconstruction as a process of national (and global) realignment, Eric Williams's (1944) work, and the huge contemporary literature on the economics of race need to be reintegrated into the curriculum.

Race and democracy. Orlando Patterson's concept of "freedom" is premised on a thorough analysis of slavery; abolitionism was a central factor in actualizing democracy and indeed propelling concepts of popular sovereignty forward (Keck and Sikkink 1998). Some signals of this complex of problems include Du Bois's (1935) account (again!) of the U.S. Civil War and Reconstruction as a failed attempt to break the world historical democratic bottleneck, and the continuing presence of racial dictatorship in the form of structural racism (Feagin 2000), as evidenced in reparations controversies and lawsuits. In general, continuing racial pluralism and the equalization of "life chances" across racial lines are effective indexes of the presence of democracy.

Race/gender as co-constitutive in modernity. Here I mean sex-based enforcement of racial subjection and its consequences (like hybridization) in colonial and slavery-based settings, and the generalized subjection of women's bodies in racial oppressions of the most varied types (Stoler 2002), all of it carrying forward in one way or another to the postcolonial, "emancipated" world, as well as sex-based resistance, women's resistance, from then to now.

Whiteness as a central theme. What does it mean to think of whiteness as non-normalized? This is still a relatively new and difficult subject. To see "white" as a *negative* category? To experience whiteness as a *beleaguered* identity? How should we understand ethnicity *within* whiteness? Are whites a racial group? Is there white subjectivity in the same sense as there is black or Latino subjectivity?

Re ethnicity: when does it trump, and when does it get trumped by, race? Nonracialized subjects/groups are always racializable. Hitler had to make my dad pull down his pants to check if he was a Jew (my dad was a refugee from the Holocaust), but that did not keep the *Volkischer Beobachter* from printing a hook-nosed caricature of "the Jew" on every page. The Brits still racialize the Irish when they need to, and so did the Americans in the nineteenth century. The Bosnian Serbs racialized the Bosnian Muslims, reinterpreting an ostensibly religious distinction racially. The Hutu and Tutsi racialize each other; Jews and Arabs in Israel and Palestine (cousins whose languages and appearances deeply overlap) do the same. That is going in one direction, from ethnicity to race. Going in the other direction, from race to ethnicity: in the liberal (and some radical) versions of antiracism, race will become ethnicity, a more benign version of difference, by and by, when the age of sweet tolerance arrives. But in the meantime, what do we do with the persistence of ethnicity *within* racial categories, as noted earlier? What do we do when ethnic divisions become quasi-racial chasms, as in Rwanda or Srebrenica?

A Final Note

This essay is far from a fully worked-out program for the revitalization of the racial curriculum in the contemporary U.S. academy. To formulate adequately a "new racial studies" pedagogy will require a much more systematic effort than is possible here. What is intended instead is an overview of at least some of the thematic considerations that would be involved in such an endeavor. I hope that this brief sketch will at least contribute to the effort to revitalize the racial curriculum as the twenty-first century advances.

Part II
Comparative Racial Studies

Babylon System:
The Continuity of Slavery

From the very day we left the shores
Of our father's land
We've been trampled on. Oh now,
Now we know everything. We got to rebel.
Somebody got to pay for the work
We've done. Rebel!

—*Bob Marley*

It's all there in "Babylon System" by Bob Marley. The song condemns the uncompensated labor that was slavery. It demands repayment or reparations. It includes the metaphor of the "winepress" drawn from the Book of Revelations: "We've been trodding on / the winepress much too long," Marley sings. But where the "winepress" in the Bible is the place where souls are refined, presumably by the treading of God, in "Babylon System" it is the slaves who both labor and are themselves trampled. It is not God but the system that presses upon them, that oppresses them, squeezing out of them the wine of freedom. They must rebel to regain it: "Got to rebel, got to rebel now," Marley sings. Babylon is a system built upon slavery.

In this essay I examine slavery as a continuing problem. I understand slavery in a broad sense, as the archetype of unfreedom. Although slavery has always existed, predating all other forms of coerced labor, I focus here on modern slavery, the system of Atlantic slavery—racial slavery—that came into being with the European conquest of the Americas and the sub-jugation of Africa.

This is obviously only a very partial treatment of the problem of slavery. Slavery was not only an Atlantic system but was and is a worldwide phe-nomenon. It is not only ancient but is also contemporary. Beyond ancient Greece and Rome, Africa and the Middle East, China and India, the Turkic lands and the Balkans, beyond the trans-Saharan slave trade (which con-tinued well into the twentieth century), enslavement continues today in numerous forms that I do not consider here: traditional chattel slavery in Mauretania and Sudan, sexual slavery and trafficking in women and girls across much of the world, enslavement of child labor and child soldiers in Asia and Africa. No list could ever be complete.

My principal concern here, though, is the legacy and lessons of the Atlantic slave system. This was a system of racial slavery on an enormous scale, perhaps the largest and longest sustained coercive displacement of human beings in history (although one must say "perhaps" because there are a lot of contenders for this title). The essay proceeds as follows: navigat-ing through the main controversies, I define slavery as a paradigmatic com-bination of exploitation and oppression, the very archetype of human unfree-dom. Next I consider the racialization of slavery, a pattern of slavery both characteristic and constitutive of the modern era. I then discuss abolition-ism, the pattern of opposition and resistance to slavery. Abolitionism was an extremely broad social movement, a model from which we can still learn.

Attention then turns to the continuity of slavery after the gradual tri-umph (obviously not total) of abolition across the length of the nineteenth century. Since I see the legacy of slavery in the ongoing unfreedom that suf-fuses the entire planet, it is obviously impossible to present a detailed dis-cussion of all these continuities here. I am content to offer two exemplary cases, one transnational and one domestic. The first of these is the global crisis of debt peonage, which I argue amounts to a form of contemporary racial slavery in the sense of exploitation/domination, enforced unfreedom, directed at peoples "of color," that is, the inhabitants of the world's "South." The second case considered here is the prison-industrial complex. In the brief discussion I can manage here I add my voice to the radical criminology tradition going back at least to Georg Rusche and Otto Kirchheimer (1939) and continuing in the work of Christian Parenti (1999), Angela Davis (1998), and many others.

A final comment addresses the ongoing problem of unfree labor. Here I point out the tenacity of "wage slavery," the disguised but still dominant system of slavery, the "Babylon System."

Slavery is the *paradigmatic combination of exploitation and oppression*. It is the foundational moment of unfreedom, and thus the reference point for all freedom struggles, all opposition to greed and cruelty.

Slavery cannot be effectively theorized either as ownership/chattelization of human beings nor as alienation/theft of identity. Much as we tend to think about it as possession of a property interest in another person, slavery cannot be reduced to this concept. From the huge literature on this, I will offer only a few reasons why this is true.

First, as even slave owners know, there is no way to control completely another human being. People determinedly resist full objectification as property; even "contented" slaves do so. Property interests in humans are always more contingent than they are even in animals, not to mention inanimate objects. The mere ability to kill an enslaved person says nothing about one's ability to control her or him, for "free" persons can also be killed, and freedom is often experienced as more precious than life itself. Most centrally, the slave owner relies on the capability of the slave, her understanding, as well her capacity to labor. Hence the very value of the slave depends on her nonreducibility to a complete object; a part of her identity escapes chattel status (Hegel 1807).

Further evidence of this is visible in the coercion that accompanies enslavement: some form of capture of persons is required to set up a slave system, and some form of imprisonment is needed to maintain it. Even if the slave comes to see himself as "naturally" a slave and is loyal and obedient, even if the slave is born into slavery and has never known any other status, even if the slave is "naturally" construed (and "naturally" understands himself) as the property of his master (Aristotle 1959), the coercive component of the system is still not obviated: the slave still must be induced to work, must be restricted to certain activities, and so on.

A final note on nonreducibility concerns the commodification not of the person, but of labor. In *The Great Transformation* (1944), a trenchant analysis of capitalism's origins, Karl Polanyi included labor on a short list of what he called "fictitious commodities," items that could not be included in market exchange because they could not be produced on market demand. This point has relevance beyond chattel slavery; indeed Polanyi intended it to apply most pointedly to what we would now call "free labor"—that is, "wage slavery." But incidentally it demonstrates the limits of all claimed property rights in other persons, since it is almost always the slave's ability to labor that constitutes her value for the master.

Just as slavery cannot be understood as chattelized humanity, neither can it be grasped as "natal alienation," which is the account that Orlando Patterson (1982; see also 1998), drawing on Max Weber, offered of the phenomenon. The idea that a person can be entirely deprived of her identity and continue to exist in a state of pure alienation—Patterson's "social death" concept—runs into some of the same contradictions that overtake the chattel concept. Total alienation entails total inertness, rendering the slave useless. To function as a slave and thus to have value for the master, the slave's alienation cannot be more than partial. The various rituals Patterson details— the renaming, the stripping off hair and clothes, the maimings and brandings—are all evidence of barbaric efforts to deprive the slave of identity. But they can never fully transcend the symbolic.

Of course, the concepts of chattelization and "natal alienation," though limited and partial, have immense value as well, for they demarcate the parameters of slavery. Though they are counterposed to one another—Patterson's account is at pains to reject the chattel concept, for example—if we take the two prototypes of objectification and identity deficit together as a sort of contradictory and dualistic model of enslavement, then we get the beginning of a workable concept of the meaning of slavery: it becomes the archetype of unfreedom. Remembering at the same time that humans tend to resist both the degradation of being "owned" by another and of being stripped of their "true identity" by another (J. Butler 1997; Sartre 1965) provides at least the bare outlines of a more complex model of slavery. We may not know what freedom is, but at least we can know that slavery is the absence of freedom.

Slavery has always existed and maybe always will exist, but my principal concern here is with *racial slavery*. What is the relationship between slavery and race? How was slavery racialized?

From a host of scholars, such as C. L. R. James (1938), Eric Williams (1944), and W. E. B. Du Bois (1935), from the work of modern historians of Africa and the Americas such as Walter Rodney (1981), John Thornton (1998), Paul Lovejoy (1983), and Emília Viotti da Costa (1982), we know that racism did not create slavery, but that slavery created racism. Ancient slavery was not racial (racism did not really exist before the dawn of the modern epoch) and was not necessarily even ethnic.

The slavery that interests me here evolved in the Atlantic system, following the path of European conquest down the west coast of Africa and across the ocean, and moving from the Mediterranean to the Atlantic islands (the Azores, Madeira, the Canaries) to the Caribbean and Brazil. As an enterprise, slavery developed (generally speaking) from plunder to plantation agriculture, from mining to farming. In this process the demand of conquerors and settlers for mass labor steadily increased as European dominance expanded: natives were wiped out in the Antilles and vastly reduced in the mainland by brutal labor practices and disease. Impoverished Europeans were enslaved by indenture but could not meet the labor demand; their subjugation proved politically and physically impractical. Hence the turn to Africa.

Even before the African slave trade was well established, proto-racial discourse was routinely employed to explain relations with the indigenous peoples of America and Africa. The racial ideology that developed over the period from, say, Henry the Navigator (mid-fifteenth century) to Shakespeare's Caliban (early seventeenth century) was hardly consistent or coherent. It was more a congeries of elements—religious, customary, practical—than a formal set of ideas. It was greatly shaped by earlier European experiences with such "others" as Jews and Muslims, and by the experiences of the Crusades, the Inquisition, and the Reconquista. It was marked by debates everywhere, but notably under the imperia of Spain and Portugal, about the religious propriety of enslavement (Todorov 1984; Cohen 1998). Whatever coherence it had (or lacked), the crude distinction between Europeans and others served a preeminent purpose: to manage empire, to extract labor, to subordinate the "others."

Slavery, then, was racialized as a practical matter, consistent with the requisites of European domination in Africa and the Americas (and to some extent in Asia too, but once again we cannot go there now).

Slavery was only racialized over some time and with difficulty: early practices of indentured labor overlapped with it; many early crews of ships, many armies of conquistadores, many expeditionary forces sent against Maroon and *quilombo* communities, many slave catchers and *pombeiros* in Africa and *bandeirantes* in Brazil were themselves black.

Then there was the whole issue of miscegenation, which is to say racially transgressive sex, rape, family life, gender dynamics, and so on. This certainly made racial classification problematic (Stoler 1991; Hodes 1999). Combined with these developments, practices of manumission and patterns of creolization blurred the lines between slave and "free," and between white and "other." Revolutionary wars freed many black people, beginning with the North American revolution and culminating in the U.S. Civil War (which Du Bois saw as an attempt to complete the American Revolution). The massive upheaval of the Haitian revolution threatened the Atlantic system profoundly and was also deeply linked to the French Revolution and the rise to hemispheric dominance of the United States. Anticolonial struggles in most of the Spanish colonies touched off significant abolitionist and antiracist impulses as well. So while slavery and racialization largely reinforced each other, they also sometimes came into conflict with each other.

A parenthetical note here: Slavery did not only create racism; it also created capitalism. Not from scratch, of course, because early forms of capitalism had existed in the medieval Italian city-states, and indeed in the ancient world. But the world-bestriding system that has dominated the past half millennium could scarcely have come into being without the massive infusions of resources plundered from around the Atlantic basin. Without the new forms of trade and commodities in trade that slavery provided, the greatest of which was the slaves themselves ("fictitious commodity" or no), without the silver and the gold mined by slaves in Potosí and the Gold Coast and hundreds of other sites (Ladurie et al. 1990; J. Cole 1985), without the sugar of Brazil and then of Haiti and Cuba, Jamaica and Barbados (Mintz 1995), the economic ascent of Europe would not have been possible. And if we are to believe James and Williams, the very labor processes that would ultimately spark the industrial revolution were pioneered in the *engenhos* of Brazil and the sugar mills of the Caribbean (see also Moreno Fraginals 1976). This is what Marx, that old abolitionist, called "the turning of Africa into a warren for the commercial hunting of blackskins." This topic—the contributions of racism to capitalism—is unfortunately beyond the scope of the present paper (but see Winant 2001).

By giving rise to *opposition and resistance,* slavery also made possible modern democracy and modern culture. Before slavery was seriously challenged in the range of movements and discourses that were to culminate in the abolitionist movement, even bourgeois democracy was largely restricted to the propertied classes. Not the idea of the rights of man, not the idea that governments "derived their just powers from the consent of the governed," but the practical implementation of such ideas, or at least the beginning incursions of the popular strata into the process of self-government, can all be traced to the struggles against slavery.

Opposition to slavery was also crucial to the gradual diffusion of modern culture, to the onset of the "dialectic of enlightenment" (Horkheimer and Adorno 1972). The early theorists of the Enlightenment, hearty participants in the ascendance of Europe, viewed their continent as the homeland of reason, and troubled themselves very little with the problem of slavery. To Hegel, Africa was without history and therefore largely outside the zone of the spirit; Locke was an investor in a British slave-trading firm; from Kant and Jefferson came the view that the Negroes' inferiority justified their subjection (Eze 1997; Count 1950).

The irony of this is that it was precisely black people—and abolitionism in general—that brought reason to those who arrogantly claimed to be its sole practitioners. Of course, abolitionism was a broad coalition, a social movement ample enough to include opponents ranging all the way from armed Africans of both the new and old worlds, anticolonialists, and nationalist movements of all types (sometimes explicitly revolutionary ones), through religiously based antagonists (for example, many Quakers and Methodists), to democratically oriented political groups (like trade unionists and socialists, though by no means all of them). The abolitionist movement even included modernizing capitalist reformers.

Black people participated as political actors in the abolitionist movement; it was the one place where they could acquire political "voice." Indeed blacks took leadership in some (though not all) situations where antislavery agitation and organization were undertaken (P. Goodman 1998; Anstey 1975; Toplin 1972; Peabody 1996). Abolitionism was thus an effort not only to fulfill the political promise of democracy but also to extend the cultural logic of Enlightenment.

As both a political and a cultural movement, then, abolitionism played a central role in opening up society. Opposing the injustice of slavery was involved in various ways with challenging racial hierarchy, although many, of course, did not make that connection. Nevertheless abolition fomented such democratic concepts as popular rule and popular sovereignty, which we now take for granted (even if we honor them only in the breach). It fostered notions of equality ("Am I not a man and a brother?"), even if they still remain unfulfilled.

The breakdown of slavery was the incomplete result of the actions of this very diverse coalition of opponents. These ranged from armed rebels who saw themselves as Africans in captivity (Thornton 1993), through escaping slaves and free black abolitionists, to white sympathizers who opposed slavery on religious grounds, to modernizing capitalists who preferred to rent their labor than to own it. Just as the Atlantic slave trade was the first truly multinational capitalist enterprise, just as the sugar mill or *ingenio/engenho* was the first capitalist industry, so too was abolition the first multinational social movement (Keck and Sikkink 1998).

It would be hard to explain the appearance of the popular movements that shaped us, that "flowered in this generation," as Marley said, as well as shaped earlier waves of twentieth-century activism, without taking into account the influence of abolitionism. Indeed it would be difficult to explain the rise of freedom struggles of all kinds—anticolonial and national liberation struggles, women's movements, even workers' movements—without noting their origins in antislavery movements. So what is striking about all this is the continuity between the present and this past.

How far are we from slavery today? How much of a connection is there between the African slave trade and the peonage, indebtedness, and coerced and sweated labor imposed today on the world's "South"? How closely do the plantation system of the antebellum and Jim Crow period, the pattyrollers (Hadden 2001; Williamson 1986), the lynch law of the 1890s, the convict leasing and chain gangs of pre–World War II Dixie resemble present-day patterns of social control deployed in ghettos, barrios, reservations, and prisons?

These questions demand answers. Such contemporary movements as the anti–World Trade Organization initiative (of Seattle, Genoa, and elsewhere) and the call for reparations for the injustices and crimes of slavery and the slave trade (articulated at the Durban UN World Conference Against Racism and elsewhere) are the driving forces raising these issues; it is their militance, their critique, that obliges us to develop a deeper understanding of the problem of slavery.

From the rise of Europe to the present, the pattern of northern racialized rule has continued unbroken, though of course subject to many variations and regroovings; it has culminated today in what Samir Amin (2001) has called "global apartheid." From the dawn of the African slave trade to Brazil, from the enactment of the "codes noirs" in French St. Domingue, from the Virginia Assembly's passage of its first Slave Code in 1705, the surveillance and enforcement of racial boundaries have been of primary importance throughout the Americas. By means both formal and informal, labor processes and the price of labor must be regulated, and discipline be maintained among the subordinate.

The Global Crisis of Debt Peonage. Such themes as plunder, sweated or superexploited labor, and the transition from chattelized mass labor to debt peonage have to be considered at both the micro- and macrosocial levels.[1]

At the *micro*level, whether they were previously subject to enslavement or merely "captured" by repressive systems of indebtedness and peonage, most of the world's peasants, natives, sharecroppers, and agricultural workers fell under (or remained under) the lash of superexploitative agrarian economic regimes from the time that chattel slavery was abolished. These systems continue even today in much of the planet's rural South, although widespread migration, both from the countryside to the city and from the world's South to its North, has advanced so significantly (especially since the end of World War II) that rural superexploitation and peonage have been widely transformed into urban superexploitation and subemployment. Yet in the city, too, both in the world's impoverished "South" and its ruling "North," survival in the informal economy is often a form of peonage (Bonacich and Appelbaum 2000; Edin and Lein 1997; Portes, Castells, and Benton 1989).

At the *macro*level, large-scale and endemic indebtedness is pervasive throughout the global South. Africa, Latin America, and Southeast Asia have experienced significant debt crises at several moments in the post–World War II era, notably in the 1980s. But the present regime is particularly onerous, especially in its impact on the poorest nations, and most especially in Africa. As this is written (2002), mean annual African debt/annual GNP ratios have reached the obscene level of 125 percent. The corresponding figures for Latin America are 42 percent, and for Asia, 28 percent, considerably less but hardly trivial. These are 1998 figures; that is, they are for the height of the recent economic expansion that, despite some bubbles bursting (especially in Asia), still had "trickle-down" effects for HIPCs (Heavily Indebted Poor Countries) that rely on export earnings to pay their international debt.

Indeed the form taken by international indebtedness resembles nothing so much as sharecropping or equivalent forms of post-abolition debt peonage reimagined on a global scale. If we consider the trajectory of debt from the onset of the post "oil shock"/Eurodollar debt crisis of 1982 to the present, we see that the debtor nations of the South repaid their original principal many times over and yet simultaneously incurred roughly the same amount of new debt. Indeed for some countries the combined amounts of old and new loans exceed by tenfold the quantity originally borrowed (Toussaint 1999). According to Saskia Sassen:

> African debt service payments reached $5 billion in 1998, which means that for every 1$ in aid, African countries paid 1.4$ in debt service. . . . [T]hese ratios are far more extreme than what were considered unmanageable levels in the Latin American debt crisis of the 1980s. The IMF asks HIPCs to pay 20 to 25% of their export earnings toward debt service. In contrast, in 1953 the Allies *cancelled* 80% of Germany's war debt and only insisted on 3 to 5% of export earnings debt service. These are also the terms asked from Central Europe after Communism. (2001; emphasis added)

The racial dimensions of this question must be recognized with particular seriousness, since as Sassen notes, European countries, even the defeated World War II enemy Germany, were not confronted with terms nearly so exiguous. When does this start to count as a new form of slavery?

Assaults on the world's poor via the global financial system can readily be understood in terms of racism: the world's poor are largely peasants and superexploited workers, dark-skinned sharecroppers and peons of a global corporate plantation. Transnational Simon Legrees now seek to sell their southern darkies the water they drink, the crops they have traditionally planted and harvested, and the weapons their corrupt governments will use to kill the peons of bordering countries, or to kill those of the "wrong" ethnicity within their own borders. The debt and its policing by the International Monetary Fund through "structural adjustment policies" result in the death of millions every year. Not only the debt but every form of development, indeed every economic relationship, is deleteriously affected: international aid programs, investment both foreign and domestic, migration patterns, social programs, education, health, and so on. Health care or AIDS medicines for these subhumans? Not unless they can pay our fees at the country club!

The Prison-Industrial Complex. In considering the perpetuation of slavery, I now turn from the global to the U.S. domestic scenario. Not entirely coincidentally, the term *big house* has two meanings. All through the Americas in slavery days it meant the master's house. Gilberto Freyre, for example, titled his best-known book on the Brazilian racial system *Casa Grande e Senzala* (The Big House and the Slave Quarters; in the book's English translation the title is rendered as *The Masters and the Slaves* [Freyre 1933]). But of course there is in the United States another usage for the term *big house:* it means the prison.

The Thirteenth Amendment to the Constitution ended slavery "except as a punishment for crime whereof the party shall have been duly convicted." This loophole effectively preserved slavery within the United States as the preferred mode of punishment. It gave rise to all sorts of cruel and exploitative practices in the past: notably convict leasing (A. Lichtenstein 1996; Mancini 1996) and chain gang labor (Colvin 1997).

Contrary to popular belief, these types of punishment remain in use today, notably in private, corporate-run prisons, and in the use of prison-based, quasi-enslaved labor: in manufacturing, service provision, and administrative work, for example. Microsoft, Boeing, TWA, Victoria's Secret, and CMT Blues (which makes blue jeans for Lee Jeans and numerous other companies) are some of the companies using low-cost prison labor for everything from manufacturing aircraft components and lingerie to booking travel reservations.

Even the university is involved. For example, many U.S. universities contract with the Sodexho-Marriott company for food service provision in dining halls, snack bars, and so on. Sodexho owns the Corrections Corporation of America, the largest of eighteen major private prison corporations in the United States. University purchases of prison-produced services have drawn numerous student protests.[2]

The overall system, the prison-industrial complex, offers a whole series of supports both for inequality in the system of income and wealth distribution, and for the coercion of subaltern groups. Economically, imprisonment is an alternative to unemployment, or rather (given the increasing use of quasi-enslavement—extremely low-waged work—in prison) a way of keeping wages low. Politically, the threat of prison, the threat of reduction to slavery, helps maintain the system's capacity for subjection and exploitation. The rate of black male involvement with the prison-industrial complex (that is, the proportion of black males currently in prison, on probation, or otherwise sub judice) has steadily climbed to its now astounding level of one in three (Mauer 1999). Just as slavery was in the past, so incarceration (that is, constitutionally sanctioned slavery) remains in the present: an everyday demonstration of the cruelty, greed, and unfreedom that are basic to capitalism's ability to function. As Christian Parenti, author of *Lockdown America*, writes:

The repression of the criminal justice system . . . is about two things: creating political obedience and regulating the price of labor. That is what the
repression of the capitalist state has always been about, from the enclosures
and the Atlantic slave trade, to the many bloody wars against organized
labor, to the militarized ghetto of 2001. Capitalism was born of state
violence and repression will always be part of its genetic code. (2001)

Unfree Labor. Parenti's comment serves to remind us that capital has
learned that in the main it is more profitable to rent labor than it is to own
it. But only "in the main"; there are other indispensable forms by which to
coerce labor that resemble slavery more closely. And the "learning process"
continues: as a number of social and economic historians have illustrated,
the transition from enslaved to waged labor was extremely difficult and indeed is still in progress (Engerman 1999; Goldfield 1997; Roediger and Foner
1989).

The development of a system of "free" labor, and the fully capitalist class
relations it characterized, evolved in good measure from the slavery-based
systems of coerced mass labor that preceded it. Marx certainly demonstrated
that the "freedom" of the waged worker is only the freedom to sell her
labor—which is to say her time, which is to say half her waking life—herself, rather than for it to be sold by someone else. Since freedom does not
extend to the working day, the term *wage slavery* is not a neologism but a
relatively accurate characterization of everyday labor relations, especially
where work is less skilled and more akin to the mass labor of early and industrial capitalism.

Early "free" workers on both sides of the Atlantic strenuously sought to
distinguish themselves from the "unfree" workers who supplied their workplaces in Bristol, Manchester, Lyons, Amsterdam, Boston, and Lisbon with
primary materials like tobacco, cotton, or sugar. Since the days of chattel
slavery ended, "free" workers have struggled to protect themselves from the
competition of workers whose unfreedom is more explicit but not entirely
different from theirs. This is the premise of "split labor market" interpretations of racism (Bonacich 1972; Bonacich 1976).

But in the world of the World Trade Organization and NAFTA, of increasingly globalized systems of exploitation and domination, it may be more
necessary than ever to counter those "splits" with new recognitions of unity.
It may be particularly useful to realize that the exploitation and domination
experienced around the world today were forged in the system of slavery.
Slavery was after all the first transnational capitalist enterprise.

Think of the "Joe Six-pack" type who goes off to work each morning with a bumper sticker on his car that reads (in bitter jibe at Disney's seven dwarfs) "I owe, I owe, so off to work I go." He is expressing in these few words, however unconsciously, his ongoing vulnerability, his identity with maquiladoras in GM plants in Ciudad Juarez, sweatshop workers at sewing machines in New York's Chinatown, and makers of computer chips in Saigon. They are all wage slaves.

Of course, to say this is to run the risk of ignoring the very serious distinctions in status between the situations of "northern" workers—often white, male, unionized, citizens, protected by some form of labor regulation, and so on—and those of "southern" workers who are nonwhite, undocumented, or perhaps chained to a carpet loom somewhere. Yet in ending this essay I would prefer to stress the commonalities that extend across all these conditions. Chief among these is the legacy, indeed the continuity, of slavery, the "Babylon system."

The Modern World Racial System

As the world lurches forward into the twenty-first century, there is widespread confusion and anxiety about the political significance, and even the meaning, of race. In this essay I argue that far from becoming less politically central, race defines and organizes the world's future, as it has done for centuries. I challenge the idea that the world, or the national societies I briefly consider in comparative light, is moving "beyond race." I suggest that the future of democracy itself depends on the outcomes of racial politics and policies, as they develop both in various national societies and in the world at large. This means that the future of democracy also depends on the *concept* of race, the meaning that is attached to race. Contemporary threats to human rights and social well-being—including the resurgent dangers of fascism, increasing impoverishment, and massive social polarization—cannot be managed or even understood without paying new and better attention to issues of race.[1]

The Modern World Racial System

The global racial system we have now is obviously not the first one we have ever had. The racial dimensions of modernity itself have been widely acknowledged. The Enlightenment's recognition of a unified, intelligible world, the construction of an international economy, the rise of democracy and popular sovereignty, and the emergence of a global culture were all deeply racialized processes. To understand how race was fundamental to the construction of modernity is of more than historical interest: it also explains much about the present. Notably, it demolishes the commonly held belief that racism is largely a thing of the past, the idea that after the bad old days of white supremacism and colonial rule, there has occurred in our own time a belated resolution to the "race problem."

Before addressing the present, let us recall that past. What are the origins of the world racial system? How have the enigmatic specters of racial difference and racial inequality been loosed on the world?

The Origins of Race and Racism

The early modern history of race is full of precedents for the horrors of our own age. The tension between slavery, on the one hand, and nascent democracy, on the other, structured the lengthy transition to the modern world. Resistance against slavery contributed crucially to the broader redefinition of political rights for which early advocates of democracy yearned and fought. Indeed the violence and genocide of earlier racial phenomena prefigured contemporary atrocities like the Holocaust, "ethnic cleansing," and totalitarianism.

These points raise a host of pressing questions: How racial was nascent capitalism? Were the politics and cultural groundwork of modernity premised on racial distinctions? Did the generally limited democracy of the "North" (or the "West") consist in part of an application of the principles of colonial rule to the "mother countries"? In what ways did early forms of resistance to racialized forms of rule—as seen in abolitionism and slave revolts, for example—energize the worldwide impetus toward democratization? In what ways did antiracism itself become an archetypal democratic movement? Did the resistance to slavery, which grew into antiracism, ultimately do more than fight for the human, social, cultural, and political rights of racially subordinated groups? Was it not also crucial in permitting the acquisition of those same rights by whites? In other words, is the modern, inclusive form of democracy, to which we have become accustomed, itself the product of global struggles against racism?

The abolition of African slavery was the great rehearsal for the "break" with white supremacy that took place in our own time. Abolition was made possible by three momentous social changes: the triumph of industrial capitalism, the upsurge of democratic movements, and the mobilization of slaves themselves in search of freedom. Abolition was not completed with the triumph of the Union in the American Civil War and the passage of the Reconstruction amendments to the Constitution. Only when Brazil, the last country to free its slaves, did so in 1888 did the first crucial battle in the centuries-long war against white supremacy draw to a close.

But abolition left many emancipatory tasks unfinished. New forms of racial inequality succeeded slavery. Even after slavery had been ended, democracy was still partial. Racialization continued to define the mechanisms of authoritarian rule and to distribute resources on a global scale. Racial thought and practices associated subordinated status almost irrevocably with distinct types of human bodies. This ranking of human society by race still enabled and justified world systemic rule. Generalized processes of racial stratification continued to support enormous and oppressive systems of commercial agriculture and mining. Thus, until the mid-twentieth century the unfulfilled dreams of human rights and equality were still tied up with the logic of race.

The "Break"

Although there was always resistance to racist rule, it was only in the period after World War II that opposition to racial stratification and racial exclusion once again became major political conflicts. Civil rights and antiracist movements, as well as nationalist and indigenous ones, fiercely contested the racial limitations on democracy. These movements challenged the conditions under which racialized labor was available for exploitation in the former colonies as well as the metropoles. They extended the antifascist legacy of World War II and articulated comprehensively with the geopolitical conflicts of the cold war. They rendered old forms of political exclusion problematic and revealed a panoply of mainstream cultural icons—artistic, linguistic, scientific, even philosophical—to be deeply conflictual. They drew on the experience of millions who had undergone military mobilization followed by an embittering return to a segregated or colonized homeland. Such movements recognized anew their international character, as massive postwar labor demand sparked international migration from the world's South to its North, from areas of peasant agriculture to industrial areas. These enormous transformations manifested themselves in a vast demand to complete the work begun a century before with slavery's abolition. They sparked the worldwide "break" with the tradition of white supremacy.

As the tumultuous 1960s drew to a close, the descendants of slaves and ex-colonials had forced at least the partial dismantling of most official forms of discrimination and empire. But with these developments—the enactment of a new series of civil rights laws, decolonization, and the adoption of cultural policies of a universalistic character—the global racial system entered a new period of instability and tension. The immediate result of the break was an uneven series of racial reforms that had the general effect of ameliorating racial injustice and inequality but also worked to contain social protest. Thus, the widespread demands of the racially subordinated and their supporters were at best answered in a limited fashion; in this way a new period of racial instability and uncertainty was inaugurated.

Some National Cases

The break was a worldwide phenomenon, but it obviously took very different forms in particular national settings. Racial conditions are generally understood to vary dramatically in distinct political, economic, and cultural contexts. In this essay I comment, necessarily briefly, on four national case studies: the United States, South Africa, Brazil, and the European Union (considered as a whole). Examined in greater detail in other work now available in book form (Winant 2001), these cases were chosen because they are crucial variants, important laboratories, where new racial dynamics are being developed.

By offering these brief overviews of particular cases of post–World War II national racial formation, I am suggesting that the break is a global backdrop, an economic, political, and cultural context in which parallel racial conflicts are being worked out nationally. Because each country's racial dynamics are unique, each one's pattern of racial formation after the break has varied as well. Yet the political imperatives of racial reform have been inescapable. As in the past, racial politics have manifested not only a local distinctiveness but a global interrelationship.

The United States

How permanent is the "color-line"? The activities of the civil rights movement and related antiracist initiatives achieved substantial, if partial, democratic reforms in earlier postwar decades. These innovations continue to coexist, however, with a weighty legacy of white supremacy originating in the colonial and slavery era. How do these two currents combine and conflict today?

Massive migration, both internal and international, has reshaped the U.S. population, both numerically and geographically. A multipolar racial pattern has largely supplanted the old racial system, which was usually (and somewhat erroneously) viewed as a bipolar white-black hierarchy. In the contemporary United States, new varieties of inter-minority competition, as well as new awareness of the international "embeddedness" of racial identity, have greater prominence. Racial stratification varies substantially by class, region, and indeed among groups, although comprehensive racial inequality certainly endures. Racial reform policies are under attack in many spheres of social policy and law, where the claim is forcefully made that the demands of the civil rights movement have largely been met, and that the United States has entered a "postracial" stage of its history.

The racial break in the United States was a partial democratization, produced by the moderate coalition that dominated the political landscape in the post–World War II years. The partial victory of the civil rights movement was achieved by a synthesis of mass mobilization, on the one hand, and a tactical alliance with U.S. national interests, on the other. This alliance was brokered by racial "moderates": political centrists largely affiliated with the Democratic Party, who perceived the need to ameliorate racial conflict and end outright racial dictatorship, but who also understood and feared the radical potential of the black movement.

There was a price to be paid for civil rights reform. It could take place only in a suitably deradicalized fashion, only if its key provisions were articulated (legislatively, juridically) in terms compatible with the core values of U.S. politics and culture: individualism, equality, competition, opportunity and the accessibility of "the American dream," and so on. This price was to be paid by the movement's radicals: revolutionaries, socialists, and political nationalists (black, brown, red, yellow, and white), who were required to forego their vision of major social transformation or to face marginalization, repression, or death if they would not.

The radical vision was an alternative "dream," Dr. King's dream let us call it, a dream in which racial justice played the central part. To be "free at last" meant something deeper than symbolic reforms and palliation of the worst excesses of white supremacy. It meant substantive social reorganization that would be manifested in egalitarian economic and democratizing political consequences. It meant something like social democracy, human rights, social citizenship for blacks and other "minorities."

But it was precisely here that the "moderate" custodians of racial reform drew their boundary line, both in practical terms and in theoretical ones (Steinberg 1995; Singh 1998). To strike down officially sanctioned racial inequality was permissible; to create racial equality through positive state action was not. The danger of redistribution—of acceding to demands to make substantive redress for the unjustified expropriation and restriction of black economic and political resources, both historically and in the present—was to be avoided at all costs.

Civil rights reform thus became the agenda of the political center, which moved "from domination to hegemony" (Winant 1994a). The key component of modern political rule, of "hegemony" as theorized by Gramsci most profoundly, is the capacity to *incorporate opposition*. By adopting many of the movement's demands, by developing a comprehensive and coherent program of "racial democracy" that hewed to a centrist political logic and reinforced key dimensions of U.S. nationalist ideology, racial "moderates" were able to define a new racial "common sense." Thus they divided the movement, reasserted a certain stability, and defused a great deal of political opposition. This was accomplished not all at once but over a prolonged period from about the mid-1950s to the mid-1980s.

This partial reconfiguration of the U.S. racial order, based on real concessions, left major issues unresolved, notably the endurance of significant patterns of inequality and discrimination. But the reform that did occur was sufficient to reduce the political challenge posed by antiracist movements in the United States. Certainly it has been more successful than the intransigent strategy of diehard segregationists—based in the slogan of "massive resistance" to even minimal integration—would have been.

Yet the fundamental problems of racial injustice and inequality, of white supremacy, of course remain—moderated perhaps, but hardly resolved.

So in the U.S. context, race not only retains its significance as a social structural phenomenon but also continues to define North American identities and life chances, well after the supposed triumph of the "civil rights revolution." Indeed "the American dilemma" may be more problematic than ever as the twenty-first century commences. For achieving this moderate agenda has required that the civil rights vision be drawn and quartered, beginning in the late 1960s and with ever greater success in the following two decades.

The tugging and hauling, the escalating contestation over the meaning of race, have resulted in ever more disrupted and contradictory notions of racial identity. The significance of race ("declining" or increasing?), the interpretation of racial equality ("color-blind" or color-conscious?), the institutionalization of racial justice ("reverse discrimination" or affirmative action?), and the very categories—black, white, Latino/Hispanic, Asian American, and Native American—employed to classify racial groups were all called into question as they emerged from the civil rights "victory" of the mid-1960s.

Not by any stretch of the imagination can this situation justify the claim that racial injustice has largely been surpassed in a post–civil rights era. Yet such views have become the new national "common sense" in respect to race, acquiring not only elite and academic spokespeople but also widespread mass adherence, especially among whites. As a result, the already limited racial reform policies (affirmative action) and the relatively powerless state agencies charged with enforcing civil rights laws (EEOC) developed in the 1960s are undergoing new and severe attack. The argument is now made that the demands of the civil rights movement have largely been met, and that the United States has entered a "postracial" stage of its history. Advocates of such positions—usually classified as "neoconservative" (but sometimes also found on the left)—ceaselessly instruct racially defined minorities to "pull themselves up by their own bootstraps," and in callous distortion of Martin Luther King Jr.'s message, exhort them to accept the "content of their character" (rather than "the color of their skin") as the basic social value of the country (Steele 1990; Thernstrom and Thernstrom 1997).

In a notable recent example, the Supreme Court moved in the *Sandoval* case to repeal even the inadequate civil rights reforms of the 1960s.[2] Here as elsewhere, by adding a purpose or "intent to discriminate" requirement to antidiscrimination law, the Court makes it almost impossible to get relief from discrimination. As critical legal theorist David Kairys (1994) has argued, this amounts to creating different equality rules for whites and nonwhites, because where whites claim to have been harmed the Court does not care about intent or purpose.

After the dust had settled from the titanic confrontation between the movement's radical propensities and the "establishment's" tremendous capacity for incorporative "moderate" reform, a great deal remained unresolved. The ambiguous and contradictory racial conditions in the United States today result from decades-long attempts simultaneously to ameliorate racial opposition and to placate the *ancien régime raciale*. The unending iteration of these opposite gestures, these contradictory practices, itself testifies to the limitations of democracy and the continuing significance of race in the United States.

South Africa

In the mid-1990s, South Africa—the most explicitly racialized society in the late twentieth century—entered a difficult but promising transition. The apartheid state had of course been committed to a racialized framework of citizenship, civic exclusion, and law in general; the postapartheid constitution incorporates the principle of nonracialism originally articulated in the ANC-based Freedom Charter of 1955. Yet the country still bears the terrible burden of apartheid's sequelae: persistent racial inequality exists across every level of society. The legacy of segregated residential areas combined with a highly racialized distribution of resources of every sort combine to urge moderation on political leadership. White fears must be placated in order to sustain the country's economic base and minimize capital flight. Whites continue to hold controlling positions throughout the economy; the handful of blacks who have made their way into the corporate and state elites understand very well the price the country would pay for a radical turn in policy.

Yet this is a state committed to racial equality and to promoting black advancement, individually and collectively. Can the postapartheid state stabilize the process of political, social, and economic integration of the black majority? Can it maintain an official nonracialism in the face of such comprehensive racial inequality? How can the vast majority of citizens—excluded until so recently from access to land, education, clean water, decent shelter; debarred from Africa's wealthiest economy; and denied the most elementary civic and political rights—garner the economic access they so desperately need without reinforcing white paranoia and fear? How can the postapartheid state facilitate the reform of racial attitudes and practices, challenging inequality, supremacism, and the legacy of racial separatism without engendering white flight and subversion?

Both the antiapartheid movement and the new government's policies were shaped by global concerns as well as by local ones. Internal political debates reflect changing global discussions around race and politics. Just as the South African Black Consciousness Movement drew on the speeches and writings of Malcolm X and Aimé Césaire in its understanding of racial oppression, just as the antiapartheid movement used international antiracist sentiment to build momentum for sanctions on the old regime, so too the current government is both guided and constrained by international pressures and issues.

Internal politics also bring international resources to bear: through the postwar era, the antiapartheid movement drew much of its resources and ideas from an international antiracist movement, largely linked to an international trend to support decolonization. Since the 1994 election, however, international constraints have limited the sphere of action of the new democratic government. Critics of affirmative action policies, for example, emphasize the danger of undermining efficiency in the name of redistribution, much as critics of redistributive policies deploy neoliberal economic arguments to reject nationalization; in each case, they invoke international discourses that are nonracial in form, yet have racial implications in practice. The South African state continues to face a considerable challenge from both left and right: will it be possible to reconstruct South Africa by building not only a democracy but a greater degree of consensus, of citizenship and belonging? To what degree can a policy of "class compromise" forestall the dangers of social upheaval and capital flight (Webster and Adler 1999)?

Understanding these processes requires viewing South African racial debates in global perspective and exploring the ways in which local actors seek to change the terms of engagement as they restructure national politics. The 1994 elections changed the racial character of the state, although many white civil servants remain in place. Affirmative action policies, to which the ANC-led government is committed, could reorganize racial distribution of incomes, if not wealth. Yet in the context of a global debate over affirmative action and in the face of the threat of the flight of white capital and skills, the process of reform has been far slower than many South Africans, white and black, expected. This dilemma remains unresolved: how can democratic nonracial institutions be constructed in a society where most attributes of socioeconomic position and identity remain highly racialized?

Brazil

Brazil presents significant parallels, both historical and contemporary, to other American nations, including the United States. These similarities include Brazil's history of slavery and black inequality, its displacement and neglect of a large indigenous population, its intermittent and ambiguous commitment to immigration, its incomplete democracy, and its vast and increasingly urban underclass (disproportionately black). Brazilian racial dynamics have traditionally received little attention, either from scholars or policy makers, despite the fact that the country has the second largest black population in the world (after Nigeria). Its postemancipation adoption of a policy of "whitening," which was to be achieved by concerted recruitment of European immigrants, owed much to the U.S. example and also drew on nineteenth-century French racial theorizing (Skidmore 1993).

Amazingly, the "myth of racial democracy" still flourishes in Brazil, even though it has been amply demonstrated to be little more than a fig leaf covering widespread racial inequality, injustice, and prejudice (Hasenbalg and Silva 1992; Hanchard 1994; Andrews 1991). The Brazilian racial system, with its "color continuum" (as opposed to the more familiar "color-line" of North America), tends to dilute democratic demands. Indeed, Brazilian racial dynamics have made it difficult to promote policies that might address racial inequality. Public discourse resolutely discourages any attempt to define inequality along racial lines; the former president, Fernando Henrique Cardoso, was the first even to broach the subject seriously, although vociferous denials, both official and informal, certainly persist. If politicians do point out racial inequalities, they challenge the myth of racial democracy and are subject to charges that they are themselves provoking racial discrimination by stressing difference.

Reliable research on racial stratification and racial attitudes in Brazil remains scarce (Telles 1992, 1994; Twine 1997; Datafolha 1995). A whole range of political questions thus remains mysterious. Consider the example of voting rights: illiterates could not vote until 1985, but there are no reliable data on the proportion of illiterates who were black, and thus the extent to which black Brazilians have been disenfranchised through this century remains uncertain, though it is undoubtedly large.

The 1980s saw the emergence of the Movimento Negro Unificado as a force to be reckoned with—though by no means as strong as the 1960s U.S. civil rights movement. The MNU represented a new development. It used the 1988 centennial of the abolition of Brazilian slavery, as well as the 1990–91 census, to dramatize persistent racial inequalities. As in South Africa, this phase of the black movement took its reference points partly from international antiracist struggles, often drawing on examples, symbols, and images from the civil rights and antiapartheid movements.

In the 1990s, a range of racial reforms was proposed in Brazil—largely in response to the increasingly visible *movimento negro*. To enact these reforms, to prompt the state to adopt antiracist policies, however, required far greater support for change than was available. The political dilemma was familiar: blacks needed organized allies, in the party system, among other impoverished and disenfranchised groups, and on the international scene. Yet in order to mobilize, they had also to begin asserting a racialized political identity, or little collective support for racial reforms could be gathered. How can blacks address this dualistic, if not contradictory, situation? How can Afro-Brazilians assert claims on the basis of group solidarity without simultaneously undermining the fragile democratic consensus that has begun to emerge across many constituencies? How can democratic institutions be built alongside policies designed to address racial inequalities without undermining a vision of common citizenship and equality? These questions remain important in the opening decade of the twenty-first century.

The European Union

The past few decades have established that, indeed, "the empire strikes back."[3] Racially plural societies are in place throughout Europe, especially in former imperial powers like the United Kingdom, the Netherlands, France, and Spain, but also in Germany, Italy, the Scandinavian countries, and to some extent in the East. The influx of substantial numbers of nonwhites during the postcolonial period has deeply altered a dynamic in which the racial system and the imperial order had been one, and in which the "other" was by and large kept outside the walls of the "mother country." As a stroll around London, Frankfurt, Paris, or Madrid quickly reveals, those days are now gone forever. Yet the response to the new situation too often takes repressive and antidemocratic forms, focusing attention on the "immigrant problem" (or the "Islamic problem"), seeking not only to shut the gates to Maghrebines or sub-Saharan Africans, Turks or Slavs (including Balkan refugees) but often also to define those "others" who are already present as enemies of the national culture and threats to the "ordinary German" (or English, or French, and so on) way of life. This rationale for racial exclusion and restriction in Europe has been analyzed as "differentialist": its distinction from the meritocratic logic of discrimination in the United States has been linked to a generally lower European interest in issues of individual equality and a relatively greater concern with the integrity of national cultures (Taguieff 2001; Wieviorka 1995).

Thus, the particular racial issue that must be confronted in Europe is the newly heterogeneous situation, the multiplication of group identities. Currently antidemocratic tendencies are widely visible: new right and neofascist groups are widespread. At both the state and regional levels the agenda of immigration restriction is gaining adherence, jeopardizing mobility of employment or residence, and sometimes stigmatizing religious or other cultural practices. Conflicts over racial pluralism and citizenship have taken on new intensity, with crucial implications for the character of democracy.

The dynamics of integration raise a wide range of questions about future European racial logics. Conflicting principles of citizenship—jus sanguinis versus jus soli—are deeply embedded in the distinct European national makeups, and their resolution in a common cultural/political framework will not come easily (Brubaker 1992). Relations with ex-colonies vary, raising serious questions not only of immigrant access and economic ties between the old empires and the new Europe but also giving rise to serious anxieties about "security" and "terrorism." Popular antiracist sentiments stimulated the formation of many multiculturalist and pluralist organizations, particularly in the early 1980s. But over the past decade they have largely ceased to function as mass mobilization initiatives in support of democracy. So, while the slogan "Touche pas mon pôte" (Hands off my buddy) no longer summons tens of thousands into the street in defense of the democratic rights of racially defined minorities, the transition to racial pluralism is still very much underway.

Toward New Racial Dynamics

To understand the changing significance of race in the aftermath of the twentieth century, the century whose central malady was diagnosed by Du Bois as "the problem of the color-line," requires us to reconsider where the racialized world came from, and where it is going. In the settings studied, the break that began with movement activity after World War II, and that was contained from the late 1960s onward by political reforms, has not been consolidated. Just as earlier stages of modern racial history failed to resolve many issues, so too does the present epoch. At the end of the century the world as a whole, and these national cases as well, are far from overcoming the tenacious legacies of colonial rule, apartheid, and segregation. All still experience continuing confusion, anxiety, and contention about race. Yet the legacies of epochal struggles for freedom, democracy, and human rights persist as well. To evaluate the transition to a new world racial system in comparative and historical perspective requires keeping in view the continuing tension that characterizes the present.

Despite the enormous vicissitudes that demarcate and distinguish national conditions, historical developments, roles in the international market, political tendencies, and cultural norms, racial differences often operate as they did in centuries past: as a way of restricting the political influence not just of racially subordinated groups but of all those at the bottom end of the system of social stratification. In the contemporary era, racial beliefs and practices have become far more contradictory and complex. The "old world racial system" has not disappeared, but it has been seriously challenged and changed. The legacy of democratic, racially oriented movements, such as the U.S. civil rights movement, antiapartheid struggles, SOS-Racisme in France, the Movimento Negro Unificado in Brazil, and anticolonialist initiatives throughout the world's South, is thus a force to reckoned with. My aim in this essay has been to trace the parameters of this situation.

It is impossible to address worldwide dilemmas of race and racism by ignoring or "transcending" these themes, for example, by adopting so-called color-blind policies. In the past the centrality of race deeply determined the economic, political, and cultural configuration of the modern world; although recent decades have seen a tremendous efflorescence of movements for racial equality and justice, the legacies of centuries of racial oppression have not been overcome. Nor is a vision of racial justice fully worked out. Certainly the idea that such justice has already been largely achieved—as seen in the "color-blind" paradigm in the United States, the "nonracialist" rhetoric of the South African Freedom Charter, the Brazilian rhetoric of "racial democracy," the emerging "racial differentialism" of the European Union—remains problematic.

What would a more credible vision entail? The pressing task today is not to jettison the concept of race but instead to come to terms with it as a form of flexible human variety.

What does this mean in respect to racism? Racism has been a crucial component of modernity, a key pillar of the global capitalist system, for five hundred years. So it remains today. Yet it has been changed, damaged, and forced to reorganize by the massive social movements that have taken place in recent decades. In the past these movements were international in scope and influence. They were deeply linked to democratizing and egalitarian trends, such as labor politics and feminism. They were able both to mobilize around the injustices and exclusion experienced by racially subordinated groups, and simultaneously to sustain alliances across racial lines. This is background; such experiences cannot simply recur. Still, the massive mobilizations that created the global break that followed World War II have certainly reshaped our world. Were these movements fated to be the last popular upsurges, the last egalitarian challenges to elite supremacy, to racial hierarchy? Surely not. In the countries I have discussed, and in transnational antiracist networks as well, these earlier precedents still wield their influence. They still spark new attempts to challenge racism.

At the same time, new political and intellectual leaders have come onto various national stages in recent years, arguing that the worst racial injustices (of the United States, Brazil, South Africa, etc.) are now firmly relegated to the past, and that the problem of racism can now be viewed as essentially solved. So why maintain affirmative action policies? Why direct resources toward immigrants, victims of segregation and apartheid, the (disproportion-ately dark-skinned) poor? Don't we already have equality now?

Will race ever be "transcended"? Will the world ever "get beyond" race? Probably not. But the entire world still has a chance of overcoming the stratification, the hierarchy, the taken-for-granted injustice and inhumanity that so often accompany the race concept. Like religion or language, race can be accepted as part of the spectrum of the human condition while it is simultaneously and categorically resisted as a means of stratifying national or global societies. Nothing is more essential in the effort to reinforce demo-cratic commitments, not to mention global survival and prosperity, as we enter a new millennium.

Reaching the Limits of Reform: Postapartheid South Africa and Post–Civil Rights United States

The city of Durban hosted the UN-sponsored World Conference Against Racism in August–September 2001. The conference was the third in a series of WCARs: the two preceding conferences had occurred while the apartheid regime was still in power, and indeed were devoted to mobilizing and articulating world opposition to the apartheid system. The very fact that the third WCAR could take place in a democratic, postapartheid South Africa, now led by the African National Congress, the party/movement that had spearheaded the freedom struggle, was an inspiration to the thousands of delegates from antiracist nongovernmental organizations (NGOs) from all over the world. I was honored to be one such delegate.

In a world largely bereft of effective emancipatory movements, ANC-led South Africa continues in many ways to be a source of hope. Yet the country is also deeply divided between the moderate reformers, most prominently President Thabo Mbeki, and those with more radical tendencies also located within the ANC, who criticize the government for maintaining much of the economic legacy of the apartheid system. The radicals seek a more thoroughgoing redistribution of resources. The unequal distribution of land, water, jobs, and housing is undoubtedly the most central problem facing the country. A particularly contentious area is the government's policy of privatizing a variety of state-owned utilities such as electricity and telephone services.

These crucial sectors of the economy have been costly to maintain under public ownership and are simultaneously coveted by international investors. Of course, the curtailment of redistribution as well as the privatization of pubic utilities both come at the expense of the (largely black) South African working class and poor. In August 2001, no doubt stimulated by the presence of thousands of WCAR delegates and the intense media attention the UN conference brought to South Africa, opposition factions within the ANC staged a two-day nationwide protest (billed as a "general strike") and headed by the Congress of South African Trade Unions (COSATU), itself a mainstay of the ANC during both its opposition and governing periods. The protesters I saw in Durban were particularly incensed by the ANC government's Growth, Employment and Redistribution (GEAR) Program, which they said gave extremely short shrift to redistribution. Marchers and protesters focused their demands on basic needs such as food, water, energy, and housing. They pointed out that these continued to be unavailable or inadequate for millions while the white middle and upper classes who benefited from apartheid still occupied privileged positions in an ANC-governed South Africa.

In response to the protests the government argued for realism and accommodation of international pressures. President Mbeki urged South Africans to be patient in the interest of stabilizing the economic situation and allowing long-term democratizing and egalitarian reform to proceed incrementally. He argued that capital flight must be discouraged, and that the country needed to attract new investment. He defended privatization as a means to open up new avenues for investment, to reduce state expenditures, and to create new opportunities for taxation, economic growth, and redistribution in the longer term.[1]

These conflicts over the future of South Africa, these difficult dilemmas in which the ANC is caught—both as governing party and as opposition-oriented social movement—express in condensed form the uncertainties of transition from racial repression to racial democracy.

In April 1993, an extended rebellion took place at the maximum security prison in Lucasville, Ohio. Hundreds of prisoners took part; ultimately nine prisoners and a guard were killed as state police retook the prison and the rebellious prisoners negotiated a surrender. Five of the prisoners involved in the uprising were eventually sentenced to death. Staughton Lynd writes about the Lucasville revolt:

The single most remarkable thing about the Lucasville rebellion is that white and black prisoners formed a common front against the authorities. When the State Highway Patrol came into the occupied cell block after the surrender, they found slogans written on the walls of the corridor and in the gymnasium that read: "Convict unity," "Convict race," "Blacks and whites together," "Blacks and whites, whites and blacks, unity," "Whites and blacks together," "Black and white unity." (1998)

Throughout the United States in recent decades, imprisonment rates for racially defined minorities have greatly increased. Nationally something like two million people are in prison. Half of the prison population is black. One in ten African American men between the ages of twenty and twenty-nine are in state and federal prisons, and if local prisons are included, the figure increases to one in seven (Mauer 1999). After the enactment of civil rights legislation in the 1960s and the black movement's decline, imprisonment is carrying out many of the same tasks that overt segregation used to perform: the regulation and intimidation of the poor, notably the black poor, is probably the most central of these. In the past it was possible to frighten black citizens away from the polling booth, especially in the South. Today felony disenfranchisement performs the same function (Uggen and Manza 2002). In the past overt doctrines of white supremacy could be publicly promulgated. Today black (and brown) working people are scapegoated by law-and-order propaganda ("Brutal Carjacking in Civic Center! Pictures at 11!"), even though actual crime rates have been declining. Perhaps most important, the threat of imprisonment leads the poor to accept low-wage work as a reasonable alternative, especially as the last vestiges of the welfare system are eliminated. The criminal "justice" system, then, regulates the labor market in some of the same ways that employment discrimination does: "Creating political obedience and regulating the price of labor," as Christian Parenti puts it, " . . . is what the repression of the capitalist state has always been about . . ." (Parenti 2001).

   This location of imprisonment at the coercive center of the U.S. system of social control and the pivotal role played by racial oppression and conflict in that system were the targets of the uprising at Lucasville. All this in a society that many (and especially many state officials) seek to describe as "color-blind"! What is remarkable about the Lucasville revolt is that the prisoners' actions gave antiracism a new and more appropriate meaning, exposing the charade of "equal justice under law" as well as the fraudulent claims that post–civil rights era America was a "color-blind society."[2]

Racism has always been an issue of democracy, an indicator—the most reliable one we have—of democracy's limitations. Just as race and racism were central to the creation of modernity, the development of capitalism, and the elaboration of Enlightenment culture, they were also key to the evolution of modern forms of democracy. In fact there is a powerful *dialectic of democracy and race*, in which race plays a contradictory role: On the one hand, democratic political logics are elaborated over the heads of racially defined "others" who are deemed unworthy of political participation. But on the other hand, the movements that challenge racial oppression—and that challenged slavery in an earlier time—have greatly advanced the entry of the popular strata, the masses, into politics. Just as white people benefited from the abolition of slavery—not only black people but also white people—so too do white people, and indeed people of every racial identity, benefit from the lessening of racism. It is not often recognized that democracy in the modern era was conceptualized as the opposite of slavery, that citizenship and social identity were for many centuries conceived in racial terms (and in many ways they still are thought of that way), and that the first transnational social movements were antiracist movements.[3]

Since World War II the connection between race and democracy has become much more explicit than it ever was before, chiefly because antiracist and anticolonialist movements around the world made it so. World War II was a worldwide racial event. It brought about a "break" with the world racial system that had existed for half a millennium or so. The racial transformation that occurred during and particularly after the war was not total, but it was still tremendously significant. It involved an exponential leap in social mobility (understood in both senses of that term: the geographic and the status-oriented) for "people of color" around the world. It included enormous (indeed worldwide) mobilizations of these racially defined "others," both military and political: colonial and postcolonial subjects, indigenous peoples, and racially demarcated national minorities were first pressed into military service and then mounted fierce political struggles for political and cultural rights in the war's aftermath.

The postwar racial break was also interwoven with themes of antifascism and cold war competition. U.S. racism was a major issue in the years of the cold war (Dudziak 2000), and South African apartheid was defended as a bulwark of anticommunism until both it and the Soviet Union were on their last legs in the late 1980s and early 1990s (Borstelmann 1993).[4]

Comparing the United States and South Africa in
Post–World War II Years

The United States and South Africa were by far the most prominent national settings for post–World War II antiracist movements. Another way of saying this is that in these two countries the battle to extend democracy across racial boundaries, to put an end to white supremacy as a political system, was the most intense in all the world (Fredrickson 1981, 1995). In both these countries, the antiracist struggle was also the core democratic struggle of the postwar years. None of this is news.

But were the antiracist mobilizations that rocked both the United States and South Africa during the post–World War II period reformist or revolutionary? How should these political conflicts be situated on the political spectrum between reform and revolution? One often encounters the phrase "the Civil Rights revolution." The struggle against apartheid, which involved both unarmed mass action and armed action, has also been interpreted as a revolutionary one.

I argue here that in both countries *political incorporation* insulated the racial state from revolutionary transformation and absorbed antiracist movements in a reform-oriented transition.[5] In the United States the political trajectory of movement challenge and hegemonic incorporation was always securely reformist; although radical and indeed revolutionary currents at times also played key roles, they suffered marginalization (and repression) as state racial policy developed from domination to hegemony (Winant 1994a). In South Africa the transition was closer to a revolutionary one, where incorporation occurred very late through a process of "pacting" in some ways resembling Latin American democratic transitions. The sociopolitical transformation that took shape in South Africa during the early 1990s was obviously far more thoroughgoing than the U.S. metamorphosis centered in the 1960s. Yet South Africa's transition toward racial democracy must still be seen as an instance of political incorporation, of racial reformism, though of a more radical type.

Although comparisons between the two countries have been legion, very little comparative attention has been paid thus far to the politics of incorporation that these two countries experienced. These two antiracist movements navigated through some very murky waters in the course of challenging and putting an end to their particular systems of white supremacy. To what extent did they succeed in "crossing Jordan"? What was the political process these movements underwent as their respective nations made the transition from officially racist to officially postracist societies? How was the cause of racial democracy advanced, and how was that cause impeded, by these transformations?

The United States

Racial democratization in the United States was dominated by a moderate and state-linked reformist coalition. The partial victory of the civil rights movement in the United States was achieved by a synthesis of mass mobilization, on the one hand, and a tactical alliance with U.S. national interests, on the other. This alliance was brokered by racial "moderates": political centrists largely affiliated with the Democratic Party, who perceived the need to ameliorate racial conflict and end outright racial dictatorship, but who also understood and feared the radical potential of the black movement.

There was a price to be paid for civil rights reform: it could take place only in a suitably deradicalized fashion, only if its key provisions were articulated (legislatively, juridically) in terms compatible with the core values of U.S. politics and culture: individualism, equality, competition, opportunity and the accessibility of "the American dream," and so on.

This price was paid primarily by the movement's radicals: revolutionaries, socialists, and political nationalists (black, brown, red, yellow, and white), who were required to forego their vision of major social transformation or to face marginalization, repression, or death if they would not. The radical vision was an alternative "dream," Dr. King's dream let us call it, a dream in which racial justice played the central part. To be "free at last" meant more than symbolic reforms and palliation of the worst excesses of white supremacy. It meant substantive social reorganization that would be manifested in egalitarian economic and democratizing political consequences. It meant something like social democracy, human rights, social citizenship in the Marshallian sense, for blacks and other racially defined minorities.

But it was precisely here that the "moderate" custodians of racial reform drew their boundary line, both in practical terms and in theoretical ones (Steinberg 1995; Singh 1998). To strike down officially sanctioned racial inequality was permissible; to create racial equality through positive state action was not. The danger of redistribution—of acceding to demands to make substantive redress for the unjustified expropriation and restriction of black economic and political resources, both historically and in the present— was to be avoided at all costs. Civil rights reform thus became the agenda of the political center, which moved "from domination to hegemony" (Winant 1994a).

The key component of modern political rule, of "hegemony" as theorized by Gramsci most profoundly, is the capacity to *incorporate opposition*.[6] By adopting many of the antiracist movement's demands, by developing a comprehensive and coherent program of racial reform policies that hewed to a centrist political logic and reinforced key dimensions of U.S. national-ist ideology, racial "moderates" were able to define a new racial "common sense." Thus they divided the movement, reasserted a certain stability, and defused a great deal of political opposition. This was accomplished not all at once but over a prolonged period from about the mid-1960s to the mid-1980s.

This partial reconfiguration of the U.S. racial order involved the making of real concessions through the passage of civil rights, voting rights, and immigration reform legislation, to name just some of the major reforms un-dertaken. The reconfiguration also left major issues unresolved: notably, significant patterns of inequality and discrimination were permitted to en-dure, either by the enactment of ineffective or tokenistic reforms, or by utter neglect (often malign as much as benign) on the part of legislatures and courts.[7]

Still, despite these clear limitations, the explicit commitment to racial reform brokered by political "moderates" located both within the apparatus of the state and in key movement organizations, and developed under several governments from the 1940s through the 1970s—from Truman through Nixon and Ford to Carter—proved generally effective at both reducing the sheer volume of overt racism practiced in the United States and simultane-ously reducing the challenge posed by antiracist movements to the political, economic, and cultural systems of the country. Certainly this reform initia-tive proved more successful at legitimizing U.S. democracy in the face of antiracist opposition than any intransigent strategy of diehard white su-premacy could possibly have been.

Yet the fundamental problems of racial injustice and inequality, of white supremacy, of course remained: moderated perhaps, but hardly resolved. Therefore, the meaning of race in the United States, and the ongoing significance of race for North American identities, also remains. Indeed, "the American dilemma" may be more problematic than ever as the twenty-first century commences. For achieving this "moderate" agenda has required that the civil rights vision be drawn and quartered, beginning in the late 1960s and with ever greater success in the following two decades.

All this tugging and hauling perpetuated and deepened anxiety and con-testation over the meaning of race rather than resolving them, and resulted in ever more disrupted and contradictory notions of racial identity. To check this in the early years of the twenty-first century, just ask yourself the following questions: Is the significance of race declining or increasing? Can we better understand racial justice and equality by using "color-blind" or "color-conscious" criteria? Can we achieve racial justice and equality by employing affirmative action policies, or do such policies constitute "reverse discrimination"? Indeed, how viable and empirically verifiable are the very categories employed to classify racial groups in the United States today: black, white, Latino/Hispanic, Asian American, and Native American? All these questions—and many others as well—were in a real sense posed precisely by the civil rights reforms of the mid-1960s.

Not by any stretch of the imagination can this situation justify the claim that racial justice has largely been achieved, or racial injustice largely surpassed, in a post–civil rights era. Yet such views have become the new national "common sense" in respect to race, acquiring not only elite and academic spokespeople but also widespread mass adherence, especially among whites. As a result, the already limited racial reform policies (affirmative action, etc.) and the relatively powerless state agencies charged with enforcing civil rights laws (EEOC) developed in the 1960s have undergone several decades of severe attack. Forceful arguments have been made that the demands of the civil rights movement have largely been met, and that the United States has entered a "postracial" stage of its history. Advocates of such positions—usually classified as "neoconservative" but sometimes also found on the left—have ceaselessly instructed racially defined minorities to "pull themselves up by their own bootstraps," and in callous distortion of Martin Luther King Jr.'s message, have exhorted them to accept the "content of their character" (rather than "the color of their skin") as the basic social value of the country (Steele 1990; Thernstrom and Thernstrom 1997).

Legislative and judicial policymaking has lurched backward, or at least wobbled, on these issues as well. As of this writing (May 2003) the Supreme Court is poised to release its decision on two crucial affirmative action cases: *Grutter v. Bollinger* and *Gratz v. Bollinger*. It is always difficult to predict, but most experts think that the Court will uphold the principle, not because of any strong commitment to racial inclusion, but because major elite institutions such as large corporations and associations of high-ranking armed forces officers have filed amicus briefs in support of affirmative action as a key factor in U.S. social cohesion (Greenhouse 2003). At the same time, the Court is in the process of repealing many of the civil rights reforms of

the 1960s, however inadequate they were to the task of achieving racial justice. In the *Alexander v. Sandoval* case (532 U.S. 275 [2001]), for example,
the Court ruled that the state of Alabama did not discriminate when it
used "English only" policies in drivers' license exams. Here, as elsewhere, by
adding an "intent to discriminate" criterion to antidiscrimination law, the
Court makes it impossible to obtain relief from all but the most egregious
and patent forms of discrimination. As critical legal theorist David Kairys
(1993, 1994) has argued, this amounts to creating different equality rules
for whites and nonwhites, because where whites allege "reverse discrimination" the Court does not care about intent or purpose.

After the dust had settled from the titanic confrontation between the
movement's radical propensities and the "establishment's" tremendous capacity for incorporative "moderate" reform, a great deal remained unresolved.
The ambiguous and contradictory racial conditions in the United States
today result from decades-long attempts simultaneously to ameliorate racial
opposition and to placate the *ancien régime raciale*. The unending iteration
of these opposite gestures, these contradictory practices, itself testifies to
the limitations of democracy and the continuing significance of race in the
United States.

South Africa

Racial democratization in South Africa was driven forward by a mass-based
opposition deeply rooted in civil society and almost entirely unconnected
to the state. Apartheid South Africa was of course the most intransigent
of all white supremacist regimes. For a long time—roughly the thirty years
between the 1960 Sharpeville massacre and the release of Nelson Mandela
from prison on February 11, 1990—only a revolutionary resolution of the
country's racial dictatorship seemed possible, since the ruling Nationalist
party was so entrenched.[8]

But the regime lost support, not only black support—it had never had
any significant black support—but also "moderate" white support. As mass
opposition increased and the apartheid regime's international (mainly U.S.-
based) backing eroded, as the cold war came to an end—removing the
regime's claim to be a bulwark against communism—the "Nats" began to
flirt with reform. They tried in vain to make concessions to their opposition
that would succeed in mollifying it: offering to extend the franchise to
"coloured" voters, for example, and to set up separate parliaments for nonwhites (though never for the black majority). But because they were unwill-

ing to accept the "one person, one vote" principle, because they were unwilling, in fact, to let go of white rule, these "concessions" all failed dismally. The political situation became more and more unstable from 1990 onward. Under pressure from business interests, trading partners, and widespread protest both internally and around the world, the regime—headed by the "moderate" Nationalist party leader F. W. de Klerk—initiated negotiations over the terms of transition. Extended maneuvering followed, but eventually a "pact" was crafted that bore interesting resemblances to various Latin American transitions away from authoritarian rule.[9]

Key to the "historic compromise" that inaugurated the shift away from apartheid and toward a new constitution and democratic elections was the willingness of Nelson Mandela himself, pressed on this point by Joe Slovo, leader of the South African Communist Party and a key figure in the ANC as well, to suspend the ANC's commitment to an explicitly socialist element of its political program: radical redistribution of privately held assets. The terms negotiated also provided whites with guarantees of political inclusion and incorporation within the new democratic system, consistent with the ANC's commitment to "nonracialism" as stated in its fundamental platform, the 1955 Freedom Charter. On the Nationalists' side, de Klerk recognized both the futility of any attempt to retain apartheid, and the desirability of a transition to the role of legal, parliamentary opposition. The Nationalists failed in their attempts to secure "group rights" for whites in the form of guaranteed seats in parliament and other similar immunizations against the "one person, one vote" formula. They also failed in attempts to stage armed provocations and insurrections against the accord between the apartheid regime and the ANC.[10]

Thus, South Africa almost reached the brink of full-scale revolution and stepped back, preferring the path of peaceful—though comprehensive—political reform. The country began its transition toward democracy with the termination of apartheid in 1994. Avoiding the trauma and bloodshed, the instability and uncertainty that revolutionary warfare would inevitably have set in motion was itself a great triumph. In many ways South Africa's dilemmas themselves produced a certain stability: confronted by vast social problems and burdened with an enormous legacy of racial inequality and oppression, the ANC government did not relinquish the commitments to political inclusion that guided it through many decades of opposition. But because it did not redistribute resources, it also did not become a target for neoimperial harassment: the familiar brand of destabilizing politics and destructive economic policy that the United States has inflicted upon other progressive initiatives in the global South, most notably in Latin America.[11]

In some respects the arduous battles of the ANC's journey to power were its greatest resource.[12] The resolute commitment to liberation from white supremacism that it nurtured among the masses of South Africans served in turn to regulate it in power: the ANC could not turn its back on the black trade unions or the community groups in the townships and provinces. These millions of newly enfranchised citizens not only elected and reelected the ANC but also expected great reforms from their party: housing, jobs, education, services, land.

On the other hand, the acquisition of formal citizenship, of *racial democracy*, created a certain political space, a cultural space, from which the South African people expected great improvements in their material lives. The newly democratic government was pressed to deliver on its more substantively difficult, more economically focused reform commitments. Though the ANC could manage significant political reforms, it could not deliver the economic progress the masses required. After 1994 the country entered a prolonged interregnum characterized by desultory redistribution, chronic conflict, and the dire predictions of failure that ongoing inequality and the persistence of structural racism necessarily engender.

Opposite to the masses whom the ANC has pledged to serve are the local and global capitalist interests who have a significant stake in the South African economy. These elites are also among the government's constituency. Indeed, some South African firms were among the most effective advocates for a transition to democracy, for the unbanning of the ANC and the release of Mandela, and for the elimination of apartheid. But in the postapartheid situation, capital has made clear not only that it will insist on the abandonment of large-scale progressive redistribution—as agreed upon by Slovo and Mandela—but that it will expect the ANC government to lead the African continent toward the neoliberal orthodoxy demanded of the global South by the "lords of humankind": the IMF, multinational lenders, the transnational corporate elite. While full-scale structural adjustment policies have not yet been imposed on South Africa, pressures have been applied for the privatization of publicly owned resources such as utilities, transport, water, and electricity, and for adherence to intellectual property conventions regarding pharmaceuticals.[13] And the government's sponsorship/acquiescence in the so-called New Partnership for African Development (NEPAD—a "free trade" scheme favored by the usual suspects: the United

States, transnational corporations, the IMF, and the World Bank) amounts to a sacrifice of the entire regional economy to neoliberal economic policies and the depredations they bring.[14]

For poor black families, lacking the wherewithal to move into the formerly all-white suburbs, promises of better schooling and housing ring somewhat hollow: millions remain in all-black townships or find themselves living in shacks in the squatter settlements that can be found on the edges of all South Africa's cities. The government has built something like one million new houses, mainly for poorer black families, but the waiting lists are very long. Applicants know they may have to wait years. Other forms of collective goods provision are also in crisis: water, electricity, and transportation are being privatized, schooling and of course health care under the shadow of the AIDS pandemic are in crisis, and unemployment remains ubiquitous as well.

Perhaps the key issue of redistribution is land reform, which has both urban and rural dimensions. It proceeds at a snail's pace, leading to occupations that have drawn the world's attention. Meanwhile South African struggles for land take place in the odoriferous atmosphere of the state-sanctioned expropriations taking place in neighboring Zimbabwe. Zimbabwe's disastrous slide into autocracy and demagogic racialism have clearly shown the ANC leadership the perils of any "command-style" land redistribution. Even if the corruption and violence of the Mugabe regime in Zimbabwe can be avoided in South Africa, preserving the good will of white property holders is the key to preserving the good will of creditors and investors in the global North.

So the conflicts and tensions confronting (and within) the ANC have become clear. At the political level, South Africa remains remarkably democratic: the government is trying to respond to South Africans' demands for expanded social services; there are substantial efforts at inclusion; formal racial barriers are down; schools and hospitals are open to all South Africans, regardless of race; affirmative action is operating in university admissions and hiring for the civil service; and South Africa's elite and middle class are becoming increasingly integrated. But class divisions and enormous inequalities still stifle the country's progress.

Debates over economic policy parallel debates over the racism and authoritarianism that still run through South African society. Under new laws that prohibit speech that incites racial hatred, a drunk white man in a bar who calls out racist insults can be punished, but in other venues where racial ideology is produced, distributed, and consumed, reforms come far more slowly: How can teachers and school staff learn to deal effectively with racially mixed classrooms? How can the police learn to work with black citizens to prevent and solve crimes rather than treating citizens as enemies? How can the media divulgate a significant antiracist message? To be sure, South African TV and radio are much improved since the days of apartheid, but conflicts abound about the racial content, the racial orientation of journalists and producers, and the overall racial politics of the media (Berger 2001).[15]

In all these areas the legacy of apartheid lives on, there is democratic conflict and debate, and the effort to democratize confronts formidable obstacles. Before the 1994 election and the transfer of power to the ANC, students of the "democratic transition" in South Africa tended to suggest that antiapartheid activists should avoid provoking a white backlash (Van Zyl Slabbert 1992; Adam and Moodley 1993). Some of these same writers are now urging more concerted efforts at redistribution and criticizing the ANC for moving *too far* to the right (Adam, Moodley, and Van Zyl Slabbert 1998). Whereas progressive students of COSATU and black trade unionism had earlier assumed that union demands for redistribution would receive sympathetic attention from the new state (Adler and Webster 1995), these same authors now recognize that the state's role has proved far more ambiguous.[16]

Still and all, the South African people have not lost hope in democracy or in the ANC. If they have been patient so far, this may be because they recognize the challenges that redistribution poses for the democratic state, or it may be because a viable and more progressive political alternative to the ANC simply has not emerged and probably cannot be created. Protest movements of considerable strength have developed, but to date their role seems confined to the important but limited task of reminding the government of its progressive responsibilities, not of replacing it.

Conclusion

The interim results of racial reform in these two countries suggest that democratic options have grown significantly from the old system of explicit and de jure white supremacy. This is particularly true in South Africa, which is arguably some kind of model for transition away from official white supremacy and for racial democratization. Whatever the limits and imperfections of the ANC as liberation movement or governing party, it deserves major credit for instituting as democratic a political system as it has done.

But even in the United States, where racial reform has been much more limited, the democratizing effects of the post–World War II antiracism movements have been striking.

The contemporary perseverance of racism (structural, institutionalized, etc.) in the two countries reflects two distinct democratic dilemmas. In the United States, racial hegemony has presented a significant stumbling block for the cause of democratization. State-based incorporation of antiracist movement demands has worked to defuse democratizing pressure. The discrediting and repression of radicals were also made a lot more possible by the "moderate" reforms instituted in the 1960s.

Comparatively speaking, the U.S. racial reforms, while significant, were a lot more limited in scope than the South African ones. On the other hand, although profound racial inequalities and injustices remain in the United States, marginalization of an overwhelming majority of blacks and other racially defined minorities is not a problem on the same scale as it is in South Africa. As a result, democratization is stalled in the United States today, while the effort to build a new movement is stalled by conditions of hegemony: incorporation, insulation, and absorption (Omi and Winant 1994, 86–87).

In South Africa, the dilemma is not racial hegemony but globalization. The ANC is in power. An opposition movement, significantly defined by antiracism, is in power! But even in power this movement is ferociously restricted by the global reach of capital. The ANC's historic compromise, its forsaking of its socialist program, was the price it had to pay to secure democracy and to end racial dictatorship. There can be little doubt that even at the high cost of abandoning its project of the progressive redistribution of national resources in the short or even medium term, the "pacted" transition was worth undertaking.

But the high price of democracy, like a long-term mortgage, has to be paid continually. The ANC has made a commitment to political pragmatism. This is both worrisome and necessary: if the ANC were not prepared to operate cautiously, the stability of the country, not to mention its advanced level of democracy, would be destroyed. So in South Africa today, social justice is stalled while the state struggles to develop, or even maintain, its commitments to the mass movement that brought it to power.

Durban, Globalization, and the World after 9/11: Toward a New Politics

The UN World Conference Against Racism was a very American event. About 40 percent of the delegates accredited to the NGO forum were North American; at Durban, one had the constant experience of running into old movement comrades and friends, as well as seeing a new and younger generation of U.S. activists coming together.

The WCAR was American in another way, too: It was anti-American. Just as the first two WCARs (1978 and 1983) were focused on anathematizing and ending the South African apartheid regime, the 2001 Durban conference sought to challenge the U.S. empire, the hegemonic position the United States occupies in a postcolonial, post–cold war, postapartheid, and post–civil rights world.

Of course, the U.S. government was well aware of this situation. The ostensibly pro–civil rights Clinton administration coquetted with the conference throughout its planning stages, worrying about the oppositional and activist orientation being developed in its various "PrepComs" and NGO statements, but at the same time hoping to moderate and co-opt the conference, to secure a role for the United States as a reform-oriented official participant. Aware of the malign implications of turning their backs on the conference, especially among their already estranged domestic constituents on the Democratic Party's left, the Clintonites were unwilling to repudiate the conference entirely. That task was left to the Bush administration, whose domestic political priorities were the converse of Clinton's. Bush was a creature of the Republican Right, a Southern president (in the U.S. sense of the term), a usurper who owed his office in large part to anti–black voting rights fraud. He sought by attacking the conference to shore up his key lower-strata "socially conservative" constituencies; he had already assured the loyalty of the corporate fat cats by enacting massive regressive income and wealth redistribution. Disowning the conference had an extra benefit for the Bushies, too: it provided a "wedge issue" to divide two key Democratic Party constituencies, blacks and Jews.

Then came September 11, and Durban was swept into the dustbin of history. What had seemed to us—the NGO delegates—such a crucial event was now yesterday's news, if people could remember it at all. A massive world crisis will do that to you.

And indeed, the 9/11 event was a rupture in U.S. politics and world politics. The actual assaults—horrifying and tragic as they were—were certainly the flashpoint of these dramatic political shifts. But it was the U.S. government's response to the attacks, the reactionary counteroffensive that Bush and his minions have undertaken against civil society both within the United States and against a range of perceived and real enemies around the world, that was decisive in launching the political crisis that democratic and egalitarian social movements now face. The emergency conditions confronting our movements derive from several sources:

- The widespread fear of "terrorism," a panicky response that the Bush regime has effectively abetted and cultivated, much as its right-wing progenitors fomented anticommunist hysteria in the cold war years (and before that, in the 1920s).
- A resurgent reactionary nationalism that continues to garner widespread popular adherence by drawing on familiar old tropes: "fortress America," "the land of the free and the home of the brave," the emergency measures necessitated by "wartime," and so on.
- A racially based identification of "the enemy" as Arabs, Arab Americans, and Muslims in general (even those, whether Muslim or not, who resemble Arabs), and beyond this, the incipient demonization of the Islamic world, which hints at a series of very old scores: the Crusades, the "clash of civilizations," the

Reconquista, and so on. A thus far minor but interesting wrinkle in this ideological complex is the Bush administration's selective co-optation of feminist criticism of the repression of women in some (but certainly not all) fundamentalist Islamic regimes.

As a result of these developments, we confront a very disturbing political situation: the near paralysis of opposition politics. The movements that seemed renascent before 9/11—notably the antiglobalization, anti-WTO movement and the resurgent antiracist movement represented by Durban, by reparations initiatives, by resistance to racial profiling, and by critiques of the prison-industrial complex—have now been put on hold. Though not completely stymied, they have been set back considerably. Denying this is whistling in the dark.

Current support for the Bush regime is driven by two factors: the sense of crisis and the failure of any credible political alternative. Rather than sinking into the slough of despond, we should be working on developing a movement-oriented explanation of the present situation. In the absence of mass opposition, ideas really count. In fact, if there were available to us a radical democratic, antiracist, antiapocalyptic alternative account—alternative to the standard rhetoric of the "A Nation Challenged" sort, I mean—the apparent "common sense" of much of the Bushies' rhetoric would be much easier to confront.

So here are some contributions toward that alternative political stance. I hope that these ideas, in concert with those of many other radical activists and intellectuals, will help reinvigorate the movement we so desperately need.

Radical globalism. In the era of the Internet, of AIDS, of diaspora, of postcoloniality, and of tidal waves of migration, globalization is not only the domain of corporations and capital; it is also a popular domain. Exclusivist concepts of citizenship are over. "Fortress" America (or Fortress Europe, or Fortress anywhere else) is an unworkable and repressive political construct. Interdependence should be recognized as a potential source of strength, not weakness. Ethnoglobality has replaced ethnonationality. Huge expatriate and postcolonial populations in the world's North represent a tremendous resource for development and democratization, if they can be afforded full citizenship rights, not demonized and superexploited. Already private remittances from "developed" countries to poor ones constitute a major source of "foreign aid," totaling about $100 billion per year.

Greed kills. One message of both Durban and 9/11 is that the world's North, for its own security, needs to terminate its ceaseless exploitation of the global South. The consumerism of "McWorld" is built on a planetary sweatshop. The global "debt trap" now engulfs not only impoverished nations but fairly developed ones like Argentina, Mexico, and South Korea. African debt/annual GNP ratios have reached the obscene level of 125 percent, and debt service in many southern countries amounts to more than 50 percent of state revenue per year. Assaults on the world's poor via the global financial system—notably the debt and its policing by the IMF through "structural adjustment policies"—result in the death of millions every year. This can readily be understood in terms of racism and terrorism: the world's poor are largely peasants and superexploited workers, dark-skinned sharecroppers and peons of a global corporate plantation. Transnational Simon Legrees now seek to sell their southern darkies the water they drink, the crops they have traditionally planted and harvested, and the weapons their corrupt governments will use to kill the peons of bordering countries, or those of the "wrong" ethnic or national identity within their own borders. Health care or AIDS medicines for these subhumans? Not unless they can pay our fees at the country club!

Colonialism is not over. The European colonial powers could not sustain their empires after World War II, a fact they sometimes had to be taught the hard way, through armed revolutions. But they had learned by the 1960s that indirect rule works better than explicit empire anyway. Setting up spheres of influence throughout the now "independent" global South allowed for a level of pillage and depredation unimaginable during the bad old days of overt colonialism. After World War II, the United States became the chief neocolonialist power. But it still carried on its decades-long schizophrenia about whether it was more properly the "big stick" imperialist or the isolationist avoider of "foreign entanglements." Defeat in Vietnam and the regime's subsequent difficulty in mounting interventions (the so-called Vietnam syndrome) show that this conflict continues in our own day, although after 9/11 and the Afghanistan triumphs, the Vietnam syndrome may well be dead: further cause for worry.

Proxy colonialism also should be mentioned, notably in the Middle East, where Israel operates as the favorite U.S. gendarme. Israel seems to have decided that this is the proper moment for an all-out war on the Palestinians, and Bush seems to have signed on. At Durban, I thought, laudable condemnation of Israeli colonialism was vitiated by real anti-Semitism.

That the Bushies used this as a poor excuse for leaving the conference does not mean that it was not a real problem.

Racism and antiracism as practice. In a recent book (Winant 2001), I have argued that racism must be understood in terms of its consequences, not as a matter of intentions or beliefs. Today, racism has been largely—though not entirely, to be sure—detached from its perpetrators. In its most advanced forms, indeed, it has no perpetrators; it is a nearly invisible, taken-for-granted, "commonsense" feature of everyday life and global social structure. This is the situation that allows U.S. courts and mainstream political discourse to overturn affirmative action, to proclaim the United States a "color-blind" society, and so on. But if we define racism as *the routinized outcome of practices that create or reproduce hierarchical social structures based on essentialized racial categories*, then we can see better how it extends from the transnational to the national to the experiential and personal, from the global debt burden to racial profiling, from Negrophobia to Islamophobia. Racism is a deeply entrenched social structure, largely congruent with the rise of capitalism, the rise of democracy (for some), and the triumph of Enlightenment concepts of identity and culture.

Since racism is so large, combating it must also be a large-scale practice. The reparations idea provides a valuable guidepost here. Reparation means repair, making whole, making good what was evil. As a sociopolitical project, reparations can be seen to extend from the large to the small, from the institutional to the personal. Clearly, abolishing the debt (not "forgiving," for who is to forgive and who is to be forgiven?) fits within the reparations logic, as does affirmative action.

Redistribution fits as well, but here we must be careful: The politics of income and wealth distribution are "double-entry" bookkeeping items. Not only the allocation of resources is involved but also the derivation of revenues. Think about the problem on the U.S. (national) level, for example: if reparations were to be paid for the crime against humanity that was African slavery (an important point from Durban), it would be important to look at both the inflow and the outflow sides of the process. On the outflow side, reparations should take the form of social investment (for a U.S. example, think of a "Marshall Plan for the Cities" or something similar). Payments to individuals or families would be problematic: slavery was far more centrally a collective wrong than an individual depredation. Its historical outcome in structural racism is the main evil we want to annul, and the negative effects of past slavery for present-day individuals are hard to assess. On the inflow side, there is a danger that reparations would be paid out of general revenues, unduly assessing present-day working people for the crimes of past colonialists and elites, perpetuating rather than attenuating racial conflicts, and allowing new variants of the "color-blind" argument to loom up in the future. An alternative revenue-oriented strategy would raise the money by means of a wealth tax, thus recognizing how many present-day capital hoards had their origins in slavery. Insurance companies indemnified slave owners if their slaves escaped or shipbound Africans revolted, for example. British slave owners were compensated for their "losses" in 1833 when Parliament abolished slavery, and North American slavocrats regained their autarchic local autonomy in the "Compromise" (which Du Bois called a counterrevolution) of 1877.

Beyond reparations, antiracist practice can be understood macropolitically in terms of social citizenship, and micropolitically in terms of acculturation and socialization. Very briefly, the concept of *social citizenship* was proposed by T. H. Marshall as the obligation of the post–World War II welfare state, the proximate stage in the achievement of popular sovereignty. Rights, Marshall argued, had been acquired by the populace in stages: first economic, then political. The time had now come for the achievement of social rights. Of course, this formulation was offered when the British flag still flew over Lagos and Singapore, and Jim Crow still flourished in the United States; it was proposed when postmodern criticism of the limits of "rights talk" (in critical race theory, for example) had not yet been made; and it certainly did not encompass the diasporic and globalized issues antiracists face today. Yet we can make use of it to think anew about political inclusion, social provision, even world citizenship.

By *acculturation and socialization* I mean the reawakening of the 1960s concept that "the personal is political" as a key principle of antiracist personal practice. No one—no matter what their racial identity is—can be free of racism in their heads or hearts; it is too deeply ingrained a social structure. Yet a great deal of thought and action has been devoted to the problem of fostering antiracist practice at the individual and experiential level. Developing these skills, fostering the interruption and interrogation of racism and extending the reach of antiracism in family, school, and cultural work, is an important dimension of the practice we want to support.

Democracy is inseparable from pluralism. Both Durban and the current world crisis (of 9/11, globalization, and the Afghan and Iraq wars) teach us once again that hegemony is inherently unstable and conflictual. But they also demonstrate that embattled hegemonies demonize their oppositions. The standard practice here is to rely on racial and religious differences to unify supporters and stigmatize critics: you're either with us or against us, a loyal subject or a "terrorist." These tactics remain effective, especially during "wartime," but they are also newly vulnerable to internal divisions. The diasporic world, the many millions of postcolonial immigrants now in the northern countries, and the legacy of antiracist and civil rights movements all potentially undermine such authoritarian appeals. The dimension of religious pluralism is especially important now. Why? Because racial and religious profiling are converging. Because Islamophobia is threatening to polarize the globe once again, this time in a nuclear age. And because religious fundamentalism—North and South, East and West—is itself a direct threat to democracy.

The body is the person. The body was a key topic at Durban, because racial identity is always about the body. At Durban, there was discussion about enslavement (ownership of one's body by another) past and present, about trafficking in women's and children's (particularly girls') bodies, about AIDS and other diseases as racial phenomena, and about the multiform linkages between sex/gender and race. It is not news that racism derives much of its energy from sexism, from the efforts of men to possess and control women's bodies. Nor is it surprising that authoritarian and antidemocratic rule takes women as its first hostages. Whether traditional or modern, whether religious or corporate, whether opposing the burka, demanding the right to abortion, or resisting the maquilas and sweatshops that dot the globe, a central thread of democratic movements—antiracist, antiglobalization, and antiauthoritarian—is the liberation of women. The right of all human beings to control their own bodies is a fundamental democratic demand.

In lieu of a conclusion. These are only tentative thoughts on the enormous challenge we—our movement, our radical democratic commitments— face in the post-Durban, and especially post-9/11, era. But this work will continue; it is part of a larger project. Numerous activists and writers are struggling with these issues. Not through any one set of ideas but through the aggregation and synthesis of many efforts to make sense of the current crisis, will we advance toward a new politics. Ultimately, while ideas may be important, what we all rely on most is the great unfulfilled desire for freedom that exists in human beings. Our task as a movement is to interpret and help organize that desire.

The New Imperialism, Globalization, and Racism

On his way to see a Broadway show in April 2003, Justin Halperin, an activist with Doctors Without Borders/Médicins Sans Frontières, stopped in for a plate of vegetable curry at a New York Indian restaurant. Little did he know he had wandered into an all-too-real "Patriot Game": a police/INS raid being carried out under the authority of the U.S. Patriot Act:

> "All of a sudden, there was a terrible commotion and five NYPD in bullet-proof vests stormed down the stairs. They had their guns drawn and were pointing them indiscriminately at the restaurant staff and at us."

After the entire restaurant had been searched and everyone inside—patrons and workers alike—had been herded at gunpoint into the dining room, five officers of the U.S. Immigration and Naturalization Service and the Homeland Security Department began checking identification, running each person's information through a wireless computer to see if they were legally in the United States, had any outstanding warrants against them, or had in any other way drawn the attention of the law.

"You have no right to hold us," Halperin and the other patrons insisted.

"Yes, we have every right," came the reply. "You are being held under the Patriot Act following suspicion under an internal Homeland Security investigation."

One of the South Asian patrons, a U.S. citizen, whispered to Halperin, "Please stop talking to them. I have been through this before. Please do whatever they say. Please for our sake..." (Halperin 2003).

Some hours later, the police and officials left the restaurant. They explained that the raid at this restaurant had been a mistake!

But raids of this sort have been going on all across the country. Is it a mistake when South Asians and Arabs are singled out for police and INS investigation and harassment? When hundreds are interned without charges for months on end? When thousands of Middle Eastern men are forced to register with the authorities and be fingerprinted (Liptak 2003; D. Cole 2002; *Agence France-Presse* 2002)?

Halperin's experience, like that of thousands of immigrants, Arabs, South Asians, and Muslims, is officially not at all about race; officially it is about "national security," defense of the "homeland," and the "war against terrorism." But unofficially and quite obviously, there is racial profiling at work here. Race offers the most accessible tool to categorize the American people politically: who is "loyal" and who is a "threat," who can be "trusted" and who should be subject to surveillance, who should retain civil rights and who should be deprived of them.

The raid on the Indian restaurant, the roundups, the registration requirements, follow a familiar pattern. Their precedents abound: in the nineteenth century U.S. nativism was anti-Irish, anti-Catholic, and anti-Asian; the Palmer raids of the 1920s targeted eastern and southern Europeans and to some extent Caribbeans; the internment of tens of thousands of Japanese Americans during World War II was based solely upon the detainees' Japanese descent; and the anticommunist hysteria that followed that war both had a significant anti-Semitic component and saw social "race mixing" as prima facie evidence of communist sympathies. Many crises, many social tensions—from recession to global conflict, from business rivalry (for example, competition from Japanese auto manufacturers) to disagreements over international relations (for example, French opposition to the Bush regime's war in Iraq)—have been translated in the United States into racial hostility toward various groups of citizens and residents both inside and outside the country. The targets of this hostility almost invariably have no substantive relationship to the conflict at hand. Yet they are singled out because of their race, because of their collective identity.

Nativism's reappearance in the United States in the aftermath of the 9/11 attacks and the U.S.-led wars in the Middle East impels us to rethink the global dimensions of racism. Today, in the twenty-first century, the well-worn techniques of racialization that have been employed so often in the past to frame so many political conflicts are being employed again. Today race provides a vital frame, a familiar fabrication with which Americans can apprehend the worldwide process that has come to be called globalization. Nativism and nationalism in the United States as well as Islamophobia are not surprisingly some of the main political/cultural framings at work.[1]

These ideologies or worldviews are also historically connected to previous waves of imperial conflict, geopolitical rivalry, and religious strife. The two Gulf wars, for example, are reminders of early patterns of U.S. conquest. The indebtedness of the poor nations of the world to the wealthy ones is a modern sequel to older patterns of exploitation: the slavery, peonage, and plunder to which poorer and less powerful peoples have been subjected.[2] The patronizing, self-righteous, and frequently violent ways in which dominant western and northern powers have justified their conquests—religiously, politically, morally—also have a long history: in Africa, the Middle East, Asia, and elsewhere. When you see the word *globalization*, think of the word *imperialism*.

Globalization is a re-racialization of the world. What have come to be called "North-South" issues are also deeply racial issues. The disparities in status and "life chances" between the world's rich and poor regions, between the (largely white and wealthy) global North and the (largely dark-skinned and poor) global South have always possessed a racial character. They are the legacy of a half millennium of imperialism. Imperial rule was thought to have ended in the decades following World War II. But is the "age of empire" really over?

This essay proceeds as follows: In the next section I argue that *globalization is a racialized social structure*. Since the termination of the old European empires in the decades after World War II, and since the fall of the apartheid regime in South Africa, global rule has been seen as operating along a North-South axis. The racial dimension of this system continues as noted. It is a system of transnational social stratification under which corporations and states based in the global North dominate the global South. This pattern of rule has largely operated indirectly, making use of economic institutions controlled by transnational corporations and states, such as the International Monetary Fund, the World Bank, and the World Trade Organization. At times military intervention has still been needed to discipline fractious elements in the global South, but such intervention has usually been temporary. After the old imperialism ended in the 1960s, after the U.S. defeat in Vietnam, intervention was undertaken with new trepidations; in particular the "Vietnam syndrome" checked U.S. military interventionism for some decades, though it hardly terminated it.

The two Gulf wars have introduced (or more properly, reintroduced) a new dimension of global domination. There are now two global axes of power and conflict: *the North-South axis and the West-East axis.* In the following section I discuss this transformation, once again emphasizing racial questions. After noting the continuing significance of the North-South divide, which has been the focus of much attention in critical studies of globalization, I then consider the historical legacy and the contemporary recrudescence of West-East imperial relations. Historically, the encounter of absolutist Europe with the Islamic world was a crucible of race consciousness. The Islamic world confronted the Christian world in the Reconquista, the Crusades, and a series of Balkan and Ottoman conflicts. The Jewish world also confronted Christian Europe: Jews were "other" as well, a more ancient "other" at that, whose distinction from Christian Europe was racialized—that is, rendered absolute and ineluctable—chiefly through the Inquisition.

These themes have found important echoes in the contemporary political panorama: "the clash of civilizations" is perhaps the most prominent of these, but the recrudescence of militant religious movements on all sides—Muslim, Christian (especially Protestant), Jewish, and Hindu—definitely invites a certain historical queasiness. In fact the amplification of religious politics represents a major recent shift in global political alignments. Beyond the irredentism that focuses on ancient or medieval defeats and takes support from literalist readings of sacred texts, politicized religion cannot avoid a tendency to differentiate human beings along absolute lines; this tendency is very susceptible to racism.

In the next section, on *global hegemony and radical democracy,* I consider the new imperialism that is emerging as the key political conflict of the twenty-first century. Despite its tremendous military strength, despite its monopolization of the world's wealth, the imposition of a new imperial order led by the United States is not likely to succeed anytime soon. Although there are some parallels between the epoch of the old imperialism and the new imperialism of the twenty-first century, there are dramatic differences as well. In good dialectical fashion these spring from the very development of globalization itself: from the unceasing movement of populations in recent decades, from the vast diffusion of information and media, from the growing experience of transnational social movements, and from opposition to the very institutions through which globalization has been developing (the WTO, IMF, and their corporate and state-based supporters).

There is a tremendous hunger for social justice throughout the world. This has given rise to a movement for participatory democracy, a grassroots politics that takes many different forms in different places. Though still in its formative stages, a new counterhegemonic political project is coming into being, based on commitments to pluralism, inclusion, and attentiveness to the needs of the "voiceless" peoples of the world. As a familiar slogan from the World Social Forum in Porto Alegre puts it, "Another world is possible."

So a global social movement is in formation, a potentially powerful counter to the new imperialism. In some final notes on *the challenge of diaspora and U.S. racial crisis*, I suggest that antiracism is one of this movement's most crucial components. Focusing mainly on the United States, I propose that the diasporic or transnational dimensions of racial/ethnonational identities, as well as continuing opposition to the structural racism endemic to the United States, present the new imperialism with serious domestic obstacles. The very racial pluralism of the United States combined with the 1960s legacy of civil rights and antiwar activism are undermining efforts to frame the new imperialism in U.S. nationalist terms or in the sociocultural terms of "the West against the rest." I argue that changing racial dynamics in the United States have the potential significantly to undermine the new imperialist project.

Globalization Is a Racialized Social Structure

After World War II, after the Chinese revolution, after the "third world" revolutions of Algeria, Indonesia, Kenya, Malaya, Vietnam, India, and the Portuguese colonies of Africa, after British decolonization in Africa, after the domestic upheavals of the 1960s in the United States and Europe, after the final fall of the apartheid system in 1994 ... Well, there was a long list of anticolonial challenges in the decades following the war's end, wasn't there? After all that (and a great deal more) it became commonplace to acknowledge the end of "the age of imperialism." What that transformation meant was of course subject to quite a bit of debate. Was it a "victory" for nationalism?—self-determination and democracy at last? Was it simply a shift from one form of elite domination (based overseas) to another (based closer to home)? Was it a transition from colonialism to "neocolonialism: the last stage of imperialism," as Kwame Nkrumah (1965) wrote? Did decolonization represent the belated appearance on the political stage of postcolonial subjects (Cabral 1974, 1976)? Had "the masses" of the global South freed themselves at last and opened a path to democracy or even socialism? Or was decolonization more accurately characterized as a new form of subalternity and resistance? Had it not produced a new set of political tensions?—subaltern elites torn between their insurgent roots and their enforced subservience to the still-dominant North, and subaltern masses facing their continuing powerlessness with a mixture of patience and discontent?[3]

Seen on a world scale, the postcolonial, North-South tableau was not really all that "post": not so much beyond the colonial pattern, although of course the "independence" of Africa and Asia (and the last Caribbean and Mesoamerican colonial territories) now implied indirect rule from the North rather than direct administration from Whitehall or the Élysée. The old empires continued in innumerable ways. The borders they had drawn now demarcated "independent" countries. The old colonial languages remained in use: English, French, and Portuguese served as lingua francas in Nigeria, Côte d'Ivoire, and Mozambique. Some old-style colonial practices persisted, for instance, the post-1967 Israeli occupation of the West Bank and Gaza. Commerce and trade, and even international telephone links, passed through the old "mother countries."[4] When "international peacemakers" were needed (and could be found), they were frequently organized by the relevant ex-colonial power.[5] In these varied ways, then, the old empires continued as legacies of a ponderous and millennial past.

So, too, the racial legacies of the imperial epoch continued. The terms of trade at the start of the twenty-first century are no longer the same as those of, say, the nineteenth: postimperial powers do not explicitly monopolize exports or demand trade concessions as did their predecessors, for example. Rather than send their troops to dictate policy, break strikes, or enforce the superexploitation of labor, they use financial instruments: the threat to withhold credit if strikes are not broken, or perhaps if education and public health budgets are not cut. Using intermediaries like the IMF, they control commerce, finance, labor practices, and social policy in a manner nearly as complete and every bit as onerous in the twenty-first century as British or Portuguese colonial policy was in the nineteenth.

Today soy cultivation in Brazil, oil extraction in Cabinda and the Ogoni region, and labor practices in Ciudad Juarez, Jakarta, or Calcutta are matters of concern in corporate headquarters in St. Louis and New York, as well as on Wall Street and at IMF headquarters in Washington.[6] Northern involvement in southern "independent" countries' environmental, social, and labor policies and practices has created—or perhaps I should say reproduced—a worldwide pattern of employment discrimination, violence, morbidity, impoverishment, pollution, and unequal exchange that shares a great deal with its colonial antecedents. This global system of social stratification correlates very well with racial criteria: the darker your skin is, the less you earn; the shorter your life span, the poorer your health and nutrition, the less education you can get. This too is a legacy of empire, a continuity of empire.

"Oh, but that's not racism! It's not intentional discrimination, just good business!" Of course, similar statements were made in the "enlightened" phases of old European colonialism, when tutelary objectives were advocated by colonial offices and "the white man's burden" was very much on officials' minds. One would like to think that today we are beyond the naive view that to carry out racist practices one must *intend* to treat people differently according to their racial identity, but of course that is still the racial "common sense," especially in the United States. If we are to be serious in our understanding of racism, then, we must grasp that it is the *practices themselves* that count. Racism has to be comprehended in terms of its consequences, not as a matter of intentions or beliefs. Today, racism has been largely—though not entirely, to be sure—detached from its perpetrators. Indeed, in its most advanced forms it has no perpetrators; it is a nearly invisible, taken-for-granted, "commonsense" feature of everyday life and global social structure.

This is true in the U.S. empire, and it is true about racism at home. One might almost imagine the Americanization of racism on a world scale, but that formulation paints racism with too unvarying a brush: racism takes different forms all over the world, but it has a general pattern. Justin Halperin encountered a form of this modern variable racism for a moment, as the workers (and proprietors) of that Indian restaurant encountered it every day, first in their home countries—India, Mexico, Guatemala, the Philippines—and then in the West Forties in Manhattan: racism is central to the empire.

The North-South Axis and the West-East Axis

The two Gulf wars have deeply affected the global context in which racial conflict takes place. Although the 1991 war was organized by the United States and undertaken to preserve oil reserves in a U.S. sphere of influence, it was legitimized by the United Nations and carried out by a large bloc of nations. Some noncombatant nations financed the war, and others were subsidized (or bribed) to fight or at least stay neutral. Under these complex conditions the first Gulf War did not yet signal a split in the tacit postimperial consensus I have discussed. It was a quasi-imperial intervention, which in an earlier time might have been termed "gunboat diplomacy." In 1991 it could still be seen as exceptional. Rather than a harbinger of a new imperial age, it was a "police action." For all the carnage of Gulf War I, the spanking of Iraq did not extend to occupation, its capital was not seized, and its ruler was allowed to retain his throne.[7]

The second Gulf War, however, has been a very different matter. It was undertaken under the flimsiest of pretexts by the United States, which sought to consolidate its access to petroleum supplies, to shore up the political position of its regional gendarme (Israel), and to increase its quotient of domination in the Middle East. The war commenced without international legitimation, after the blessings of the UN Security Council were sought and refused. The United States invaded Iraq anyway, acting nearly unilaterally, and quickly seized Baghdad. The previous ruling party was outlawed, and planning got under way for the creation of a puppet regime. Prolonged occupation will be required. Popular resistance is already apparent, though still disorganized.

Gulf War II was not centrally about Iraq, which was no more than an apparently tempting target. The invasion and occupation of Iraq were a gambit in a larger scheme to throw U.S. weight around, especially in the oil-rich Middle East. U.S. ideologues have frankly admitted that they aim to operate a twenty-first-century imperialism.[8] This war was undertaken as a conscious deviation from established U.S. foreign policy. It was launched in blithe disregard of the "Vietnam syndrome," which previously had proscribed extended U.S. military engagement overseas. In place of that limited but real constraint, which had tacitly restricted U.S. interventionism to short-term commitments or nonhostile use of troops (as "peacekeepers"), the Bush II regime planned more sustained military action. Bush established and extended U.S. military bases throughout the former Soviet Central Asian states, Afghanistan, the Horn of Africa, and the Persian Gulf. He also adopted a policy of "preemptive" assault where only future—not present—threats were perceived, particularly where "weapons of mass destruction" (WMD) were being sought or acquired by a nation or group deemed to be hostile (Allen and Gellman 2002).[9] These two policies—a "forward basing" strategy combined with the arrogation of the right to intervene "preemptively" where no attack had occurred—constitute the military pillars of a new imperial initiative. When combined with the U.S. demand for and dependence on Middle East oil, the demonization, sometimes denied but sometimes flagrant, of Arabs both at home and abroad, the critical attitudes toward Islam put forward by the U.S. Christian Right—the core of Bush's political base—the West-East axis of the new U.S. imperialism is apparent (Goodstein 2003).

With imperialism comes colonialism. Though Bush and Co. assured the world to the contrary, claiming that U.S. forces would be welcomed as liberators, the country's present condition is more akin to subjugation than liberation. Self-rule is not around the corner; the domination of Iraq and exploitation of the country's resources are well underway, under the auspices of the U.S. military and favored U.S. corporations. In just a few months a full-scale U.S. imperialist operation has been mounted in the heart of the Middle East, in a core state within the larger Arab nation (Amin 1978).

With colonialism comes racism. There is nothing new about this; the notes being struck are familiar. The United States affords itself a civilizing mission in the Arab world, the Muslim world, much as the British and French did in the past. Although the president and secretary of state sometimes praise Islam as a religion of peace, it is more often seen as a cloak for barbarism and terrorism. Islam has been equated with terror in the West; this is particularly true in the United States after the September 11, 2001, attacks. The flood of periodical ink and broadcast sound bites devoted to the problematic and mysterious essence of Islam—political Islam, fundamentalist Islam, sex and gender under Islam, the putative "backwardness" of Islam in comparison to the enlightened and democratic West, the tutelary role of Christianity and obligation of proselytization in the Islamic world, and so on—signals a regression in the West, and particularly in the United States, to orientalism at its worst (Said 1978). It hardly needs repeating that like the nineteenth-century phenomenon Edward Said analyzed so influentially, twenty-first-century orientalism is also a discursive set of variations on the theme of imperial rule: the tutelary mission of the West is proclaimed—in the values of "freedom," "democracy," "pluralism," "secularism," and so on—while underneath the surface the old agendas advance: most notably political-military power and the capture of natural resources.

So when the NYPD and the INS/Department of Homeland Security agents detain and harass the patrons and workers at a New York Indian restaurant, these are some of the policies they are carrying out:

- Racial profiling. They do not operate this way in French restaurants in New York.
- Immigration restriction. Immigrants are the chief target. This is an old story and dilemma, because immigrants provide cheap labor.

- Surveillance. The action in the restaurant was carried out by a combination of mainstream and secret police; the latter are building dossiers not only on immigrants but on everyone. Does the name Stasi ring a bell? This stuff is also unconstitutional, if anybody cares.
- Harassment of low-wage labor. Racism generally fortifies and deepens exploitation, which means it is different at different class levels. The NYPD and INS do not carry out raids of this type at Morgan Stanley or Microsoft, which have plenty of South Asian staff too.

Thus the West-East conflict in part supplants the North-South one. The spectacle of the United States and its servile media juxtaposing a putatively civilized "West" to a demonized and ascriptively "barbarous" (if not pagan) "East," I suggest, now takes precedence (whether temporarily or in a long-term way remains to be seen) over the North-South conflict we had grown used to. However, I would not want to say North-South issues have flown away. Do not forget that there were also Mexicans and Filipinos working in the Indian restaurant where Halperin was dining.

No, it is not that North-South issues have been resolved or that they have somehow disappeared. They are just not as present, not as visible, right now. With Gulf War II in the headlines, these issues are on the back burner.

The West-East global axis, like the North-South one, is a fundamentally racialized world social structure. West-East was always a key axis of global modernity. Its resurrection in the twenty-first century as an elemental conflict in the global system cries out for interpretation within the cultural and political frameworks of the present.

Historically the West-East divide was about religion in a different way than the North-South difference was. Starting in roughly the sixteenth century, the North-South division of the newly encompassed globe was understood as distinguishing Europeans from "the others": the primitives, the subhumans, the polytheistic and animistic heathens. So the world was seen from the Europe of conquest and nascent empire; so it was seen from the home base of the "lords of humankind" (Kiernan 1969). The West-East schism, however, predated that by more than half a millennium. It was about Christian Europe versus the Muslims and the Jews, who were rivals (especially the Muslims) for both sacred and profane dominion, and impediments (especially the Jews) to the millennial and chiliastic goals of Christianity. The race concept had not crystallized in thought or social practice at the time of the Reconquista (roughly from the eighth century until the fifteenth), nor in the era of the Crusades (roughly from the end of the eleventh century to the middle of the thirteenth). The Inquisition, founded in 1229, began as an effort—obviously quite fierce—to police doctrine, and only some centuries later, in the sixteenth century, developed a concept of Jewish identity that was racial to all intents and purposes.[10] In the Crusades a protoracial imagery was also invoked vis-a-vis Muslims, for example, in Pope Urban II's call (1095) for the first crusade:

> O what a disgrace if such a despised and base race, which worships demons, should conquer a people which has the faith of omnipotent God and is made glorious with the name of Christ! With what reproaches will the Lord overwhelm us if you do not aid those who, with us, profess the Christian religion! (Thatcher and McNeal 1905, 513–17)[11]

Thus in important ways these epochal struggles prefigured the racialization of humankind and demarcated the boundaries (let us call them the ethnonational boundaries) of the premodern world system, at least in respect to Europe, North Africa, and western Asia.

When the Reconquista terminated, the Maghreb was securely Muslim, and the Iberian Peninsula was fully Christian (Roman Catholic). The Crusades were ultimately lost by the Europeans, with the Middle East remaining under Muslim rule. In eastern Europe the Ottoman Empire was defeated at the second siege of Vienna (1683), and a permanent if tremulous frontier between Islamic and Christian (Eastern Orthodox—later Roman Catholic as well) peoples was established in the Balkans. The Inquisition (and the Crusades) decimated the Jews throughout the Middle Ages but did not eradicate them.[12] By this time, however, the North-South motif was well established in European imperial activity. The extensive "rehearsals" of practices of racial categorization that had been carried out in Europe's earlier relations with Muslim (and Jewish) others was already being transposed to "other others": Native Americans, sub-Saharan Africans, South Asians, and Pacific Islanders. The theory and practice of racialization were seriously underway as well: racial identity and racial difference, as well as racial inequality and hierarchy, were not only being codified in law, science, business, politics, and imperial administration, but were also being "managed" in everyday experience throughout much of the world. Soon enough the meaning of race would receive a thorough treatment in the key Enlightenment texts. The harnessing of such themes—racial, ethnonational, and religious difference, the menace of "otherness"—to the purposes of empire is thus a very old story. Like the Freudian "return of the repressed," they have found important echoes in the contemporary political panorama: "the clash of civilizations" (of which more below) is perhaps the most prominent of these, but the rise of a theocratic Protestant evangelism in the United States also counts. In fact the politicization of religion all around—in Koran-waving Islam as well as Bible-belting Protestantism and ultraorthodox Judaism, in rising Hindu nationalism and recent battles in the Balkans, in (the former Soviet) Central Asia, in Afghanistan, in the Philippines, in Africa, and elsewhere—represents a major recent shift in global political alignments. Beyond the irredentism still festering in memories of ancient or medieval defeats nurtured over centuries, beyond the literalist readings of sacred texts on the part of fundamentalists of different faiths, there is a disturbingly racist dimension to politicized religion: the "other" is a lesser being, an obstacle to God's will. This racism is a lot more apparent today than it was in 1683.[13]

Global Hegemony and Radical Democracy

Comes now the new imperialism. So is this the "clash of civilizations"? Is it a new Reconquista, a new crusade as radical Islamists would argue, a new Inquisition, a new 1683? Is Islam to be thrown back again, not at the gates of Vienna but at those of Baghdad? Or is the present situation very different from that of the Middle Ages? Is there something problematic about the "clash" thesis?

Good questions, to which only tentative answers can be given. Although the West has made war in the Islamic heartland, there are still limits. There is no prospect for a generalized military assault against the Muslim world—which is what the Crusades were. But there is an effort underway to define the West-East conflict as a new epochal conflict in the manner of the cold war. In the United States this is called the "war on terror," and in political Islam it is sometimes reviled as a new "crusade" that must be met with "jihad." Still, the new imperialism is not a "clash of civilizations," despite the Bushies' tacit (or not so tacit) embrace of that Huntington thesis (1996). It is a clash, all right, but principally a geopolitical one centering on issues of race and class. It is a conflict *within* civilizations—or cultures—not among them. The terms and conditions of this new imperial conflict are just now being defined in practice.

From the standpoint of its organizers and theorists in Washington, the new imperialism is an attempt to generate a *global hegemonic project* for the twenty-first century. It is a bid to reassert quasi-global rule on the part of the imperial U.S. politburo, which finds itself newly beleaguered and deeply threatened not so much by armed resistance as by demands for global redistribution of resources and wealth. Highly militarized but somewhat devoid of political vision, nostalgic for clear-cut conflict on the cold war pattern, this new initiative repudiates the preceding period's limited but real commitment to sociopolitical reform, reasserts and justifies the metropole's unprecedented appetite for scarce resources and wealth, and dismisses large segments of the world's population as undeserving of economic well-being, political self-rule, or cultural recognition. Its project is principally framed as a national undertaking, in which "all true Americans" participate, and which stigmatizes opponents as outsiders or even traitors.

So the new imperialism is nationalistic in a reactionary way, a retro way. Though willing to operate unilaterally outside U.S. borders, the new imperial project nevertheless seeks allies and partners, if for no other reason than utility. A small number of other nations have proved themselves "willing" to collaborate with the United States—in a strictly subordinate role, let it be noted—in its attempt to reassert a global hegemony. For the present, however, imperial headquarters is confident enough to confront not only the global South and East but also to tangle with former allies like France and Germany, allies who are "unwilling."

From the standpoint of its opposition, challenging the new imperialism is a *global democratic project*. This is an effort to reclaim the traditions of participatory democracy and sociopolitical pluralism in the postcolonial and postsocialist era. Generating this opposition involves building regional alliances and trade agreements (such as MercoSur in South America) and initiating progressive redistribution of resources at the national level where possible—even in the face of IMF-based structural adjustment policies and other pressures for austerity.[14] Most centrally, challenging the new imperialism means organizing and theorizing a popularly based global democracy movement, already visible in some important institutions and mobilizations such as the World Social Forum (2001–03), the UN World Council Against Racism gathering in Durban (2001), and the Seattle (1999) and Genoa (2001) protests against the WTO. This movement opposes "free trade"/

unequal exchange, environmental depredation, the superexploitation of labor, and, perhaps most important, the onerous debt peonage under which the global South staggers year after year (Stiglitz 2002). It advocates global redistribution of wealth and income, custodianship and protection of the earth's resources, and respect for cultural diversity. It incorporates religious, labor, community, women's, racially based, and environmentalist organizations from all over the world. And it vindicates participatory democracy as the core political value of our era.

These conflicts have so far been defined primarily as North-South ones, and secondarily as localized or national conflicts. They still dominate the framework of opposition, for they have been the source of active mobilization for a decade or more now. But in the wake of the 9/11 events and the Afghan and second Gulf wars, and after the articulation by the Bush II regime of an explicit doctrine of preemptive war making, democratic activists and theorists have begun to turn their attention toward the problem of resurgent imperialism.

A global democratic project will have to address not only the needs of the global South and of various local and national grassroots constituencies but also those of the global East. Democratic rights must be developed "from below" in the societies of the Middle East, South Asia, and East Asia: Palestinian self-rule, restoration of democracy in Myanmar, secular and political pluralism in India, democratic transition in China, Pakistan, and Indonesia.... This is a long list.

It is important to distinguish the counterhegemonic project of participatory democracy from the cloak of democratic advocacy with which the new imperialist project has sought to cover itself. When convenient, the United States has repeatedly sought to frame its interventions—especially in the Middle East and Asia—as undertaken in pursuit of democratic objectives. But after decades of sponsoring or supporting military coups throughout the region (in Iran, Pakistan, Indonesia, and elsewhere), after numerous direct interventions (in Lebanon, Vietnam, Afghanistan, Iraq, and elsewhere), after maintaining cozy alliances with brutal dictatorships in numerous countries in the region (Marcos's Philippines, Rhee's Korea, Suharto's Indonesia, and the Shah's Iran, among others), it hardly becomes the United States to present itself as a tribune of democracy today.

Progress toward participatory democracy can perhaps be made using mass struggles committed to nonviolent principles, such as are now becoming visible in Iran and have some tradition, despite everything, in the Philippines, Palestine, Myanmar, Indonesia, and elsewhere. Unquestionably the development of "eastern" democracy will involve some "western" elements: challenging theocratic rule and supporting religious pluralism, and extending and defending women's rights. It will also involve democratic redistribution of mineral wealth and revenues, most especially that of oil. If this sounds utopian, consider the extent to which present ownership of these resources is a leftover from the days of British and French colonial rule.

The Challenge of Diaspora and the U.S. Racial Crisis

A global democratic project must assert the rights and help develop the political capacity of those in the global South and global East: people who are excluded from political participation, superexploited, and subjected to institutionalized violence. But any serious challenge to the new imperialism cannot confine itself to the global South and East. It will have to address the parallel conditions and demands of those within the metropole. As in the past, race and racism play a crucial role in challenging the limits of democracy there.

There is a resemblance between the post–World War II dismantling of the old imperialism and the reform of state racial policies in the United States during the same period. Elsewhere I have written extensively about the worldwide racial "break" or rupture set in motion during and after the war (Winant 2001). In the postwar period antiracist and anticolonial movements interacted extensively (Dudziak 2000). Consider Dr. King's denunciation of the Vietnam War in this regard, a position that was seen as controversial at the time. Similarly, postcolonial reform regimes and post–civil rights era racial policies exhibit numerous similarities: both achieved the incorporation of a range of movement demands (generally the more mainstream or moderate ones) in state policy; both also experienced the inclusion (or co-optation) of former insurgents and movement leaders in postcolonial and post–civil rights state apparatuses (in government executives or leaderships, as legislators and officials, etc.).[15]

There are significant consequences of this pattern of "contentious politics" (McAdam, Tarrow, and Tilly 2001), reform, and incorporation. The price movements pay for winning reforms is demobilization. In addition the more radical demands and sectors of oppositional movements are likely to be marginalized if not repressed after significant reform takes place.

In this essay I have discussed the consequences of the termination of the old empires and the transition to a model of indirect rule after World War II. This is what is generally called globalization: the North-South patterns already mentioned, the role of the IMF, SAPs, the WTO, "free trade," and so on. But what about the metropolitan side of the parallel? What have been the consequences of movement incorporation and racial reform in the United States? Everyday accounts of race and racism—such as those available from the mainstream media, from political leaders, and even in university settings—tell us that the racial crisis that engulfed the United States a few decades ago has passed. This is the new "common sense": that little remains of the organized black movement that confronted Jim Crow in the South and rose up in anger in the ghetto "riots" during the mid-1960s, that reforms have been made, that racial attitudes have shifted, that far from espousing white supremacism (which was certainly the norm before World War II and far from uncommon even in the 1960s), most whites today call themselves "color-blind." Officially the United States has entered the age of "diversity."

Yet at the same time, by almost every conceivable indicator researchers can bring forward, the same racial inequalities—or shall I say the same "structural racism"?—that existed in the past persist today: modified here and there perhaps, but hardly eliminated and only slightly reduced in scope, especially in terms of black-white disparities. This is not the place to inventory the data, but whether we look at wealth/income (in)equality, health, access to/returns to education, segregation by residence or occupation, rates of surveillance or punishment by the criminal "justice" system, or many other indicators that compare racial "life chances," we find patterns strikingly similar to those of the past (Feagin and McKinney 2002).

So today the parallel between postwar anti-imperial movements and antiracist ones continues, as the new imperialism confronts an ongoing demand for greater democracy in the global South and East, while post–civil rights racial hegemony confronts an ongoing demand for greater democracy in the U.S. "homeland."

In the era of globalization, however, U.S. racial hegemony faces a formidable new problem in the "homeland": the problem of *diaspora*. After World War II, after CNN, after the Internet, after tidal waves of migration from South to North, from East to West, and from the countryside to the city, globalization is not only the domain of the imperial state and the transnational corporations; it is also a popular domain. As a result, the United States, like other national societies of the global North and West—the UK, France, Germany—is a lot less homogeneous at the start of the twenty-first century than it was in the heyday of classical imperialism or the era of de jure racism. Despite incessant governmental and civil society–based campaigns on behalf of "patriotism" and nationalism, the flag, the pledge of allegiance, and so on, U.S. national identities are a lot more "diverse" (to use the post–civil rights era parlance once again) than they ever were before.

The United States is a settler nation; it has always been a destination for immigrants. In the post–World War II period, and especially since the immigration reforms of the 1960s, immigration from Asia, Africa, South Asia, Latin America, and the Middle East—from the global South and East—expanded greatly.[16] This contrasted significantly with earlier patterns, which from the founding of the United States until the later nineteenth century were dominated by less restricted European immigration and always had a profound nativist and racist dimension. The patterns of immigration to the United States have always reflected the pressures that global political and economic conditions placed on potential migrants, but at the same time U.S. immigration has been organized quite pervasively by national racial policies and practices (Jacobson 1998; Smith 1997).

Diaspora is a Greek term that was originally applied to the scattering of the Jews. Peoples have always been dispersed, and mass migration has always existed, but in the modern era it expanded on a worldwide scale as transportation capabilities, slavery and colonialism, capitalist labor requirements, and war making (which displaces great masses of people) reached new heights. While the old empires, slave traders, and developing capitalist enterprises effectuated the displacement and migration of great masses of people (principally for purposes of labor extraction and settlement), an alternative, "grassroots" form of globalization also developed during the "age of empire": notably in the African diaspora but also in the diasporas of numerous peoples driven or drawn away from their native countries by economic or political pressures. Both these processes of global demographic transformation—one driven "from above" and the other organized "from below"—reached their apogees during and after World War II. In consequence of that war a vast demographic shift took place, impelled by wartime mobilization, by labor demand during and after the war, and by the rearrangement of the world political landscape that followed the war. Numerous post–World War II diasporas appeared or were reinforced: African, Caribbean, Filipino, "offshore Chinese," South Asian, and many others. These were greatly facilitated by improved transportation, by the new global reach of communications media, and by the creation of "migration chains" between sending and receiving communities often far apart.

By now there are very substantial migrant communities in the United States, as there are throughout the global North and West. The sociopolitical identities of these groups, as well as the economic and cultural roles they play in their own diasporic/transnational communities, are becoming crucial factors in the developing conflict for global hegemony. Not yet two years after the 9/11 attacks, Islamophobia—the current principal form of U.S. nativism—may already have deeply alienated U.S. Muslims. Unconditional U.S. support for the Israeli occupation of the West Bank and Gaza has forced many Muslims in the United States, as it has many throughout the Muslim world, to see the United States as an enemy of human and civil rights for Arabs. Terrorist attacks on the part of radical Islamist groups, carried out in various countries, have reinforced the polarization between the U.S. regime and popular democratic aspirations, especially in the Arab lands.[17] Racial profiling of Muslims, of Arabs and Arab Americans, as well as of South Asians and others happens in numerous ways: mosques are surveilled, immigration restrictions are stepped up, "voluntary" registration campaigns are mandated, arbitrary and secret detentions occur, and the definition of "terrorism" is expanded to include many activities that for non-Muslims are fully protected forms of political speech or social service. Recall Halperin's account of the raid on the Indian restaurant in New York.

On the other hand, the threat of "terrorist" attacks on civilians is disturbing and real enough after 9/11, even if it is being used for political purposes in Washington. In the enormous and varied diasporic communities in question—Indian, Pakistani, Palestinian, Iraqi, Iranian, and so on—there are millions of people who are highly integrated into U.S. society, who have developed their individual and group identities along the familiar "ethnic" or "hyphenated American" lines, and who do not expect their normal lives to be called into question at the workplace, in their children's schools, when they travel, or in other ways as well. The vast majority of Muslim Americans of Middle Eastern or South Asian descent do not accept a radicalized political Islam, remain loyal to the United States, and share the democratic values the country professes (Zaman 2002). In fact, like other expatriate and postcolonial populations in the United States and elsewhere in the world's North and West, these diasporic minorities represent a tremendous resource for development and democratization, if they can be afforded full citizenship rights, not demonized, harassed, or superexploited. Already private remittances from "developed" countries to poor ones constitute a major source of "foreign aid," totaling over $100 billion in 2001.[18]

So when we ask, what civilizations are clashing? we quickly discover that what has been labeled the "clash of civilizations" is as much a series of domestic political conflicts over issues of nationalism, citizenship, nativism, and racism as it is a global conflict: North-South or West-East. Once again in the United States, racial, ethnonational, gender-based, and also class-based issues are politically resurgent. Rather than some epochal "clash"—aka "the war on terrorism"—on the order of the Crusades or Reconquista, today the sociopolitical status of diasporic groups—whether recent immigrants or well-established ethnonational minorities—has become a prominent political issue. Will they receive the protections that the "open society" claims to extend, that the Constitution guarantees, and that the civil rights–era reforms advanced still further? Or will they be subject to the racist harassment of the Patriot Act and its successors? Recall again Halperin's account of the raid on the Indian restaurant in New York.

It may be somewhat surprising to hear that "the clash of civilizations" is occurring no less in Washington than in the Middle East! Just as significant democratic, secular, and modernizing tendencies are confronting political Islam in the Middle East and on a world scale (Zaman 2002), for example, so too are powerful theocratic tendencies, notably Protestant evangelical but also Catholic and Jewish ones, gaining significant influence in Washington, despite their antidemocratic and antisecular views.[19] Indeed the Bush regime is under continuing pressure from these religious-political currents to toughen its stand *even more* on their key issues: particularly gay rights and abortion rights (Hallow 2003).

What of overall U.S. racial dynamics in the time of the new imperialism, the post–civil rights era? I have argued that the Bush regime's policies have definite racist dimensions both at home and abroad. Although it is not possible in this essay to explore these in depth, it seems fitting to complete my discussion of the new imperialism with an overview of this insufficiently recognized problem.

The new imperialism has made a definite turn toward militarism as an instrument of global policy. Yet who does the fighting, and who pays for the war effort? The U.S. armed forces are predominantly composed of working-class youth. They are far more racially "diverse" than the higher (or even intermediate) reaches of the nation's occupational structure. While the upper-income and wealth-holding strata are doing their best to avoid taxation, they are leaving the burdens of financing military spending to the same working- and lower-middle-class families whose kids do the fighting. Simultaneously the Bush regime is hollowing out the social programs from which working-class and racially defined minorities most benefit: education, health care, housing, transportation, child care, not to mention welfare.

To the extent that it can be considered a comprehensive social policy, the new imperialism has thus far displayed a tendency toward ferocious anti-statism. The one exception to that has been its rampant militarism, but even there cuts are being made in veterans' benefits. In fact, the Bush regime's unprecedented proclivity for regressive redistribution of wealth has been described by one of this policy's chief advocates as predominantly a strategy for drastically reducing the size of government.[20] Defining racism as a practice, then, understanding it in terms of its consequences—as discussed earlier—leads to the inescapable conclusion that the new imperialism is a racist policy not only globally but locally, not only abroad but at home as well. As a comprehensive social policy it has decidedly deleterious effects on the life chances of racially defined minorities within the United States. It is racially discriminatory.

The shifting racial demography of the United States will have significant effects on national politics. Racially defined minorities are increasing in electoral influence. Whites are losing their majority status in much of the United States. Whites are now a minority in California; they will soon be a minority elsewhere as well. Many of the large West Coast, Gulf Coast, and East Coast cities are becoming more diverse in racial terms. The suburbs remain largely white but are becoming more racially diverse as well. The country is being racially resegregated by cities, states, and regions and is also being restratified across the whole system of wealth and income distribution. These tendencies are creating new areas in which racial conflict may emerge.

For example, within two decades the public educational system will be largely composed of nonwhite students. What will be the implications of this for educational policy, school finance, staffing, structure, and curriculum? Around the same time a majority of the labor force will no longer be white, and the population and labor force will be older. The retired population will have a majority of whites, while the younger working population will have a majority of nonwhite workers. What will happen to the social security system when whites' retirement is financed largely by nonwhite workers? What will happen to the structure of taxation when it becomes a means of financing global militarism based disproportionately on the tax outlays of diasporic/transnational minorities?

Already white politicians opposed to immigration are having difficulty winning elections as their constituencies become darker. In 1994 the Republican Party pushed for the adoption of Proposition 187 in California. Voter approval of this anti-immigration measure (which had definite nativist tendencies) consolidated Latino voters' support for the Democratic Party. Currently the fastest growing racially defined minority group,[21] Latinos now outnumber blacks nationally; their political allegiance will prove more and more crucial in coming elections. East Asian, South Asian, and Middle Eastern diasporic communities are also increasing in size.[22]

White political opposition to affirmative action is also coming under increased fire, as an emerging coalition of universities, corporations, the military, and minority voters looks to the Democratic Party to defend it.[23] Changing racial demographics may also reshape the politics of crime and punishment in the coming years. Support for the death penalty, once hugely popular, seems to be waning, and efforts are underway to reform drug-oriented mandatory sentencing laws, which emphasize victimless crimes, discriminate against racially defined minorities (for many whites, drug problems are defined as health issues requiring treatment, not prison), and are very costly to state budgets (Mauer 1999). As the number of minority voters (and minority taxpayers) increases, the politics of punishment may become more humane.

Although it seems to be riding high at the moment, the Bush II regime can also be seen as carrying out a somewhat desperate effort to preserve a moribund social order, both global and national. The new imperialism is the global dimension of the regime's foreign policy. It is an effort to reassert U.S. global hegemony based largely on military superiority. Domestically the regime remains dependent in crucial ways on a dying (or at least decadent) form of white racial nationalism, despite its sporadic attempts to portray itself as ecumenically embracing Islam and operating a domestic policy of "compassionate conservatism."

Opposing the somewhat frightening spectacle of an arrogant and clumsy giant—a modern Gulliver trying to subdue by force the growing ranks of the world's alienated Lilliputians—is a developing counterhegemonic project. At its core is the principle of participatory democracy. Still in its preliminary stages, still limited largely to grassroots and insurgent movements, both in the global South and East and in the northern metropoles, still reeling from the demise of much of the socialist ideal, still trying to regroup after post–World War II reformism successfully incorporated many progressive movements, still lacking official support beyond some hopeful preliminary gestures in Latin America (notably in Brazil) and in Europe (in a few "unwilling" EU countries), the movement for participatory democracy nevertheless possesses one great resource: the vast support of millions all around the world. A luta continua!

Part III
Racial Theory

One Hundred Years of Racial Theory

In the past few decades the significance of race has been called into question. Social and political change have overtaken the concept, which until quite recently had retained a relatively stable set of meanings, both in social theory and in popular consciousness. To be sure, racial meanings have never been solid and fixed. Racial identities are themselves not immutable; they have always been reinvented and reinterpreted. The very concept of race itself only came into being with the dawn of the modern world system and the rise of capitalism in the sixteenth century. Still, the use of racial categories to locate individuals and groups socially and politically, the association of physical appearance (so-called phenotype) with cultural identity, social status, and political interest did begin to permeate the world about half a millennium ago.

Once racial identity was an established component of human identity—which is to say after the rise of Europe, the conquest of the Americas and the subjugation of Asia, and the establishment of the African slave trade—race came to seem an ineluctable, ineffable component of self and society. The *social fact* of race, once loosed upon the world, could not be removed from it. And because race was understood to be not merely a social but also a *natural fact*, a physical difference among human beings, its significance and permanence as a demarcation among human groups was rarely, if ever, questioned. No matter how named, no matter how varied and varying, racial categories had found a permanent home in the world.

How then to grasp the problem of racial theory? How may we take stock of the meaning of race in all its historical and comparative vicissitudes? The extent of the literature on the race concept alone, not to mention the mountains of empirical studies that focus on racial issues, presents difficulties for any attempt at theoretical overview and synthesis. A wide range of concepts from both the classical and modern traditions can readily be applied to racial matters. Variations among national and cultural understandings of the meaning of race cry out for comparative approaches. World history has been racialized at least since the rise of the modern world system; racial hierarchy remains global even in the postcolonial present; and popular concepts of race, however variegated, remain in general and everyday use almost everywhere. Thus, any effective theory of race seems to require, at a minimum, comparative historical and political components, some sort of sociology of culture or knowledge, and an adequate microsocial account as well.

Over the past few decades both interest in racial matters and the pace at which racial dynamics have been changing worldwide have increased dramatically. Controversy over the meaning and significance of race was greatly heightened after World War II. The war itself had significant racial dimensions and left a legacy of revulsion at racism and genocide. The social movements and revolutionary upsurges that succeeded the war and brought the colonial era to an end also raised the problematic of race to a new level of prominence. The civil rights movement in the United States and the anti-apartheid mobilization in South Africa are but the most prominent examples of this. As it gained its independence, the postcolonial world was quickly embroiled in the competition of the cold war, a situation that placed not only the legacy of imperial rule but also the racial policies of the superpowers (especially those of the United States) under additional scrutiny. Another consequence of the war was enormous migratory flows from the world's rural South to its metropolitan North; in these demographic shifts "the empire struck back," pluralizing the former "mother countries" (Centre for Contemporary Cultural Studies 1982). All these developments raised significant questions about the meaning of race.

Origins of the Race Concept

Can any subject be more central or more controversial in social thought than that of race? Although prefigured in various ways by ethnocentrism and taking preliminary form in ancient concepts of civilization and barbarity (Snowden 1983), citizen (or *zoon politikon*) and outsider/slave (Hannaford 1996; Finley 1983), the concept is essentially a modern one. Yes, the Crusades and the Inquisition and the Mediterranean slave trade were important rehearsals for modern systems of racial differentiation, but in terms of scale and inexorability the race concept began to attain its familiar meanings only at the end of the Middle Ages.

At this point it would be useful to say what I mean by *race*. At its most basic level, race can be defined as a *concept that signifies and symbolizes sociopolitical conflicts and interests in reference to different types of human bodies*. Although the concept of race appeals to biologically based human characteristics (so-called phenotypes), selection of these particular human features for purposes of racial signification is always and necessarily a social and historical process. There is no biological basis for distinguishing human groups along the lines of "race," and the sociohistorical categories employed to differentiate among these groups reveal themselves, upon serious examination, to be imprecise if not completely arbitrary (Omi and Winant 1994).

The idea of race began to take shape with the rise of a world political economy. The onset of global economic integration, the dawn of seaborne empire, the conquest of the Americas, and the rise of the Atlantic slave trade were all key elements in the genealogy of race. The concept emerged over time as a kind of world historical bricolage, an accretive process that was in part theoretical but much more centrally practical.[1] Though intimated throughout the world in innumerable ways, racial categorization of human beings was a European invention. It was an outcome of the same world historical processes that created European nation-states and empires, built the "dark satanic mills" of Britain (and the even more dark and satanic sugar mills of the Brazilian Reconcavo and the Caribbean), and explained it all by means of Enlightenment rationality.

But this is not to say that the European attainment of imperial and world-encompassing power "gave rise" to race. Indeed, it is just as easy to argue the opposite: that the modern concept of race "gave rise to," or at least facilitated the creation of, an integrated sociopolitical world, a modern authoritarian state, the structures of an international economy, and the emergence over time of a global culture. We must recognize all these issues as deeply racialized matters.

The Social Study of Race Has Been Shaped by Large-Scale Political Processes

The "Classics"

When we look at the treatment of racial matters in social theory, we find the concept present from the beginning, though often in an inchoate, undertheorized, or taken-for-granted form. Herbert Spencer, the usual example cited as the ur-sociologist, reads as a biological determinist today, preoccupied as he is with human evolution and the ranking of groups according to their "natural" characteristics.[2]

Marx's orientation to themes we would now consider racial was complex. His denunciation in *Capital* of the depredation, despoliation, and plunder of the non-European world in pursuit of "primitive accumulation,"[3] and his ferocious opposition to slavery both commend him. But his insistence that the colonized precapitalist societies would ultimately benefit from their enmeshment in the brutal clutches of the European powers hints to present-day readers that he was not entirely immune to the hierarchization of the world that characterized the imperial Europe of his day.

Weber's treatment of the concept of *ethnie* under the rubric of "status" (a relational category based on "honor") presages a social constructionist approach to race, but in Weber's voluminous output there is no serious consideration of the modern imperial phenomenon, there are numerous instances of European chauvinism,[4] and there is an occasional indulgence in—let us call it—racialist meditation.[5] Durkheim too ranks the world Eurocentrically, distinguishing rather absolutely between "primitive" and "civilized" peoples based on the limited ethnology available to him; he also muses somewhat racialistically.[6]

It is not my purpose to chide these masters. Far from it: they acquit themselves well when compared to the rank-and-file pundits, and even the *bien philosophes* who were their contemporaries. They can hardly be expected to have remained totally immune from the racial ideology of their times. But that is precisely the point: social theory arose in an imperialist, Eurocentric, and indeed racist era, both in Europe and in the United States. In its "classical" early statements, it was racially marked by the time and place of its birth.

Across the Atlantic

It was largely in the United States that the early sociology of race first forsook the library for the streets, partaking in the great empirical efflorescence that marked the field's establishment in that country. There was an inescapable association between the discipline's development in this period (the early twentieth century) and the rise of pragmatism in U.S. philosophy and progressivism in U.S. politics during the same epoch. It is not hard to understand why race was promoted to a more central social concern as the discipline acquired a foothold—indeed, its headquarters—in the United States.

After all, this was a country where African slavery was still an artifact of liv-ing memory, where the frontier had only recently been declared "closed," where immigration was at a flood stage, and where debates over the propri-ety of imperial activity (in the Philippines, for example) were still current.

At the beginning of the twentieth century, a nearly comprehensive view of the race concept still located it at the biological level. On this account, races were "natural": their characteristics were essential and given, immut-able. Over the centuries such approaches had accomplished a wide range of explanatory work. Both the defense of slavery and its critique (abolition-ism) had appealed to "natural" criteria in support of their views. In a similar vein the holocaust visited upon indigenous peoples, as well as the absorp-tion of large numbers of former Mexican, Spanish, and Asian subjects through war and coercive immigration policies, had been justified as "natu-ral," inevitable forms of human progress.[7] Even after emancipation and the "closing of the frontier" in the United States, scientific arguments still sum-moned "natural causes" to the defense of hierarchical concepts of race. In the late nineteenth and early twentieth centuries the impact of social Dar-winism was enormous (not merely on Herbert Spencer), and the arguments of eugenics also acquired great support.

But as the world racial system underwent significant shifts in the early twentieth century, and as labor demands grew more complex and the agenda of democratization gradually assumed greater importance, biologistic racial theories became increasingly obsolete. The resurgence of anticolonial move-ments in Africa and Asia (a century after the success of such movements in the Americas), the spreading of democratic demands to countries consid-ered "backward" and "uncivilized," and the increased mobility (both geo-graphic and economic) of ex-slaves and former peasants during and after World War I all motivated the gradual but inexorable development of a more sophisticated social scientific approach to race.

The two early-twentieth-century examples of pathbreaking racial theo-rizing that require mention here are, first, the pioneering study by W. E. B. Du Bois of black life in Philadelphia (Du Bois 1899), and the extensive body of work on racial matters that formed a crucial component of the Chicago School of sociology. Both these pioneers were oriented by the pragmatism that was the most original, and remains the most important, contribution of North American social theory.

Du Bois's *The Philadelphia Negro* sought both to make a significant advance over previous knowledge (overwhelmingly ignorant and stereotyped) about black life and U.S. racial dynamics,[8] and to build on a solid base of empirical

data a powerful and strategic argument for the democratization of race relations in turn-of-the-century America. Though slightly marred by concessions demanded of Du Bois by his patrons, the work still stands, an entire
century later, as a magisterial survey of the unique racial dementia of the
United States: the country's foundational involvement with African enslavement and the permanent consequences of that involvement. In addition to
his pathbreaking approach to racial theory, particularly evident in his concept of "the veil" and his understanding of racial dualism (Du Bois 1903b),
Du Bois's early work is notable for its relentless empirical commitments and
independent application of pragmatist philosophy to the social enterprise
(West 1989), both theoretical and practical. As Elijah Anderson points out
in his introduction to the centennial reissue of *The Philadelphia Negro* (Du
Bois 1899), the tendency to attribute these innovations to more "mainstream" sociologists for many years banished Du Bois from his rightful place
in the disciplinary canon.

The large body of work on race produced by the researchers of the Chicago School also demonstrates the influence of pragmatism and progressivism. Oriented by a "social problems" approach and consciously viewing
the city of Chicago as a social laboratory, the Chicago sociologists authored
a group of studies focusing on crime, poverty, "slums," and so on, all problems that were frequently seen racially. Although they were not entirely
immune to the racism of their day, the approaches that developed in Chicago were notable for their attentiveness to their empirical subjects and for
their generally democratic orientation. Moving from the preliminary work
of Ernest Burgess, through the great creativity and comprehensiveness of
W. I. Thomas and Florian Znaniecki's massive study,[9] the Chicago engagement with the problematic of race culminated in the work of Robert E.
Park on the macrodimensions of race (Park 1950).[10] There was also an important micro side of the Chicago tradition, which proceeded from George
Herbert Mead and deeply informed Herbert Blumer's work on the symbolic
dimensions of race (Blumer 1958). Perhaps most important, the work of
the Chicago sociologists broke definitively with the racial biologism that
had characterized earlier treatments, asserting with increasing clarity the
position that race was a socially constructed, not "naturally" given, phenomenon.[11] The influence of this view on crucial later treatments of race
throughout the social sciences—for example, Gunnar Myrdal's *An American Dilemma* (1944) and St. Clair Drake and Horace Cayton's magisterial
work (1945)—was enormous. The Myrdal study would not even have
come into being, much less exercised the tremendous political influence it

did (Southern 1987; Jackson 1990), without vast assistance from Chicago-trained scholars.[12]

Contemporary Approaches to the Race Concept

The same dynamics that prompted the Americanization of sociology and sparked the shift from classical theorizing to empirical research were also at work in the development of contemporary approaches to race. Once again, pressing sociopolitical issues drove the theoretical vehicle forward.

Social argument could only properly challenge biologistic positions after the race concept had been fully reinterpreted sociohistorically. Given the onrushing European disaster of fascism, the task of elaborating a democratic and inclusionist theory of race fell largely to U.S. scholars from the 1930s onward.[13] Here the social work carried out by the Chicago scholars and their successors, and the continuously powerful voice of Du Bois, combined with the insights and research of a growing number of progressive racial observers. To name but a few other important influences, the Boasian shift in anthropology, which refocused that discipline from physical to cultural preoccupations and had widespread effects in popular culture, was certainly significant. The association of fascism with eugenics—a movement that had developed strong bases both in Britain and the United States as well as in Germany—forced choices upon democratically and progressively inclined publics, both intellectual and political. The "retreat of scientific racism" was the result of these unsavory connections (Barkan 1992). Marxist accounts of race became more prominent as a function of the upsurge of communism (a leading, though not unproblematic, antiracist influence, especially in the 1930s and 1940s). The growth of important black movements, both political and cultural,[14] also strongly affected the racial "public sphere" in the interwar period. And the liberal democratic ethos, strongly invoked in the United States by the wartime work of Myrdal (1944), exercised tremendous influence.

The Post–World War II Challenge

In the post–World War II period, the concept of race was more comprehensively challenged than ever before in modern history. Decolonization spread through the global South, sometimes achieving its emancipatory aims by peaceful or at least largely political means, and sometimes requiring prolonged warfare to dislodge the occupying northern (aka white) power. Migration and urbanization of previously impoverished ex-colonials and former peasants—largely "people of color"—landed millions of dark faces in the world's metropoles. These newly urbanized groups soon mobilized and pressed for their political and social rights, contesting entrenched customs and institutionalized patterns of white supremacy and racism in numerous countries. Especially in the United States, the hegemonic postwar nation, these racially based movements took the political center stage.

These new demands for inclusion, in turn, induced serious crises in national political systems. As racial regimes steeped in discriminatory or exclusionist traditions were pressured to innovate and reform, social approaches to race were also transformed. A great (although quite belated) interest in patterns of discrimination and prejudice developed.[15] Interest in the dynamics of racial inequality grew at the international level.[16] Not only the mainstream sociology but also the radical sociology of race advanced, spurred on by the new movements as well as by dissatisfaction with the pace and scope of reform (Blauner 1972; Ladner 1973).

While an obvious advance over earlier views, postwar racial theory was subject to numerous limitations both in its moderate and its radical versions. Most problematic was the tendency toward *reductionism:* the three main theoretical tendencies all subordinated the race concept to some supposedly more objective or "real" social structure. *Ethnicity*-based theories were generally the most mainstream or "moderate." They saw race as a culturally grounded framework of collective identity. *Class*-based theories understood race in terms of group-based stratification and economic competition. *Nation*-based theories perceived race in the geopolitical terms largely given by the decolonization process so prominent in the postwar era. They focused attention on issues of peoplehood, rootedness, and race unity, as well as citizenship and rights. As is common in theories linked to nationalist movements, substantial currents of irredentism permeated these theories.[17]

As the twentieth century (whose "problem is the color-line," as Du Bois had famously written) drew toward its end, these approaches to the race concept also neared their limits. They were informed by and oriented to the pressing sociopolitical problems of their time, notably racial prejudice and discrimination (especially state-sponsored discrimination). After these grievances had been forcefully raised in many countries by antiracist movements, they were generally at least ameliorated by democratic and inclusionist efforts at reform. Although hardly eliminated by shifts in state racial policy, racial injustice became less visible as a result of these reforms, and overt racism was generally stigmatized. In such a situation the racial theory that sought to explain such phenomena slowly became obsolete. Thus are we left at century's end with a range of unanticipated, or at least theoretically unre-solved, racial dilemmas.

The Limits of Contemporary Racial Theory

The inadequacy of the range of theoretical approaches to race available in sociology at the turn of the twenty-first century is quite striking. Consistent with the argument presented in this essay, this theoretical crisis can be seen as reflecting the continuing sociopolitical crisis of race. In particular, the *persistence of racially based distinctions*, distinctions that state-based racial reforms were supposed to overcome, poses major problems for racial theories inherited from the earlier post–World War II years.

Ethnicity-oriented theories of race had suggested that the suppression of prejudiced attitudes could be achieved through contact, integration, and assimilation, and that discrimination could be ended by laws and regula-tions that made jobs, education, housing, and so on equally accessible to all. But the endurance of obstacles to integration severely undermined ethnicity-based approaches to race,[18] while assimilation into white cultural norms was hardly desirable to most racially defined minorities. Faced with these impasses in the United States today, ethnicity theories of race have devolved into "neoconservatism," which can do no better than reprove racially defined minorities for their continuing race consciousness and supposed failure to take advantage of civil rights reforms (Thernstrom and Thernstrom 1997). In Western Europe, these theories take the form of "differentialism," which repudiates the racist cultural hierarchies of the past but affirms the exclu-sionist commitments of (French, German, British, etc.) "national culture," thus upholding barriers to immigration and racial pluralism, not to mention integration (Taguieff 1988; Wieviorka 1995; Balibar and Wallerstein 1991).

Class-based theories of race had argued that racial conflict was the mode in which class conflict was "lived out" or expressed (Hall et al. 1978). This suggested that racial stratification and intergroup competition were fairly well defined in the postwar world (Bonacich 1972, 1976; Gordon, Reich, and Edwards 1982; Reich 1981). If the inequality among racially defined groups was to be overcome, it would require not only interracial solidarity but also race-conscious programs designed to remedy the *effects* of discrimi-nation. Such programs, put into place in many countries and under various names, have come to be known under the rubric of "affirmative action." But two factors have undermined the plausibility of this account. First, a grow-ing inequality *within* racially defined minority groups weakens group cohe-sion both politically and culturally; this undermines the case for affirmative action. Second, enduring white commitments to racial privilege—that is, persistent racism—largely trump interracial working-class solidarity, defeating whatever potential for economic redistribution such programs as affirmative action may have offered. Thus class-based theories of race have in practice been vitiated by the failure of the socialist (or social democratic, or New Deal) vision in the present epoch.[19]

Nation-oriented accounts of race have been called into question by the combined weight of international and intranational heterogeneity. In a postcolonial era that has witnessed tremendous migration, that offers unprecedented ease of movement, and that boasts of communicative powers (mass media, particularly music and film, but also telephonic and computer-based resources) unimaginable even a few years ago, the nation-based dimensions of racial solidarity have atrophied. Trans- (or perhaps post-) national forms of racial correspondence persist but now take the form of *diasporic* identities of various kinds (Kilson and Rotberg 1976; Appadurai 1996; Lemelle and Kelley 1994). At this point, however, transnational racial solidarity generally lacks the kind of political commitment and organization once displayed under the banners of pan-Africanism or the "nonaligned" movements. In this situation, nation-based theories of race have devolved into crude and "retro" forms of cultural nationalism, informed more by mysticism than by social analysis.[20]

Notes toward a New Racial Theory

If the earlier theoretical accounts have atrophied, and a new approach is needed, what would be its outlines? As the century draws to an end, a convincing racial theory must address the persistence of racial classification and stratification in an era officially committed to racial equality and multiculturalism. The present moment is one of increasing globalization and postcoloniality. It is a time when most national societies, and the world as a whole, are acknowledged to be racially multipolar, and when "hybridity" is frequently recognized as a key feature of racial identity. Today, in marked distinction to the situation that obtained before World War II, most states and members of state elites claim to oppose discrimination, deny their continuing adherence to racialized views of their populations, and even present themselves as "color-blind" or "differentialist." How and why do racial distinctions endure in such changed circumstances?

Any minimally adequate theoretical response to this question must include recognition of the *comparative/historical dimension of race*. The mere fact that we are discussing race here and now (in a post–civil rights, post–cold war, postcolonial period) itself imposes significant theoretical constraints and opportunities. As I argued earlier, earlier racial theories too were products of their times and places. We remain in a similar situation today.

A second dimension in which any successful theory must operate is the ability to range over, and hopefully to link, the *micro and macro aspects of racial signification and racialized social structure.* Such a multileveled and interconnected account is a general obligation of social theory in the present.[21] It is a duty incurred by any attempt to conceptualize the continuing significance of race. A notable and intriguing feature of race is its ubiquity, its presence in both the "smallest" and the "largest" features of social relationships, institutions, and identities.

A third theoretical dimension involves recognition of the *newly pervasive forms of politics* in recent times. This may be regarded as a racially conscious conception of action or agency. In the United States, much of the impetus behind the reconceptualization of politics that has occurred in recent decades was derived from racially based and indeed antiracist social movements. The democratizing challenge posed after World War II to "normal" systems of domination and power, "accepted" divisions of labor, and "rational-legal" means of legitimation had inescapable racial dimensions. Racially based movements, then, and the "second-wave" feminism that followed and was inspired by them, problematized the public-private distinction basic to an older generation of political theory and political sociology.[22] This has been recognized in new approaches to political sociology, such as "political process" models (McAdam 1982; Morris and Mueller 1992). It also appears in the revival of interest in pragmatist sociology, in symbolic interactionism, in "constitution" theories of society (Joas 1996; Giddens 1984), and in the belated revival of interest in the work of Du Bois (West 1989; Lewis 1993; Winant 1997).

For the past few decades these themes have been developed in a body of theoretical work that goes under the general heading of *racial formation theory.* As one of the founders of this approach, I must acknowledge from the beginning the lack of consensus as well as the overall incompleteness of this theoretical current. Still, I submit that racial formation theory at least begins to meet the requirements for a social account of race, one capable of addressing the fin de siècle conditions enumerated here.[23]

To summarize the racial formation approach: (1) It views the meaning of race and the content of racial identities as unstable and politically contested; (2) It understands racial formation as occurring at the intersection/conflict of racial "projects" that combine representational/discursive elements with structural/institutional ones; (3) It sees these intersections as iterative sequences of interpretations ("articulations") of the meaning of race that are open to many types of agency, from the individual to the organizational, from the local to the global.

If we are to understand the changing significance of race at the end of the twentieth century, we must develop a more effective theory of race. The racial formation perspective suggests some directions in which such a theory should be pursued. As in the past, racial theory today is shaped by the large-scale sociopolitical processes it is called upon to explain. Employing a racial formation perspective makes it possible to glimpse a pattern in present global racial dynamics.

That pattern looks something like the following: in the period during and after World War II an enormous challenge was posed to established systems of rule by racially defined social movements around the world. Although these movement challenges achieved some great gains and precipitated important reforms in state racial policy, neither the movements nor the reforms could be consolidated. At the end of the century the world as a whole, and various national societies as well, are far from overcoming the tenacious legacies of colonial rule, apartheid, and segregation. All still experience continuing confusion, anxiety, and contention about race. Yet the legacies of epochal struggles for freedom, democracy, and human rights persist as well.

Despite the enormous vicissitudes that demarcate and distinguish national conditions, historical developments, roles in the international market, political tendencies, and cultural norms, racial differences often operate as they did in centuries past: as a way of restricting the political influence not just of racially subordinated groups but of all those at the bottom end of the system of social stratification. In the contemporary era, racial beliefs and practices have become far more contradictory and complex. The "old world racial order" has not disappeared, but it has been seriously disrupted and changed. The legacy of democratic, racially oriented movements and anticolonialist initiatives throughout the world's South remains a force to be reckoned with.[24] But the incorporative (or if one prefers this term, "hegemonic") effects of decades of reform-oriented state racial policies have had a profound effect as well: they have removed much of the motivation for sustained, antiracist mobilization.

In this unresolved situation, it is unlikely that attempts to address worldwide dilemmas of race and racism by ignoring or "transcending" these

themes, for example, by adopting so-called color-blind or differentialist policies, will have much effect. In the past the centrality of race deeply determined the economic, political, and cultural configuration of the modern
world. Although recent decades have seen a tremendous efflorescence of
movements for racial equality and justice, the legacies of centuries of racial
oppression have not been overcome. Nor is a vision of racial justice fully
worked out. Certainly the idea that such justice has already been largely
achieved—as seen in the "color-blind" paradigm in the United States, the
"nonracialist" rhetoric of the South African Freedom Charter, the Brazilian
rhetoric of "racial democracy," and the emerging "racial differentialism" of
the European Union—remains problematic.

Race will never be "transcended." Nor should it be, for it is both the
product of a long history of oppression and of an equally extensive history
of freedom struggle. The race concept is a product of human oppression, but
it is also a key marker of human variety and difference, of collectivity and
solidarity.

Will the world ever "get beyond" race? Probably not. But the entire world
still has a chance of overcoming the stratification, the hierarchy, the taken-
for-granted injustice and inhumanity that so often accompany the race
concept.

Accomplishing this is continuing work; it is also service, conflict, art,
play, and love. Understanding race and overcoming racism are part of the
permanent effort to comprehend and accomplish human emancipation and
freedom. Like some strangely qualitative asymptote, freedom is approached
but never quite reached. It is born of desire and understanding. It is as much
about having a dream—think of Dr. King's dream—as it is about continually renewing the effort to overcome injustice and inequality, exclusion and
repression. We shall overcome.

For centuries, racial politics has been central to this endeavor. Ultimately, the deepest meaning of race is its link to the great unfulfilled desire
for freedom that exists in human beings. Our task as a movement is to interpret and help organize that desire.

Racial Dualism at Century's End

Racial Dualism

Race matters: whether we in the United States—and in many other countries as well—wish this to be the case or not. The United States: What is it? A nation built on the soil of conquest, battened on the theft of human beings. Yet it is not only this. The United States was also created out of the doctrine of natural rights, whose restrictive application was continually eroded by the struggles of the excluded: first the European "others," and then the other "others," down to our own day. Throughout U.S. history, racial conflicts continually shaped and reshaped the categories into which identities—all identities—were classified. The racial struggles at the heart of U.S. society, the racial projects whose clash and clangor leap off the pages of today's headlines as they have for centuries, have created the politics and culture of today. Race matters: yet race today is as problematic a concept as ever.

Over the past few decades, the way we in the United States think of race has changed once again, as so often in the past. I shall argue in this essay that we are now in a period of universal racial dualism.

Once, U.S. society was a nearly monolithic racial hierarchy, in which everyone knew "his" place; under racial dualism, however, everyone's racial identity is problematized. "How does it feel to be a problem?" Du Bois famously reported being asked (Du Bois 1903b). The racial dualism he discerned was, of course, that of black people, who, he argued, were forced to live simultaneously in two worlds. His insight, which at the beginning of the twentieth century addressed black experience in a society of all-encompassing white supremacy, continues to apply, but the situation he analyzed has now become considerably more complicated. Today the racial anxiety, uncertainty, conflict, and tension expressed by the term *racial dualism* affect everyone in the United States, albeit in different ways.

Monolithic white supremacy is over, yet, white power and privilege live on. The overt politics of racial subordination has been destroyed, yet it is still very possible to "play the racial card" in the political arena. Blacks and other racially defined minorities are no longer subject to legal segregation, but they have not been relieved of the burdens of discrimination, even by laws supposedly intended to do so. Whites are no longer the official "ruling race," yet they still enjoy many of the privileges descended from the time when they were.

The old recipes for racial equality, which implied creation of a "colorblind" society, have been transformed into formulas for the maintenance of racial inequality. The old programs for eliminating white racial privilege are now accused of creating nonwhite racial privilege. The welfare state, once seen as the instrument for overcoming poverty and social injustice, is now accused of fomenting these very ills.

What racial dualism means today is that there are now, so to speak, two ways of looking at race, where previously there was only one. In the past, let us say the pre–World War II era, everyone agreed that racial subordination existed; the debate was about whether it was justified. Theodore Bilbo and Thurgood Marshall—to pick two emblematic figures—shared the same paradigm, perhaps disagreeing politically and morally, perhaps even representing the forces of evil and good respectively, but nevertheless looking at the same social world.

But today agreement about the continuing existence of racial subordination has vanished. The meaning of race has been deeply problematized. Indeed, the very idea that "race matters" is something that today must be argued, something that is not self-evident. This in itself attests to the transformation that racial dualism has undergone from the time of *Souls* to our own time.

On the one hand, the world Du Bois analyzed is still very much with us. We live in a racialized society, a society in which racial meaning is engraved upon all our experiences. Racial identity shapes not only "life chances," but social life, taste, place of residence. Indeed, the meaning of race, the racial interpretation of everyday life and of the larger culture, polity, and economy, has been so finely tuned for so long and has become so ingrained that it is now "second nature," a "common sense" that rarely requires acknowledgement.

As our racial antennae are tuned and retuned, race becomes "naturalized." As an element of "human nature," race partakes of the same degree of reality today—so it seems—as it did at the end of the nineteenth century, when biologistic theories of race held sway, and eugenics was advocated by supposedly enlightened and progressive thinkers. Indeed, if race is so much a part of "common sense," if it is so involved in the production of person, culture, state, and nation, if racial identity is so recognizable, so palpable, so immediately obvious, then in practical terms at least, it becomes "real." The sociological dictum that if people "define situations as real, they are real in their consequences" has its truth (Thomas and Thomas 1928, 572).

On the other hand, though, this "reality" is a rank illusion. It is patently inadequate, if not wholly false, to understand human experience, individual or collective, in racial terms. Indeed, it is difficult even to specify the meaning of race beyond the most superficial notions. When we seek to delineate the principles underlying racial categorization, we encounter tremendous obstacles. Not only ordinary individuals but even specialists—say, anthropologists or sociologists or geneticists—cannot present a convincing rationale for distinguishing among human groups by physical characteristics. Our "second nature," our "common sense" about race, it turns out, is deeply uncertain, almost mythical.

Consider: in the United States, hybridity is universal; most blacks have "white blood," and tens of millions of whites have "black blood." Latinos, Native Americans, Asian Americans, and blacks, as well as whites, have centuries-long histories of contact with one another; colonial rule, enslavement, and migration have dubious merits, but they are all effective "race mixers" (F. J. Davis 1991; Forbes 1988). Of course, even to speak in these terms, of "blood," "mixture," or "hybridity," even to use such categories as "Asian American," "Latino," or "white," one must enter deeply into the complexities of racial discourse. Such language reveals at once the sociohistorical embeddedness of all racial ideas. For these are merely current North American designations, and hardly unproblematic ones at that. They are not in any sense "true" or original self-descriptions of the human groups they name. Nor could any language be found that would avoid such a situation.

Race matters, then, in a second sense: it matters not only as a means of rendering the social world intelligible but simultaneously as a way of making it opaque and mysterious. Race is not only real but also illusory. Not only is it common sense, it is also common nonsense. Not only does it establish our identity, it also denies us our identity. Not only does it allocate resources, power, and privilege; it also provides means for challenging that allocation. Race not only naturalizes but also socializes. The ineluctably contradictory character of race provides the context in which racial dualism—or the "color-line," as Du Bois designated it—has developed as "the problem of the twentieth century."

Racial Dualism as History

The racial dynamics of conquest, of colonization, and of enslavement placed an indelible stamp on U.S. society. Racialization (Omi and Winant 1994; Roediger 1991) affected every individual and group, locating all in the hierarchy of the developing herrenvolk democracy (Takaki 1993; van den Berghe 1967; Roediger 1991). The herrenvolk, of course, were the white men of a certain standing or class, the only ones deemed worthy of full citizenship rights.

For centuries, white supremacy went almost entirely unquestioned in the political mainstream. This fact established the overall contours as well as the particular political and cultural legacies of racial subordination and resistance. It eliminated or at best severely limited the political terrain on which racially defined groups could mobilize within civil society, thus constituting these groups as "outsiders." It denied the existence of commonalities among whites and nonwhites—such as shared economic activities and statuses, shared rights as citizens, even on occasion shared humanity—thus constructing race, at least in principle, in terms of all-embracing social difference.

Not only did racialization tend to minimize differences among people considered white, but it also homogenized distinctions among those whose difference with whites was considered the only crucial component of their identities. Over time, then, this "white versus other" concept of difference created not fixed and unchanging racial identities—for these are always in flux—but the potentiality, the social structure, indeed, the necessity of universally racialized identities in the United States. Elsewhere Omi and I have described this process (drawing on Gramsci 1971) as *racial war of maneuver:* a conflict between disenfranchised and systematically subordinated groups and a dictatorial and comprehensively dominant power (Omi and Winant 1994).

In a war of maneuver, the principal efforts of the subordinated are devoted to self-preservation and resistance. They are anathematized; they lack social standing or political rights. In respect to social action, their options are generally reduced to withdrawal into exclusive (and excluded) communities, to subversion (Bhabha 1994), and, occasionally, to armed revolt.

In a schematic account of this type, there is an inevitable tendency to render the dynamics of racial oppression as more homogeneous than they actually were. But, of course, racial war of maneuver is not static, not frozen. At various moments, for example, under the impact of the Haitian revolution or the pressures of abolitionism, and in the interregnum of Reconstruction, the power of white supremacy waxed or waned considerably. Its component parts—its ideology and instrumentalities—evolved and changed over time. Furthermore, what is true of oppression is true for resistance: both everyday, small-scale forms of opposition (Scott 1986) and large-scale challenge, such as armed revolt and institution-building among free blacks, varied significantly with the conditions of racial war of maneuver. Nor should the account of racial war of maneuver be confined to black-white dynamics alone. Efforts to subordinate Native American nations (Cornell 1988; Rogin 1975), Mexicans (Montejano 1987), and Asians (Okihiro 1994; Takaki 1990) through warfare, expropriation of land, exclusion, denial of political rights, and superexploitation all fit into the general pattern of racial war of maneuver. Regional and temporal variations in these conflicts (Almaguer 1994) do not diminish the general applicability of this concept. Although I cannot detail these processes here, I have discussed them elsewhere (Winant 1994a), and they have been extensively treated by others (Du Bois 1935; Foner 1988; Williamson 1986; Takaki 1993).

Paradoxically, white institutionalization of racial difference, white refusal to grant such basic democratic rights as citizenship, access to the legal system and the vote, and white resistance to the participation by racially defined minorities in civil society permitted—and, indeed, demanded—the organization and consolidation of excluded communities of color. Because it had so comprehensively externalized its racial others, racial war of maneuver helped constitute their resistance and opposition. It set the stage for its own destruction because, over centuries, whites forced nonwhites to forge their own identities, to draw on their own profound cultural and political resources, to suppress their differences, and to unite outside the high walls of a supposedly democratic society whose rights and privileges were systematically restricted on the basis of race.

Racial war of maneuver can be linked to the racial dualism discerned by Du Bois. If in the present we have no trouble understanding racism as a relation with both macro- and microsocial dimensions, as something that necessarily operates at both the institutional and social structural levels on the one hand, and at the levels of identity and experience on the other (Omi and Winant 1994), it is not anachronistic to discern that dynamic in earlier historical moments. What for whites was a fierce and pathological rejection of the possibility that they might harbor traits identified with various racial "others" was for nonwhites a quasi-terroristic requirement that they anticipate and strive to protect themselves against the "violence of representation" (Armstrong and Tennenhouse 1989), not to mention the physical violence, directed against them by members of the ruling race. Psychohistorical approaches to U.S. racial dynamics have long investigated these processes (Drinnon 1985; Rogin 1975; Williamson 1986).

Thus, racial dualism was in part an adaptation, a resistance strategy of the oppressed, the excluded, the terrorized, under the conditions of racial war of maneuver. This recognition is clearly present in Du Bois, although by the time *Souls* appeared the seeds of the breakdown of this centuries-long racial regime were already germinating; indeed, Du Bois himself is the chief cultivator of those seeds, the key agitator for a very different strategic orientation, a racial war of position.

In the United States a *racial war of position* came into being gradually in the twentieth century, taking full shape only in the years following World War II. Gramsci explains war of position as political and cultural conflict, undertaken under conditions in which subordinated groups have attained some foothold, some rights, within civil society; thus, they have the leverage, the ability to press some claims on their rulers and on the state (Omi and Winant 1994). Du Bois was the crucial early theorist of the transition to racial war of position, as well as the key strategist of black movement politics in that transition. His conflicts with Washington, and later with Garvey, can be understood in terms of his commitment to politics, his ceaseless struggle for black access to civil society—in other words, his effort to create a racial war of position. Like Horatio at the bridge, Du Bois stands between the old and new racial orders, fighting tenaciously at the cusp of historical transition. Among modern theorists and activists, the only figure to whom he can be compared is Marx, who also ushered in almost single-handedly a new way of thinking about the world, and who, like Du Bois, made his new manner of thought into a distinct kind of political practice.

Racial Dualism as Politics

Once a foothold in civil society was achieved, it was only a matter of time until full-scale political struggle over race emerged. The sources of the modern black movement have been extensively analyzed (Morris 1984; Branch 1988; Carson 1981; Zinn 1985; Omi and Winant 1994; Kluger 1977; J. Grant 1968) and need not detain us here. For present purposes, the important thing is that the movement transformed the American political universe, creating new organizations, new collective identities, and new political norms; challenging past racial practices and stereotypes; and ushering in a wave of democratizing social reform. This "great transformation," which at first affected blacks but soon touched Latinos, Asian Americans, and Native Americans as well, permitted the entry of millions of racial minority group members into the political process. It set off the "second wave" of feminism, a new anti-imperialist and antiwar movement, movements for gay and disability rights, and even for environmental protection. The black movement deeply affected whites as well, challenging often unconscious beliefs in white supremacy and demanding new and more respectful forms of behavior in relation to nonwhites.

In transforming the meaning of race and the contours of racial politics, the movement shifted the rules of participation and organizing principles of American politics itself. It made identity, difference, the "personal," and language itself political issues in very new ways.

Once racial politics had taken the form of war of position, once basic political rights had been achieved, racial dualism ceased to be an exclusively black or minority response to white supremacy. The "normalizing" quality of white (and male) identity, which in the past had tended to render whiteness transparent and to equate it with U.S. nationality itself, as in the phrase "a white man's country," necessarily experienced a certain erosion as nonwhites and women acquired a significant degree of admission into mainstream institutions and began to exercise their voices and rights from inside, rather than from outside, the terrain of democratic politics.

By the mid-1960s, popular support for the main principles of the "civil rights revolution" had been secured, and legislation passed. An alternative viewpoint to the exclusionary framework of racial war of maneuver, to the archaic principles of overt white supremacy, had been institutionalized, and in legal terms (or in respect to what Weber would call "formal rationality") something that could be described as "equality" had developed.

But no more than that. Substantive equality had not been achieved. White supremacy had not been vanquished. Indeed, as soon as civil rights legislation and equal opportunity policies were initiated, they started to erode under reactionary pressures. Because a significant breach had been opened in the armor of white supremacy, it was not expedient for the forces of "racial reaction" (Omi and Winant 1994) to seek a return to overtly exclusionary policies. Instead, they sought to reinterpret the movement's victories, to strip it of its more radical implications, to rearticulate its vision of a substantively egalitarian society in conservative and individualistic terms. *Equality* has had many meanings since the nation was founded; it was hardly unprecedented to redefine it in terms of formal and legal standing rather than in terms of redistribution of resources, compensation for past wrongs, or forceful efforts to reshape the material conditions of minorities. In retrospect, we can see that to have undertaken these measures would have involved as revolutionary a change as the Reconstruction measures did (Du Bois 1935; Foner 1988), for it would have required not only the dismantling of segregated neighborhoods, workplaces, and schools but the transformation of the status of white workers as well. Substantive equality would have meant massive redistribution of resources; it would have clashed with fundamental capitalist class interests; it was never even on the table.

The seeds of racial reaction were thus already present in the ideological choices open in the 1960s: moderate tendencies that espoused integration and "color-blind" racial policies, and radical positions that advocated black (or brown, or red, or yellow) power, in other words, racial nationalism. While each of these positions had something to recommend it, neither was sustainable by itself, and no synthesis between them seemed possible. Integrationist views held open the possibility of a class-based alliance between minority and white poor and working people, a position that Martin Luther King Jr. was espousing in the last year of his life (Garrow 1988). In ideological terms, though, integrationism tended to liquidate the specifically racial dimension of the movement that had spawned it. Nationalist perspectives had the opposite problem: though they could assert the irreducibility of racial differences, they lacked the ideological equipment to forge alliances across racial lines, particularly with whites. The few groups that possessed the ability to walk the line between racial nationalism and radical multiracial class politics—such as the Black Panther Party—were undone by repression and by their precarious hold on an impoverished and volatile membership.

Thus, the rise to power of neoconservatism, which inherited and rearticulated the "moderate" tendencies that emerged from the movement. Indeed, already in the mid-1960s such voices were heard decrying the tendency toward "positive discrimination" (M. Gordon 1964); by the mid-1970s a leading neoconservative could produce an influential tract titled *Affirmative Discrimination* (Glazer 1978), and an important intervention of 1978 claimed that race was "declining in significance" (Wilson 1980).

Among ordinary whites similar fragmentations occurred: reacting to perceived losses in their racially privileged status but unable to identify with the more radical successors to the movement, unable in the aftermath of the civil rights era to espouse white supremacy but excluded and condemned by a racial politics that paid little attention to class, most whites came to support a conservative and individualistic form of egalitarianism, advocating a supposedly "color-blind" (but actually deeply race-conscious) political position. This was the white "politics of difference." This synthesis acquired particular force as job losses and stagnating incomes cut deeply into whites' sense of security. It gathered strength as the lower strata of the black and Latino communities were plunged into deeper poverty by massive cutbacks in welfare state programs, education, and federal assistance to the cities. When the inevitable moral panics about crime, drugs, drive-bys, and teenage pregnancy ensued, they fueled the white flight to the right. In a thoroughly corporate culture, no countervailing arguments (against corporate greed and deindustrialization, for example) acquired so much as a foothold in the mainstream political discourse.

Meanwhile blacks, as well as other racially defined minority groups, were convulsed by new conflicts over group identity. Class divisions and various strains of resurgent cultural nationalism disrupted the black community and drove some blacks, both elite and everyday folk, in strongly conservative directions. Latinos, Native Americans, and Asian Americans experienced different, but parallel, schisms. Even those whose "whiteness" retains problematic elements, such as Arab Americans and Jews, were newly confronted by conflicts over where their political and moral allegiances lay in the post–civil rights era.

These examples need not be extended further. The point is clear: a new racial paradigm, tension-ridden, uncertain, and unstable, came into being. This paradigm combined the pre–World War II inheritance of white supremacy, which survived in significant measure, with the legacy of the 1960s movements, themselves based on a centuries-long tradition of resistance to conquest, enslavement, and racial oppression.

So all the social practices that enforced black racial dualism in 1903 continue today: the segregation of minority (and particularly black) communities (Massey and Denton 1993), the discriminatory and regressive allocation of underemployment, undereducation, and other forms of substantive inequality to members of these communities, and the general cultural subordination that accompanies white supremacy.

Nevertheless, we are not in 1903. Massive transformations have occurred in the U.S. racial system, particularly over the past half century. From the mid-1950s to the early 1970s, an important wave of racial reform swept across the land, altering not only racial policy but also racial identity, redrawing the American political and cultural map and refueling oppositional currents that had lain dormant in the United States for decades, such as feminism and anti-imperialism. Strictly, of course, this was not a "new" movement at all but rather an upwelling of oppositional forces that abided, that had their origins in the earliest moments of conquest and enslavement, and that were linked to the most epochal struggles of oppressed peoples across the globe for emancipation and justice.

From the 1960s to the present, then, both black people and the nation as a whole have been riven by a thoroughgoing and deep-seated struggle: the antagonistic coexistence, the contradiction, of the two great forces of white supremacy, on the one hand, and of the movement for racial and, indeed, broader social justice, on the other. It is this convulsion, this contradiction, that constitutes racial dualism at century's end.

I anticipate various objections to the line of argument that race no longer operates as a simple signifier—as it largely did in Du Bois's day—absolutely locating one in a certain largely homogeneous community or another. Was white supremacy ever truly that monolithic? Did not Du Bois's narrative already expose its delusions of absolute racial difference? And hasn't "the movement" accomplished at least this much: that it has made possible a greater "crossing over," a greater cultural hybridization, a greater awareness of the presence of "others" who are also subjects, who also have rights, who can act politically, and so on? Furthermore, isn't the designation of "duality" suspect for various reasons? Does it not privilege whites, for instance, by suggesting that there are whites and there are "the others"? In racial terms, shouldn't I be talking about "pluralism" rather than dualism?

And what about the other dimensions of politics and identity? What about gender and class? These dynamics shape politics and culture today in ways very different from the manner in which Du Bois—feminist and socialist though he was—encountered them nearly a century ago. Even if we think about their impact on racial identity and politics, on the problematic theme of racial dualism today, they appear to play a fragmenting role: pointing to many fissures, not just two.

Without question, there are weaknesses in my use of the racial dualism framework in a revised, contemporary form. Although I think these objections can be all be answered, for now I want simply to stress the effectiveness of this approach in illuminating the charged and contentious sociohistorical context in which racial politics is framed in the United States at century's end. I have shown how the concept helps us understand the peculiar and contradictory character of large-scale, macrolevel racial politics at century's end. I should like now to apply it to small-scale, microlevel racial politics.

Racial Dualism as Identity

As the civil rights legacy was drawn and quartered—beginning in the late 1960s and with ever greater success in the following two decades—the tugging and hauling, the escalating contestation over the meaning of race, resulted in ever more conflicting and contradictory notions of racial identity. The significance of race ("declining" or increasing?), the interpretation of racial equality ("color-blind" or color-conscious?), the institutionalization of racial justice ("reverse discrimination" or affirmative action?), and the very categories—black, white, Latino/Hispanic, Asian American, and Native American—employed to classify racial groups were all called into question as they emerged from the civil rights "victory" of the mid-1960s. These racial signifiers are all ambiguous or contradictory today. We cannot escape the racial labels that U.S. society comprehensively assigns to all within it; this has been the fate of "Americans" since Europeans arrived on these shores. Yet, less than ever can we identify unproblematically or unself-consciously with these designations, for they are riven—as we ourselves are fissured—to an unprecedented extent by the conflicts and contradictions posed by the political struggles of the past decades.

How do these conflicts and contradictions shape the various racial identities available today? Without hoping to be anything more than schematic, I will now offer some observations on the racial "politics of identity" at century's end. As the entire argument I have presented here should suggest, I do not share the denunciatory attitude toward "identity politics" so evident on both right and left today (Gitlin 1993; see also Newfield 1993). In my view, the matrices of identity are ineluctably political, for they involve interests, desire, antagonisms, and so on in constant interplay with broad social structures.

Yet, the critics do have one thing right: if my account here rings true, there can be no "straightforward" identity politics. Our awareness of the pervasiveness of racial dualism today should serve to check claims of unmediated authenticity, whether hegemonic or subaltern. Appeals to "traditional values," to the national culture, to canonized texts that exemplify hegemonic claims must therefore be treated with the extreme suspicion that awareness of standpoint demands. Subaltern claims, as expressed, for example, through invocation of supposedly direct experiences of oppression—of the form "As a black person, I know X ...," or "As a woman, I know X ... (where X is an undifferentiated generalization about blacks' or women's experience)—are also suspect.

With these guidelines in mind, let us briefly explore the terrain of the racial politics of identity, focusing our attention on the operations of racial dualism today.

Black Racial Dualism

First, thirty years after the ambiguous victory of the civil rights movement, what does it mean to be "black"? The decline of the organized black movement in the 1970s and the wholesale assaults against the welfare state initiated by Ronald Reagan during the 1980s sharply increased divisions along class and gender lines in the black community. The divergent experiences of the black middle class and the black poor—experiences far more distant from each other than they were in the days of official segregation—make a unitary racial identity seem a distant dream indeed. A whole other set of divisions has emerged around gender, such that black men's and women's experiences probably diverge more significantly today than at any other moment since slavery days. Consequently, a coherent black politics that could reach across class and gender lines seems remote.

Divisions of class have meant that in the upper strata of the black community a portion of the ideal of substantive equality has indeed been achieved, though in the United States no black person can ever believe herself or himself to be beyond the reach of white supremacy (Cose 1993; Graham 1995; L. Williams 1991). Meanwhile the desolation of the poor increases steadily, fueled in part by the very claim that equality (formal equality, that is) has been attained, that we are now a "color-blind" society, and so on. Such rhetoric attributes black poverty to defects in black motivation (Murray 1984; Kaus 1992), intelligence (Herrnstein and Murray 1994), or family structure (L. Gordon 1994), a strategy of victim blaming that often takes aim not only at "underclass" blacks but at low-income black women in particular. Additionally, opportunity structures for blacks are changing by class and gender in unprecedented ways (Carnoy 1994; Hacker 1992).

The significance of a divided black community, and hence identity, is complex, even contradictory. On the one hand, the emergence of diverse and even conflicting voices in the black community is welcome, for it reflects real changes in the direction of mobility and democratization. On the other hand, the persistence of glaring racial inequality—that is, of an ongoing dimension of white supremacy and racism that pervades the entire society—demands a level of concerted action that division and discord tend to preclude. Racial dualism at century's end.

Other "Others"

In the 1990s, what does it mean to be "yellow" or "brown"? Before the success of civil rights (and particularly immigration) reforms in the mid-1960s, racialized groups of Asian and Latin American origin experienced very high levels of exclusion and intolerance. After 1965 these communities began to grow rapidly. Previously isolated in enclaves based on language and national origin, Koreans, Filipinos, Japanese, and Chinese underwent a new "panethnic" racializing process from the late 1960s onward, emerging as "Asian Americans" (Espiritu 1992). Accompanying these shifts was significant upward mobility for some—though by no means all—sectors of Asian America.

Similar shifts overtook Mexicans, Puerto Ricans, Central Americans, and even Cubans as the "Latino" and "Hispanic" categories were popularized (Moore and Pachon 1985). For example, the destruction of formal segregation in Texas had a profound impact on Mexican Americans there (Montejano 1987). Segregation of Latinos in the upper and middle economic strata decreased rapidly across the country (far more rapidly than that of comparable black income earners) (Massey and Denton 1993), and some Latino groups achieved or consolidated solid middle-class status (notably Cubans and to some extent Dominicans). The Mexican, Puerto Rican, and Central American barrios, however, continued to be plagued by immigrant bashing and high levels of poverty that could only be seen as racially organized (Moore and Pinderhughes 1993).

Thus, for both Asian Americans and Latinos, contemporary racial identity is fraught with contradictions. Apart from long-standing antagonisms between particular groups—for example, Cubans and Puerto Ricans, and Koreans and Japanese—significant class- and gender-based conflicts exist as

well. Tendencies among long-established residents to disparage and sometimes exploit immigrants who are "fresh off the boat," or for group ties to
attenuate as social mobility increases suggest the centrality of class in immigrant life (Portes and Bach 1985; Takaki 1990). The liberating possibilities
encountered by immigrating women and their greater proclivity to settle in
the United States rather than to return to their countries of origin suggest
the centrality of gender in immigrant life (Grasmuck and Pessar 1991).

Not unlike blacks, Asian Americans and Latinos often find themselves
caught between the past and the future. Old forms of racism have resurfaced
to confront them, as in the renewed enthusiasm for immigrant bashing and
the recurrent waves of anti-Japanese and anti-Chinese paranoia. Discrimination has resurfaced again, sometimes in new ways, as in controversies
over Asian admissions to elite universities (Takagi 1992). Yet, at the same
time, the newly panethnicized identities of Asian Americans and Latinos
have brought them face to face with challenges that are quite distinct from
anything faced in the past. Some examples of these challenges are the dubious gift of neoconservative support (Asians as the "model minority," for
example), the antagonism of blacks (Kim 1993; Omi and Winant 1993;
J. Miles 1992), and the tendencies toward dilution of specific ethnic/
national identity in a racialized category created by a combination of "lumping" and political exigency. Often more successful and accepted than in the
past but subject to new antagonisms and new doubts about their status,
Asian Americans and Latinos experience a distinct racial dualism today.

With respect to Native Americans, there is ample evidence to believe
that in the postwar period Indian nations as well came face-to-face with
a racially dualistic situation. Here, too, the old logic of despoliation still
applied: environmental destruction and land rape, appalling poverty, and
cultural assault continued to take their toll. Yet, a new, activist, and often
economically and politically savvy Native America could also be glimpsed.
Today Indians have developed techniques for fighting in the courts, for
asserting treaty rights, and indeed for regaining a modicum of economic and
political control over their tribal destinies that would have been unthinkable a generation ago (Nagel 1995; Cornell 1988).

White Racial Dualism

In the post–civil rights period, what did it mean to be white? During the
epoch of racial war of maneuver, in which exclusion was the predominant
status assigned to racially identified minorities, white identity (and particularly white male identity) was "normalized"; "otherness" was elsewhere:

among people "of color" and to some extent women. All these were marked by their identities, but under conditions of virtually unchallenged white supremacy, white men were not. Once "white egalitarianism" (Saxton 1990) had been established as the political price elites had to pay to secure mass electoral support, herrenvolk Republicanism (Roediger 1991) became the organizing principle of nineteenth-century U.S. politics and culture. Only whites (only white men) were full citizens; only they were fully formed individuals. In terms of race and gender their identities were, so to speak, transparent, which is what we mean by the term *normalized*.

Of course, for a long time many whites partook of an ethnic "otherness" that placed them in an ambiguous relationship with both established WASP elites and racially defined minorities. But by the 1960s white ethnicity was in serious decline. Large-scale European immigration had become a thing of the past; while urban ethnic enclaves continued to exist in many major cities, suburbanization and gentrification had taken their toll. Communal forms of white ethnic identity had been eroded by outmarriage and by heterogeneous contact in schools, workplaces, neighborhoods, and religious settings (Alba 1990; Waters 1990).

Nor were alternative collective identities, other forms of solidarity, readily available to whites. Class-based identities had always been weak in the United States and were particularly debilitated in the wake of the red-baiting period of the late 1940s and 1950s, the same moment in which the black movement was gathering strength. What remained was the "imagined community" (Anderson 1991) of white racial nationalism (Walters 1987): the United States as a "white man's country," and so on. It was this ideological construct of whiteness, already deeply problematic in a thoroughly modernized, advanced industrial society, that the black movement confronted in the post–World War II period.

Detached from the previous generations' ethnic ties, unable to see themselves as part of a potentially majoritarian working class with larger social justice interests, and unable to revert to the discredited white supremacy of an earlier period, most whites were ripe for conversion to neoconservative racial ideology after the civil rights "victory" in the mid-1960s. Efforts on the part of Martin Luther King Jr., Bayard Rustin, and even the Black Panther Party to forge multiracial alliances for large-scale redistributive policies and other forms of substantive social justice never had a serious chance in the national political arena.

Instead, neoconservative and new right politicians, initiated by the Wallace campaigns of the mid-1960s, appealed to white workers on the basis of their residual commitments to racial "status honor" (Edsall and Edsall 1992). Wallace, and Nixon in his "southern strategy," invoked the powerful remnants of white supremacy and white privilege. Since white identities could no longer be overtly depicted as superior, they were now presented in "coded" fashion as a beleaguered American individualism, as the hallmarks of a noble tradition now unfairly put upon by unworthy challengers, as the "silent majority," and so on. The racial reaction begun by Wallace and consummated by Reagan, which resurrected twentieth-century Republicanism from the oblivion to which the New Deal had supposedly consigned it, was thus a fairly direct descendant of the "white labor republicanism" (Roediger 1991; Saxton 1990) that had shaped the U.S. working class along racial lines more than a century earlier.

In this fashion from the late 1960s on, white identity was reinterpreted, rearticulated in a dualistic fashion: on the one hand egalitarian, on the other hand privileged; on the one hand individualistic and "color-blind," on the other hand "normalized" and white. With Reagan's election in 1980, the process reached its peak. A policy of regressive redistribution was adopted; working-class incomes, stagnant since the mid-1970s, continued to drop in real terms as profits soared. Neoconservative racial ideology—with its commitment to formal racial equality and its professions of "color blindness"— now proved particularly useful: it served to organize and rationalize white working-class resentments against declining living standards. To hear Reagan tell it, the problems faced by white workers did not derive from corporate greed for ever greater profits, from deindustrialization and the "downsizing" of workforces; rather their troubles emanated from the welfare state, which expropriated the taxes of the productive citizens who "played by the rules" and "went to work each day" in order to subsidize unproductive and parasitic welfare queens and career criminals "who didn't want to work."

Nowhere was this new framework of the white "politics of identity" more clearly on display than in the reaction to affirmative action policies of all sorts (in hiring, university admissions, federal contracting, etc.). Assaults on these policies, which have been developing since their introduction as tentative and quite limited efforts at racial redistribution (Johnson 1967), sometimes reached absurd levels. These attacks are clearly designed to effect ideological shifts rather than to shift resources in any meaningful way. They represent whiteness as disadvantage, something that has few precedents in

U.S. racial history (Gallagher 1994). This imaginary white disadvantage—for which there is almost no evidence at the empirical level—has achieved widespread popular credence and provides the cultural and political "glue" that holds together a wide variety of reactionary racial politics.

To summarize: today, the politics of white identity is undergoing a profound political crisis. The destruction of the communal bases of white ethnicity is far advanced, yet whiteness remains a significant source of "status honor." White privilege—a relic of centuries of herrenvolk democracy—has been called into question in the post–civil rights period. Yet, far from being destroyed, the white "politics of identity" is now being trumpeted as an ideology of victimization. The situation would be farcical if it were not so dangerous, reflecting venerable white anxieties and fortifying the drift to the right that now, as in the past, is highly conducive to race baiting. Today's "color-blind" white supremacy, then, embodies the racial duality of contemporary white identity.

It is not the case, however, that whites have unequivocally or unanimously embraced the right, though certainly the ideological effects of neoconservatism have been profound, particularly on economically vulnerable whites. Although a minority among whites, there are still millions who have resisted the siren song of neoconservatism, recognizing that the claim of "color blindness" masks a continuing current of white supremacy and racism.

Why? What enables any whites to adhere to the objective of substantive social justice rather than its merely formal illusions? And how deep does this commitment run? We know little about the sources of white antiracism today. Yet few themes on the domestic political horizon are more important.

Without becoming entirely speculative, it is possible to identify a few elements of white experience that have potential antiracist dimensions. Feminism and gay liberation have developed critiques of discrimination that are intimately related to the experiences of racially defined minorities. Furthermore, these struggles can trace their origins back to the black struggles of the nineteenth century as well as to those of the 1960s. Millions of white lives have been changed by these movements. Other forms of radical political experience also taught basic antiracist lessons, despite various political and ideological limitations. Here I am thinking of the great industrial organizing drives of the 1930s, the various communist currents, new left and antiwar activities during the 1960s, the farmworkers movement, the solidarity movements with Central America in the 1970s and 1980s, and, above all, the civil rights movement, in which many thousands of whites were involved (Thompson 2001).

These political struggles exercised a moral influence on whites, just as they did on national politics; that influence has perhaps waned under decades of assault from the right, but it has proved far more difficult to eradicate than its opponents expected. Beyond its fundamentally ethical character, white antiracism draws upon various material interests as well (I recognize that this distinction is not an absolute one). Among these is the difficulty of uniting all whites under conservative banners: Jews in particular (whose "whiteness" continues to exhibit fissures and cultural contradictions [Sacks 1994]) still adhere disproportionately to social and political liberalism for reasons that have been extensively analyzed. Arab Americans, paradoxically, are moving toward a similar position. Other sources of white antiracism may be located in religious institutions, the academy, and popular cultural forms, although none of these is free of ambiguity and contradiction.

In short, the problematic and volatile quality of contemporary white identities, not their consolidation, is evident at all levels of U.S. society, from the most casual conversation to the contortions and contradictions of national politics. This volatility provides ongoing evidence of racial dualism among whites.

Toward Radical Democracy

U.S. politics has plunged to the right as the aspirations of the activists and adherents of the 1960s movements have been forsaken. Indeed, the legacy of those struggles has been twisted and tortured into service as an obstacle to the achievement of real social and racial justice. Today the attempt to imagine a greater and more robust democracy, racially inclusive as well as substantively egalitarian, seems almost utopian. Yet, I submit that it is precisely that task that most cries out for thought and action. Those who wish to halt the gallop to the right need to be able to envision a convincing political alternative, if the cause of racial justice, and indeed of radical democracy, is ever to resume its advance.

Without presumption—for this task is more than the work of an essay— I would like to suggest that the recognition of widespread racial dualism in U.S. politics and culture at century's end suggests certain principles that can be applied to this effort of imagination.

To acknowledge racial dualism is to understand the malleability and flexibility of all identities, especially racial ones. One of the recognitions hard won by the movements of the 1960s—not only the racially based ones but all the so-called new social movements across the globe—was that identity is a political construct. Not carved in stone, not "sutured" (Mouffe and Laclau 1985), our concepts of ourselves can be dramatically altered by new move- ments, new articulations of the possible. It may yet turn out that the great- est achievement of the 1960s movements, sparked by the black movement, was not the political reforms they accomplished, but the new possibilities for racial identity they engendered, not just for black people but for everyone.

The right wing has in a certain sense understood the challenge of "reimag- ining" race, for it has clearly articulated a particular vision of the meaning of race in a conservative democratic society. This is the concept of "color blindness." Undeniably this vision has a certain appeal, not only as a cover for the perpetuation of white supremacy but as a plausible reinvention of fundamental elements of national ideology: individualism, an "opportunity, not entitlement" society, and so on. But this vision also has profound weak- nesses, even beyond its disingenuousness. It is authoritarian, repressive, relentlessly homogeneous. It allows little space for the further development of racially based institutions and cultural representations—"difference"— whose vitality has persevered and ramified for centuries. "Color blindness"— let us imagine it to be a genuine antiracism for a moment—assumes that if we refuse to recognize racial difference, it will disappear; it assumes that racial distinctions are inherently invidious. But this is not a convincing claim: race and racial identity are not merely produced by racism, as neoconserva- tives (as well as some on the left) might argue. They are also means of self- representation, autonomous signification, cultural (and thus social and polit- ical) practice.

All the evidence suggests that once created and institutionalized, once having evolved over many centuries, racial difference is a permanent, though flexible, attribute of human society (Winant 1994b). Racial categories can neither be liquidated ("color blindness") nor reified as unchanging features of human nature (for example, in biologistic racism). Somewhat paradoxi- cally, then, the permanence of race coexists with the necessarily contingent and contextual character of racial identity and racial difference. Racial dual- ism at century's end.

Beyond these inadequacies in neoconservative racial ideology lie the intersections between issues of race and those of class and gender. Neocon- servatism rationalizes the regressive redistribution of income, not only along racial but also along class lines. As the gap between wealth and poverty increases, its consequences become more severe, not only for racially defined minorities but also for whites. Thus far, it has proved quite effective to scapegoat impoverished minority strata as the cause of white underemployment and stagnating income levels. We can observe this strategy—which is a classical one—being extended further and further as its inadequacies become more obvious. For example, the gathering assault on affirmative action policies suggests that not only impoverished ghetto and barrio residents but also working- and middle-class minorities are now to be blamed for the white working class's failure to thrive.

It is also quite striking how much the "imagined community" of a supposedly color-blind nation also depends on the reassertion of maleness and heterosexuality. For example, the effort to restigmatize illegitimacy (Murray 1993) explicitly tries to move beyond the traditional assault on minority (and particularly black) women's supposed promiscuity and hyperfertility to stigmatize low-income white women as well. The attack on affirmative action clearly directs fire not only at racially defined minorities but at women. Attacks on gay rights also suggest the continuing resonance of discrimination. They point to the overlap of new and old civil rights struggles; they demand that we once again choose between equality and freedom on the one hand, and cruelty and repression on the other.

Neoconservative scapegoating thus has perverse consequences for many whites as well as racially defined minorities. It holds down white income levels and props up unemployment. It stigmatizes women and gays, white as well as nonwhite. And despite its "color-blind" facade, it depends on rigid concepts of racial, gender, and sexual identities that accord less and less with the authoritarian and repressive morality (Republican "family values") it seeks to enforce.

Scapegoating flourishes in large part because a radical democratic challenge to its fundamental premises has been silenced and marginalized. But must this be the case? Without presuming to write a prescription for a new antiracist political program, it is possible to identify some of the elements such a politics might encompass, based on the analysis of contemporary racial dualism presented here.

Radical democracy must compete with authoritarianism of all sorts to articulate a more open and flexible vision of politics. First, any radical democratic politics must acknowledge and accept the uncertainty and fragility of social and cultural identities (Przeworski 1986; Lechner 1988)—racial identities particularly—and the fears that threats to these identities can produce. This is necessary to avoid the temptations of neoconservatism evident not only on the right but even on the left (Sleeper 1990). A more effective approach would be informed by an awareness of the pervasiveness of racial dualism at century's end. It would evoke the ethical dimensions of identity politics (West 1991; Lechner 1988) and ask to what extent we permit our-selves to know the racialized other, both outside us and within us.

When the instabilities inherent in both minority and majority identities are acknowledged, the door to coalition politics—closed since the defec-tion to the right of the civil rights "moderates" in the mid-1960s—can be reopened. In many different settings, from school boards and city councils to ethnic studies programs, from feminist politics (often split along racial/ethnic lines) (Caraway 1991; Frankenburg 1993) to environmental issues (Bullard 1993), the absence or weakness of transracial political alliances plays into the hands of the Right. And more often than not, what obstructs the formation of these alliances is the inability to get beyond either rigid denials of racial difference or rigid conceptions of racial identity (or both). For whites, such conceptions usually involve defenses—often covert or even unconscious—of outmoded ideas of racial privilege. For members of racially defined minority groups, such conceptions usually involve appeals to flawed notions of racial/ethnic authenticity.

Our dire political situation demands that we reinvent coalition politics, not as an alternative to the "politics of difference" but as a supplement to it. A radical democratic politics would permit both plural and singular organi-zational projects, both multiracial and particular types of initiatives. There is room for the kinds of antiracist alliances now emerging in different parts of the country, alongside exclusively black or Indian or Chicano organiza-tions. Indeed, these terms are no longer adequate: many types of "black" (Afro-Caribbean, Haitian, as well as Afro-American) distinctions must be both recognized and mobilized today. Chicano (Hispano), Puertorriqueno (Nuyorican...), as well as Latino and Hispanic identifications exist, and coexist, among us.

And what about whites? It is crucial that antiracist whites take part in multiracial political activity if there is to be any effective challenge to the Right. The organizations that currently do this work are few but vital: groups like the Children's Defense Fund, the Progressive Majority, People for the American Way, PFLAG, and the Northwest Alliance, to name but a few. At this point it is difficult to see whites mobilizing independently qua whites in an antiracist fashion, for the legacy of white supremacy and the attachment to privilege is still too strong. But the time may come when this becomes a possibility, in the context of a stronger multiracial movement for radical democracy.

The account of racial dualism offered here seeks to open up political possibilities that have been shut down; I know full well that some of these ideas will be criticized as utopian, vague, and impractical. But precisely because the times are so tough, it is vital that we examine the contingency and multiplicity of our own identities. No individual belongs to "just" one socially constructed category: each has her or his multiple racial, gender, class-based, national identities, and that is just a start of the list. Nor are these categories uniform or stable; we are Whitmanesque, we contain multitudes. To recognize our many selves is to understand the vast social construction that is not only the individual but history itself, the present as history. A radical democratic politics must invite us to comprehend this.

To understand the fragility of our identities can be profoundly disconcerting, especially in the absence of a political and moral vision in which the individual and the group can see themselves as included, supported, and contributing to the construction of a better society. To counter the authoritarian interpretation of fear and uncertainty, to resist the imposition of exclusive and repressive models of order, a radical democratic politics must acknowledge those very fears and uncertainties, while at the same time offering a way to accept and interpret these emotions publicly and collectively. Racial dualism can be something desirable. Not through repression but through knowledge of the differences within ourselves can we achieve the solidarity with others that, though necessarily partial, is essential for the creation of a more just and free world.

What Can Racial Theory Tell Us about Social Theory?

In honor of Joe R. Feagin

Race is a peculiar theoretical category. While it is very much a part of every-day social life, not only in the United States but in various ways all around the world, race is also a suspect social classification. In social scientific terms and even in biological ones, the very existence of racial distinctions has been called into question.[1] Not only intellectuals but also politicians frequently dismiss the race concept as an outmoded relic of the past, an illusion. In practical terms this questioning of the reality of race gives rise to calls for "color blindness," notably in debates over social policy.[2]

Such positions would have been nearly incomprehensible a few decades ago. For centuries—beginning in the sixteenth century or so[3]—race was taken to be a given, an unimpeachable phenomenon both of society and nature, an indelible mark of human difference. Although this seeming certainty has been cast into doubt in the years since World War II, racial distinctions still correlate quite nicely with patterns of inequality and domination throughout the world. The continuing significance of race, both at the macrosocial level (say, in respect to North-South global disparities, or patterns of employment, or residential segregation) and at the microsocial level (say, in regard to the way individuals recognize their own and others' identities), might lead us to believe that far from being an illusion, race is something fundamental, unquestionable, and obvious. So palpable a distinction, so unquestionable a mark on the very body itself, must retain a fundamentally unchangeable meaning.

But that view is problematic as well. Just as the claim that race is a sort of mass illusion falls to pieces when we contemplate the momentous effects, the world-shaping consequences of half a millennium of belief in this concept, so too the argument that race is at some basic level an objective component of human identity, something "scientifically" knowable, comes apart when we take fully into account the enormous range of meanings assigned by different societies to the concept of race. Race varies, racial categories shift, new races are invented, and old ones retired. And the interpretations attached to racial identity, racial inequality, racial politics, and racial culture are subject to tremendous debate and uncertainty. Although very much present in historical and social development, although as relevant as ever to questions of human freedom and welfare, race is no more a stable and established social scientific category than it is an illusion.

This notable ambiguity, or perhaps contradiction—partly "illusion," and partly "objective reality"; partly relic of earlier benighted times, and partly world-shaping social structure—is shared by no other significant social scientific concept. Let us compare, for example, the theoretical statuses of the categories of class and gender. We may debate the determinations or parameters of class structure and class identity—for example, questioning the dynamics of mobility, the sources of inequality, or the concept of "mode of production"—but few would argue seriously that class does not exist. We might argue about gender in the same way: Is it a matter of "difference" or "inequality"? To what extent does the gender concept link the social and the biological? Is gender a matter of identity or "performance," something you *are* or something you *do*? But no one is seriously proposing that we can simply forget about gender, that it is no longer a useful theoretical and social marker.

So what is "race," then? In other work I have attempted to answer this question concisely and conventionally, to provide a straightforward definition. For purposes of clarification, I repeat that definition here in a note.[4] Yet, my goal in this essay is not to clarify the meaning of race but to explore the significance for social theory of this resilient concept. For if race is both objective and illusory, if it is *both* a way of ordering and explaining the social world *and* of making it opaque and mysterious, that is more than a peculiar phenomenon in social science. That is a compelling theoretical problem.

In other words, theoretical attention is demanded by the claim that race is not only real but also imaginary, that it is not only common sense but also common nonsense, that it both establishes our identity and denies us our identity. Further yet, once we recognize that race not only allocates resources, power, and privilege but also provides means for challenging that allocation, that race not only naturalizes societal organization but also socializes human nature in the broadest possible sense, we find ourselves facing a demanding theoretical agenda. At the least, this situation requires us to revisit some key claims in social theory.

This theoretical cloud—the difficulties of the race category—may turn out to have a silver lining. The peculiarities involved in theorizing race may provide new opportunities for theorizing a whole range of social issues and, indeed, for proposing new approaches to one of the central problems of sociological theory: the problem of "micro-macro linkages." In this essay I explore the possibilities for such a new approach, basing my ideas on the ambiguity and contrariety of race, on the simultaneous resonance of the race concept at the levels of individual experience and collective/institutional organization (or, we might say, at the micro- and macrolevels), on the continuity of racialization as a feature of modernity, on the historical flexibility of racial categories and cleavages, and on the centrality of race as a field of political contestation, as a place where state and civil society intersect. Throughout, my effort is to apply to the broad canvas of social theory the insights we have gained from studying racial theory.

This essay proceeds as follows. In the next section, I provide a general assessment of the condition of social theory's journey up to now. This consists of a brief and obviously schematic overview of the modern vicissitudes of social theory from its European roots to its situation at the turn of the twenty-first century, in the era of U.S. world hegemony. Taking note of the not-so-mysterious neglect of the dynamics of race in social theory's developing account of modernity, this section ends with a discussion of some contemporary "fault lines" in social theory, stressing "micro-macro" and political sociology models.

The following section considers the effects of introducing racial theory into this account. As already noted, the concept of race was associated with the rise of modernity (or with the rise of the "modern world system"). For centuries, understandings of race—at least as practiced by those in power—considered it to be a natural phenomenon, not a social one. This "take" on race upheld an explicit white supremacism, or more properly a number of white supremacist ideologies. Despite earlier attempts to disrupt these commitments, such as abolitionism and racial reformism of various types, and despite some radical insurgencies against white rule (notably in Haiti but elsewhere as well), white supremacism largely resisted serious challenge until the contemporary period, the era beginning with World War II and continuing today. At that point, or beginning then, there was a rupture, a worldwide "break" with the dominant viewpoint: white supremacy was called into question far more thoroughly than ever before, if not destroyed. During these recent years, as anti-fascist war was waged, as colonialism was terminated, as cold-war rivalries focused new attention on the global South, and as racial reforms (of a moderate type, to be sure) were instituted around the world, racial theory became more sophisticated. It did so of necessity, for now postcolonial, civil rights–oriented, and antiapartheid viewpoints and movements had achieved a new legitimacy. These had to be examined and explained; such is the task of all social theory. From these new "racial conditions" arose such perspectives as subaltern studies, critical race theory, and racial formation theory (my own contribution), among others.

The core claim of this essay is that these developments—both practical and theoretical—stimulated new theoretical approaches that were not confined to racial theory but extended more widely. The new world racial dynamics that succeeded World War II and the decades that followed it gave rise not only to new understandings of race but also to new approaches to social structure and agency. The outlines of a new social theory began to emerge in those years, appearing like Hegel's owl of Minerva as a by-product of the rearranged world social system, the system that racial struggle had upended, at least in part.

That new social theory—which of course draws heavily on a whole series of precursors—may be characterized, for lack of a better term, as *radical pragmatism*. In the following section of this essay I offer a series of notes on the contours of this perspective, focusing on the new approaches that it makes possible to a series of key theoretical problems: social agency, micro-macro linkages, state–civil society interaction. I cannot provide more than some preliminary comments here, but I hope to explore these themes further in subsequent work.

The final section of this essay, titled "On Pragmatism and Liberation," attempts some comments on radical pragmatism's importance not only for social theory but also for political practice. Here I also offer a tribute to the great antiracist scholar Joe R. Feagin, to whom this essay is dedicated.

Social Theory's Journey Up to Now

Leaving aside (principally for reasons of space) social theory's extensive precursors in philosophy and economics, the modern origins of this body of thought may be located in the age of revolution that encompassed the "long nineteenth century." The downfall of absolutism and the establishment of Enlightenment rationality generated new demands for explanatory systems of thought, ideas that could explain the comprehensive changes engulfing social institutions (most centrally the state), class structure and social inequality, and even concepts of social identity and everyday life. The works of Hobbes, Montesquieu, Locke, Rousseau, Kant, and most notably Hegel are the foundational documents of social theory. The main tasks of these early theorists were to presage and later to respond to the appearance of capitalism and the rise of its independent and profane (and revolutionary) class, the bourgeoisie; to wrestle with the demise of the concept of divine right and the concomitant rise of secular rule; and to assimilate and harness the dawning culture of Enlightenment, a culture that was based on scientific and critical discourse rather than transcendental religious doctrine.

To be sure, these founders of modern social theory could hardly ignore the rise of Europe or the ongoing processes of plunder, colonization, and enslavement through which European global domination was assured. An account of race was thus available from the Enlightenment's sachems, from Kant, Hegel, and Locke most notably, but presented in the work of others as well (Bernasconi and Lott 2000; Eze 1997; Count 1950). Yet, discussion of race rarely took center stage, doing so perhaps in part only after the Darwinian challenge. Even after Darwin, there was a widespread taken-for-grantedness of racial hierarchy and inequality, which was explained by biological reasons, consistent with the "natural history" approach of Enlightenment thought. The European right to dominate the world, the superiority of a putatively European racial type, was not in question. Where the problem of slavery was addressed, as in Hegel's *Phenomenology*, it was posed in respect to the practices and views of the ancients (as a more dialectical reworking of Aristotle's position, notably) rather than as a pillar of the extant system of relations with the non-European world. Even those who denounced the horrors of slavery and colonialism (Marx in particular) tended to view these systems as necessary stages in the making of the modern world.

By the later nineteenth century, social theory had divided into two main trends, the insurgent and the integrationist perspectives. The insurgents, inspired by the thought of Karl Marx, sought to harness their explanatory efforts to the interests of a subordinated group, the proletariat. The integrationists, best exemplified by Émile Durkheim, proposed an "organic" theoretical perspective that downgraded the elements of (class) conflict stressed by Marx (Tilly 1984). A third current, offered by Max Weber, combined elements of the two: while recognizing the permanence of social conflict, Weber dismissed egalitarian and revolutionary aspirations as utopian and stressed the role of social organization—in practical terms, the state—in achieving integration (aka legitimacy).[5]

What all the main "classical" theoretical currents had in common was their emphasis on *macrolevel* social institutions and relationships, whether conflictual or integrationist, in structuring society. Microlevel, experiential dynamics were present in these accounts but always in strictly subordinate ways. "Alienation," "disenchantment," and "anomie" were despondent, tragic, or perhaps rebellious responses to the onset of modernity, whether it was seen as subjection on the part of capitalism, rational legal authority, or the developing division of labor with its "organic solidarity." *Verstehen*, the understanding by the social actor of the meaning of her or his action, was the apogee of classical sociology's encounter with (what we would today call) the micro-macro linkage, but *verstehen* was really a methodological standpoint imported into sociology by Weber. Its origins lay in Wilhelm Dilthey's (and Immanuel Kant's) philosophy of the subject. Ultimately it had little to do with informing actual social practice or action; it was merely informed by it. *Verstehen* was not pragmatism.

Without dwelling on these points, it is worthwhile to note that this classical theory's emphasis on the large-scale lineaments of social structure no doubt was itself a legacy of the premodern European social order, the corporatist and hierarchical feudal system. That system understood the flow of authority down from heaven through the crown, to the nobles, and ultimately to the lowliest serf. It also assigned a patrimonial responsibility to all (well, all males, anyway) in the hierarchy: to look after those beneath them. Conversely, the exploited—the serfs and other lowly producers—fed, clothed, armed, and housed all those above them. In such a social structure, every individual, every experience, every microlevel relationship, was assigned its place and meaning. The rise of capitalism and the onset of the modern world system did not overthrow all of this system, of course; although the obligations of patrimonialism were replaced with the uncaring ideology of laissez-faire, the fundamental macrosystem of rulers and ruled, producers and owners, continued. Old regimes were swept away: the lords were replaced by the bourgeoisie, and the serfs became proletarians. Momentous as these changes were, all that was solid did not melt into air. And therefore the central problems for the classical social theory of the nineteenth century remained focused on the macrolevel: exploitation, authority, organization, conflict, solidarity.

As the axis of global power "crossed the pond," moving to North America at the turn of the twentieth century, so too did the preoccupations of social theory. Although the leading U.S. social theorists—the founders of Chicago sociology, for example, and W. E. B. Du Bois—had studied in Europe (principally in Germany), their theoretical preoccupations were derived from pragmatism, the philosophical orientation that was America's unique contribution to Western thought. Although I cannot address this complex body of ideas adequately here, I will note that it was a much more worldly, much more practical philosophical approach than the dominant European models.

Pragmatism broke with the formal and abstracted dualisms that characterized much European philosophy, for example, Cartesian mind-world dualism, and Hegelian subject-object dualism as well. From its earliest formulations by Ralph Waldo Emerson, to its more worked-out framing by C. S. Peirce and William James, to its maturation with John Dewey, pragmatism postulated the existence of active subjectivities, already present in the material world, interpreting their experience practically and morally. It was morally and politically activated by the traumatic experience of the U.S. Civil War and was deeply shaped by the democratic and individualistic sociopolitical premises that had founded the United States. Pragmatism was also profoundly disturbed by slavery and its legacy; it had been greatly influenced by abolitionism, although it was not free of the general racism that characterized the late nineteenth and early twentieth century (West 1989). And it was coming into its own in conjunction with the United States' rise to world power and capitalist power during and after the turn of the twentieth century.[6]

In contrast to Europe, the United States had no feudal past and had been founded on rejection of aristocracy. It was shaped by the contradiction between anticolonial and republican principles, on the one hand, and ongoing commitments to slavery and conquest/settlement, on the other. It was, in short, a society whose social structure was particularly unresolved (at least in comparison to those of its European progenitors) and had constantly to be reinterpreted, if not reinvented, sometimes at horrific cost. Faced with these requirements, pragmatism tended to reverse the primacy afforded in European social theory to macrolevel social institutions and relationships in structuring society: instead, it placed primary emphasis on microlevel relationships, on agency and interpretation, on experience and interaction. Obviously, pragmatist social theory did not entirely ignore the state, the economy, or such problems as inequality, any more than Marx or Weber had dismissed such microlevel issues as identity or experience. Yet, its stress on the microlevel was consistent with North American mistrust of the state, of collectivity, indeed, of class consciousness and collectivity.

Fault Lines in Social Theory

Having proposed a distinction, at least in emphasis, between macro- and micro-oriented social theory, and having tentatively linked this distinction to the tendential European versus North American split in social-theoretical orientations, I hasten to demur. It is important not to reify the micro and macro concepts. These are but convenient analytical categories, signifying no more than the emphasis social theorists place on distinct types of social relationships and actors. In reality *there is no clear distinction* between the micro- and macrolevels of society. People live out their lives and experience their identities in relation to all the big institutions: state-based, economic, cultural. Those big structures, in turn, can only operate if they are socialized, recognized, taken-for-granted in everyday life.

Yet this divide between "micro" and "macro," this "optical" distinction, remains a major fault line in social theory. It has occasioned numerous attempts to establish a credible account of the micro-macro "link," whereby large-scale social institutions might be explained as products of patterned small-scale social interactions (Alexander et al. 1987; Huber 1991). Conversely, there have been many theoretical efforts to account for individual actions and small-scale relationships as the mediated or performative manifestations of the macrolevel social institutions, the patterned system of incentives and constraints in which individuals are "embedded."[7]

Accounts that can manage the "linkage" problem as a theoretical "two-way street," however, have yet to emerge. Yet, to theorize contemporary social structure without a convincing statement of this bidirectional pattern of determination is at least difficult, if not impossible.

A highly related problem is that of *agency*. From the pragmatist point of

view individuals are "agents": they continually interpret their social relationships, their experience, and act upon them, based upon these interpretations (Mead 1938, 1962; Blumer 1969). From more classical theoretical
viewpoints, though, and from those deriving from them, such as structural
functionalism and structural marxism (Parsons 1937; Althusser and Balibar
1970), individuals are "bearers of structures": they act out imperatives imposed on them by their institutionalized locations, or at most deviate from
these mandates, in which case they not only run the risks of exclusion, punishment, or anomie but also perversely shore up the very constraints they
reject.

Each theoretical approach to the problem of agency—somewhat stylized
here but hopefully not travestied—has obvious drawbacks. How agency can
be exercised by individuals whose freedom is patently limited and constrained is not effectively addressed by the pragmatists; conversely, how
"bearers of structures" can wield any effective individuality is not obvious
in, say, the Parsonian system, or even in conflict theory such as Marxism.[8]
The failure to resolve the problem of agency, then, is another clear fault
line in contemporary social theory.

I could mention many other similar dilemmas here, but I want to return
to the accomplishments of racial theory. I hope to show in the next section
how contemporary understandings of race can at least begin to overcome
these dilemmas in contemporary social theory.

Introducing Racial Theory into This Account

As noted, world racial dynamics underwent a significant transition in the
latter half of the twentieth century. Beginning with World War II, white
supremacism was challenged more comprehensively than ever before. Both
its colonial and its metropolitan models were confronted with unprecedented
levels of opposition. The political conflicts involved in this worldwide racial
"break" on occasion attained revolutionary dimensions but more regularly
led to political reforms. Though white supremacy was too entrenched to be
entirely defeated, its administrators and beneficiaries were forced to undertake significant programs of democratization and inclusion. Thus, the system that for centuries had been largely taken-for-granted—at least by those
in power—was both deeply shaken by the worldwide racial upsurge and
also revealed by it to be surprisingly resilient. Dispossessed of its colonies,
largely divested of its formal and legal commitments to racial exclusion,

segregation, and deprivation of citizenship rights, white supremacy was not overthrown. Rather it was reinvented as "color-blind," "differentialist," and "multicultural." It became a far more armored, far more slippery political target, as it incorporated much of its former movement opposition.

Addressing this new situation required the development of a body of new theoretical work. The new insights went under various names: critical race theory, diaspora theory, postcolonial theory, subalternity theory, and racial formation theory, among others. As one of the founders of the racial formation approach, I must acknowledge its continuing lack of consensus and its great variety of internal debates, indeed, its incompleteness as a theoretical initiative. On the other hand, I also want to honor the tremendous fertility and openness of this entire range of theoretical currents.[9]

So over a few decades, a new understanding of the meaning of race had to be worked out, a concept that would draw on the accomplishments of centuries of struggle but would also cope with the adaptive capability and resilience of white supremacy. Racial theory had to address the persistence of racial injustice and inequality—as well as the embeddedness of racial meanings and identities—in an era officially committed to racial equality and multiculturalism. It had to take into account the world's increasing interconnectedness and postcoloniality. It had to acknowledge that most national societies, and the world as a whole, were racially multipolar, and that "hybridity" was now recognized as a key feature of racial identity. Politically, racial theory had to respond to a situation in which, in sharp contrast to the conditions that had obtained before World War II, most states and members of state elites now claimed (at least officially) that they opposed discrimination. Indeed, most now denied their continuing adherence to the racial ideologies and traditions of their national societies and even presented their contemporary racial attitudes and policies as "color-blind" or "multiculturalist."

Racial theory had to explain how and why and in what form racial distinctions operated in such changed circumstances. The new racial theory that emerged in response to these challenges stressed three themes. First, it argued that turn-of-the-century racial politics were rooted in a *comparative/ historical dynamic*, a racial *longue durée* that was coextensive with modernity itself; second, it viewed established patterns of *social action and social agency* as crucially shaped, both individually and collectively, by racial factors; and third, it developed the ability to range over and to link the *micro- and macro-aspects of racial signification and racialized social structure* in a new, bidirectional pattern (the heretofore absent "two-way street").

Radical Pragmatism

The tentative outlines of a radical pragmatist *social* theory, I want to suggest, can be conceived in terms of these same three elements that have been so crucial in allowing the development of a new *racial* theory. In a brief essay I cannot fully elaborate this approach, but I can offer a series of notes on the contours of this perspective.

Comparative/Historical Dimensions of Social Structure

Rather than thinking of social structure as developing from any central set of organizing relationships—the mode of production, the system of legitimation of authority, the framework of social solidarity, and so on—a radical pragmatist perspective suggests that society is organized through a process of "circular and cumulative causation" (Myrdal 1963). There is obviously no one "event" that marks the onset of modernity, no profound chasm lying between the remote past and the start of the modern epoch in which we live. All the key ideologies that were articulated, repeated, and modified to create the modern world, and all the practices that accumulated and accreted during that world's development, had their earlier incarnations. To select some central examples: protocapitalist systems for extraction of surpluses and for the organization and exploitation of labor; imperialisms with their states, their metropoles and hinterlands; and cultural representations of social identity, of course, all predated the rise of modernity. In similar fashion, we can recognize early forms of exploitation and domination (as well as protoracial categorizations, systems of gender differentialization and hierarchy, and so on) as having been present throughout these precursory forms of sociohistorical organization.

Yet, there is something different about the "modern world system," as Immanuel Wallerstein has argued extensively. This difference lies in its combination of global reach and lack of unified authoritative rule.[10] This system is a form of world historical organization that came into being beginning (very roughly) about 1500 CE. This new world historical system repeated organizational elements and social categories that had gone before, for example, slavery and resistance to it—here is Gunnar Myrdal's "circularity." Yet, it also combined and transformed these components in new ways, achieving an unprecedented synergy—Myrdal's "cumulative" dimension—in the process. The "decentered" quality of modernity is in part the result of the world system's achievement of unity by new and historically unprecedented means: capitalism, not the authority of a central politico-military power (such as Rome), brought it about; this is one of Wallerstein's central points.[11] But that "decenteredness" is also the result of innumerable experiments and experiences of resistance, both collective and individual; it is also the outcome of countless interpretive efforts, both spontaneous and organized. In short, at least as I interpret the historical sociology of the "modern world system," global social structure is the ongoing (and unstable) product of individual and collective efforts to understand and organize their experiences and relationships.

Such a claim risks dismissal as verging on the obvious, of course. Its substantiation depends on a detailed case study approach, which is not possible here. But in other work I have attempted to offer such an account of the "circular and cumulative" development of racial meanings, racial conflicts, and racialized social structures over modernity's evolution. I have noted, for example, the recurrence of revolutionary movement dynamics in resistance to racial oppression, and the recursive character of conceptions of racial identity. I have argued as well that these developing racial conflicts were not only complex *effects* of the unfolding of modernity, but that they were also key *causes* of modernity's advance (Winant 2001). That is my central point here: the comparative/historical logic of racial formation parallels the logic of modernity's development overall.[12] What Myrdal's observation about "circular and cumulative causation" means is that global social structure and "development" are a lot more open-ended, a lot more subject to political "dynamics of contention" (McAdam, Tarrow, and Tilly 2001), a lot more open to "agency" than mainstream social theory tends to recognize.

Social Action and Social Agency

The foregoing remarks already imply a great deal about the radical pragmatist concept of action and agency. As I have already noted, mainstream social theory, especially in its classical and structuralist forms, tends to lack a convincing theory of action (Joas 1996). Location in particular positions tends to be seen as mandating particular patterns of action and constraining others. Similarly, "positionality" is often understood as imparting specific forms of "consciousness." A few examples here: consider the problem of class consciousness ("in itself/for itself") in Marx, the Weberian take on politics ("the slow boring of hard boards"), and the individualist, U.S.-inflected, game-theoretic logic that dominates rational choice approaches.

In contrast the radical pragmatist approach to action/agency invokes the concept of "signifying action" (Perinbanayagam 1985). The innovation in this tradition—that of George Herbert Mead and Herbert Blumer—is the

claim that present in all social action there is always an interpretative dimension, always a discursive framework. Not only is no individual action or
agency possible without this, but no collective action, no sociopolitical
mobilization, and, indeed, no organizational or state-based action is undertaken in the absence of an explanatory and interpretive faculty.[13]

Racial formation theory develops its account in a framework quite parallel to this one, arguing that racial meanings are established and racial organization is carried out through "racial projects," which consist precisely in the
linkage of action and articulation.

> [T]he key element in racial formation is the link between signification and
> structure, between what race means in a particular discursive practice and
> how, based upon such interpretations, social structures are racially organized.
> (Winant 1994a, 4)

The "project" concept points to a flexible and contested model of racial
identity, racial politics, and indeed racialized social structure. Every racially
defined experience, identity, or discourse acts upon the social structure of
race; in similar fashion every racially oriented policy, organizational effort,
or state action necessarily involves an interpretive practice in which the
meaning of race is being signified and represented. Obviously, the significance
of this infinite variety of actions and interpretations varies enormously,
ranging from the trivial to the world historical; yet, in the outcome of these
interactions and articulations the racial system is both maintained and
transformed. The pragmatist logic of this approach is apparent here.

This radical pragmatist approach, I want to suggest, can be applied more
generally to problems of social action and agency. Such theories as Mead's,
Dewey's, and particularly Blumer's have stressed similar points, putting particular emphasis on microlevel social relationships (see the following section). Du Bois, as well, in his complex theory of racism—involving the
concept of "the veil" and the idea of "double consciousness"—develops a
parallel approach.[14] When we combine this approach to the problem of
action/agency with Myrdal's concept of sociohistorical development, we
begin to see problems of politics from a newer and far more "open" or democratic perspective. This is the subject of the next section.

Micro-Macro Linkages

Pragmatist social theory has proved effective at theorizing micro-macro
linkages as aggregations or iterations of small-scale ("micro") interactions
(Collins 1987). But it works better in making links "from the small to the

large" than in the opposite direction. Making links "from the large to the small," explaining processes of political socialization or acculturation, has generally been the province of macrolevel theoretical approaches.[15]

Certainly the standard pragmatist approach has a great deal to offer. Racial formation theory has adopted much of its version of racialization, much of its explanation of the dynamics of racial identity, from the symbolic inter-actionist account of "role-taking" that comes through Blumer from its origins in Mead. In addition there are important links between this pragmatist approach and the work of Frantz Fanon (1967), as well as with subalternity theory (Scott 1990).

Yet, valuable as this account of microlevel agency is, a more convincing approach would highlight cause-effect relationships, and micro-macro link-ages, *that work in both directions*. In other words, a more effective pragmatist approach would go beyond "iterated interaction ritual chains"—Randall Collins's model is just one of several that work "from the small to the large"; it would simultaneously recognize macrosocial determinations of microlevel experience and interaction, thus seeing the linkage as a "two-way street." Racial formation theory does this through its concept of the complex in-tersection of racial projects, which operate simultaneously at micro- and macrolevels. Supreme Court decisions, say, and friendships in a schoolyard, are in this sense both racial projects (Omi and Winant 1994). Not only that, these large-scale and small-scale instances of racialization are complexly interconnected. Individual identities and microlevel relationships both repeat and resist the racial identities and roles in which they are located. Simultaneously, large-scale, macrolevel political processes (those Supreme Court decisions, for example) are effective only to the extent that they can be socialized, ideologically interpellated (Althusser 1971), and "inhabited," so to speak, as well as enforced.

I emphasize that there is no concrete division between micro- and macrolevel social relationships. Pragmatist social theory can neither dispense with the centrality of individual interpretation and agency nor with the effectivity of institutions and collective action in its account of social structure. Pragma-tism must avow—or at least cannot avoid—the necessarily indeterminate, or unstable, character of social structure. For after all, interpretations are flexible, and cooperation can be withheld or stinted (as in the formula: "I comply but I do not obey"). Similarly, social agencies and organizations can lose their legitimacy, their "grip" on their members, the adhesion of their subjects. In such recognitions and avowals, pragmatism can take on a *radical* new applicability to the pressing tasks of social theory.

To follow this obviously political account of the significance of a radicalized pragmatism one more step: the micro-macro linkage argument so central
to an adequate social theory remains inadequate, I want to suggest, without
the explicit presence of an intermediate "level" of linkages: let us call it the
"meso" level. Here civil society and state institutions interact; here collective forms of agency operate; here movements and states shape each other.

Omi and I have argued in respect to racial politics that movements and
states pass through reiterative cycles of interactions, which we label political "trajectories." Movements "work" the state, accepting concessions in
exchange for demobilization; states in turn "learn" from movements, adapting demands into laws and policies and incorporating movement leaders as
officials and deputies, while at the same time moderating and disciplining
these same demands and leaders (Omi and Winant 1994, 84–88; see also
McAdam, McCarthy, and Zald 1996). Such is the mesolevel cycle. This
state–civil society relationship is necessarily an "unstable equilibrium"
(Gramsci 1971, 182); it requires reiteration (Myrdal's "circularity") as sociopolitical demands change. It tends both to accumulate reforms and concessions (Myrdal's "cumulative" dimension) and to attenuate and ossify over
time. The mesolevel, intermediate between "micro" and "macro," between
small- and large-scale determinations of social structure, also interacts with
both these other levels: this is a theory of social structural "linkages," after
all. Thus, state-based reforms may satisfy some but not all the (individual)
members of a social movement: the movement may then split into radical
and moderate factions; this may be a great success for state managers and
political leaders, who thus demonstrate how well they have learned how to
handle movement opposition. On the other hand, states that do not comprehensively process opposition, that do not make concessions sufficient to
pacify movement opponents, are likely to provoke new mesolevel confrontations: their hegemony is limited; they only pacify social conflicts rather
than resolving them. Such is the case with the worldwide anticolonialist and
antiracist movement upsurge of the post–World War II period. Such is the
case with the "processing" of racially based demands for democracy and social
justice with which, during these decades, many states were confronted.[16]

On Pragmatism and Liberation

In a vital new work, Joe R. Feagin (to whom this essay is dedicated) and his
coauthor Hernán Vera have revived the insights of another radical social

theorist working in the pragmatist tradition, C. Wright Mills (Feagin and Vera 2002). Meditating anew upon Mills's "sociological imagination," Feagin and Vera focus much of their attention on the practice of sociology, on the ways the discipline can work to resist oppression and to supply much needed skills and knowledge to those hungering and longing for social justice, equality, and democracy. Invoking the term *liberation* in the very title of their book, they also remind us that social theory has itself been a battleground between those who sought to interpret the world in order to change it (Marx 1978, 145) and those who sought to protect and justify existing systems of rule.

It is no accident that these scholars seek to advance the cause of liberation through sociological work. Feagin's lifework of inquiry into the problem of racism, and his decades-long commitment to antiracist activity and advocacy stand as profound testimony to the emancipatory potential of social thought and social action. Indeed Feagin's work explores the connection I have endeavored to explain in this essay: the connection between understanding the dynamics of race and racism and understanding the social structure as a whole.

In the early decades of the twentieth century, pragmatist sociology had already broken with the large-scale structural theories of the "founding fathers" of sociology. With the work of Du Bois (at the turn of the twentieth century) and in the key theoretical and empirical approaches developed by the Chicago School, an indissoluble element of democracy had entered the sociological imagination. The attention paid by Du Bois to the experience of racism, to the "peculiar sensation" of double consciousness, to "living within the veil," honored its subjects' abilities and insights into their own social world in a way no other sociologist had done before. The best work of the Chicago thinkers, notably Mead's insights into the process of socialization, the work of W. I. Thomas and Robert E. Park, and that of such Chicago students as Oliver Cox and E. Franklin Frazier, recognized the enormous powers of the social individual to make and remake her own life, her own self, her community, her society. The symbolic interactionism of Blumer was also a profoundly empowering account: of socialization processes, identity-making, and the "sources of the self." Taken as a whole, pragmatist sociology was a tremendous democratic achievement. Its accomplishments are directly tied to the work of C. Wright Mills on social and political inequality (Mills 1956; see also Mills's early work, *Sociology and Pragmatism* [1964]), to the civil rights and antiracist upsurges of the post–World War II years, to the appearance of both "first-wave" and "second-wave" feminism, and to the insurgencies of the anti–Vietnam War movement and new left of the 1960s.

Yet, pragmatist sociology was never able to articulate a full-scale social theory.[17] That work remains incomplete. But to the extent that we can determine a direction of its development, the radical pragmatist account, developed to its fullest, perhaps, in racial theory, provides more of a signpost than any other body of thought. In the various strands of that work, in critical race theory and some varieties of subaltern studies, in racial formation theory, and in liberation sociology as well, we can envision the direction in which we must move. Feagin's work, both on the overcoming of racism and on the sociology of liberation, is the best example of radical pragmatism that we have.

Conclusion

Racial Politics in the Twenty-first Century

Racial globalism, racial difference, and racial justice are among our most fundamental political challenges. The modern epoch was founded on European imperialism and African slavery. Both these systems were organized racially. The theft of labor and life, of land and resources, from millions of Africans and Native Americans, and from Asians and Pacific Islanders as well,[1] financed the rise of Europe and made possible both its subsequent mercantilism and its later industrialism. Conquest, imperial rule, and the chattelization of labor (principally but not entirely African labor) divided humanity into Europeans and "others." Ferocious and unending cultural and psychic energies were expended to sustain this schism, which was also constantly challenged and undermined in innumerable ways.

The central issue in this book is racial politics: democracy, I have argued throughout, can be pragmatically measured by the degree and scope of racial inclusion and racial justice available in a given society. Since the origins of our modern world political system lie in racial dictatorship, it should not be surprising that where racial difference is concerned, democracy continues to be in short supply. Even though reform of state racial policies has occurred in several historical "breaks"—when the abolition of slavery, decolonization, and large-scale extensions of citizenship and civil rights took place—the contemporary world remains fully mired in the same racial history from which it originally sprang.

Colonial rule and slavocracy were systems whose fundamental political character was dictatorial. By seizure of territory, by kidnapping and theft, by coercive and authoritarian rule, Europe-based imperial regimes destroyed countless lives and sensibilities. No amount of rationalization, no invocation of themes of development and uplift, no efforts at historical relativization can justify these predations or deodorize their moral stink.[2]

The destruction of the non-European world by conquest and enslavement is often seen as the theft of resources, lives, and labor, but it is rarely recognized as a *political* assault as well. But it was also that: a usurpation, an attack on the autonomy, the collectivity, and the cultural freedom of countless communities and peoples. It was even more than that: the rise of Europe was also an attack on *European* autonomy, freedom, collectivity, and so on. For beyond slavery and empire's evisceration of much of the non-European world, the ascent of these systems also involved the debilitation of the Europeans themselves. Nascent Europe was after all hardly composed of consensual regimes. Absolutist throughout and far from any sort of democracy, the rising empires of Europe forged their national and transnational identities almost entirely through extra-economic coercion. The new rulers were in many respects no more "advanced" as civilizations than the peoples over whom they came to rule (Davidson 1992). Sure, the conquerors and slave catchers were better armed, but were they more mindful, so to speak, than those whose lands and bodies they seized?

European empires did not grant political "voice" (Hirschmann 1970) either to their colonial subjects and slaves or to their subjects at home. As what remained of feudal ties shrank away in the "mother countries" of Europe, property and property alone came to confer political "voice." This property, let it be remembered, had also largely been acquired by force. What Marx called "primitive accumulation" (1967, chaps. 26–33) was a confiscation of land and labor both in Europe and outside it. In Europe the destruction of feudalism encompassed both the expropriation by the bourgeoisie of land that had been manorial or communal, and the coercive extraction of labor from the now expropriated peasantry (man, woman, and child) under conditions not vastly better than chattel slavery. Outside Europe, primitive accumulation also meant the seizure of land and labor:

> The discovery of gold and silver in America, the extirpation, enslavement, and entombment in mines of the aboriginal population, the beginning of the conquest and looting of the East Indies, the turning of Africa into a warren for the commercial hunting of blackskins, signalized the rosy dawn of the era of capitalist production. These idyllic proceedings are the chief

momenta of primitive accumulation. On their heels treads the commercial war of the European nations with the globe for a theater. It begins with the revolt of the Netherlands from Spain, assumes giant dimensions in England's AntiJacobin War, and is still going on in the opium wars with China, etc. (Marx 1967, 351)

Colonial settlers, of course, were not all slavers. Some were themselves closer to slaves than slave masters. Many were classed as bound laborers, many were in flight from starvation, war, or "ethnic cleansing." Damaged by Europe but still bearing a European identity, most colonials (the "ordinary" settlers, let us call them) would soon be further debilitated by their immersion in a racial order. Their participation in that racial system would be mandated, their own racialization ineluctable. In accepting the "psychological wage" (Du Bois 1935) that whiteness offered, they simultaneously consented to their own debasement and colluded in their own depoliticization, their own powerlessness.

So racial politics have their origins in the ravaging of the globe, in the consolidation of European rule, and in the identification, the interpellation, of all humanity along racial lines. It is a bleak picture. But not in every way. Racial politics also embody autonomy, opposition, resistance, creativity, autogestion, revolution. Without romanticizing the premodern world, precapitalist modes of production (Marx 1964), archaic economies (Polanyi 1968), "traditional" forms of rule (Weber 1994), or "mechanical solidarity" (Durkheim 1947), without dwelling on the horrors of the transition to the "modern world-system" (Wallerstein 1974–89), we must recognize that for the past half millennium, refusal of slavery, resistance to colonialism, noncompliance with racial domination, fidelity to often beleaguered cultural traditions and alternative concepts of group and individual identity, and belief in racial solidarity have been some of the most crucial sources of insurgency, some of the central passions underlying emancipatory and democratic politics, both in the United States and all around the world.

We live in history. We live in continuity with a past that includes conquest and slavery. Not far in our past are state-sponsored racial exclusion and segregation, apartheid, colonial occupation, genocide, peonage. Indeed, these phenomena are not really in the past at all! Ghettoization persists across the world from Rocinha in Rio de Janeiro to Bedford-Stuyvesant, from Soweto to the banlieues of suburban Paris and the disparagingly named "casbahs" of Marseilles and Frankfurt. Apartheid lives on in South Africa despite the efforts of the ANC-led government to undo its legacy. The West Bank is colonially occupied. U.S. military bases in the Horn of

Africa, the Dominican Republic, the Philippines (yet again!), and now Iraq
signal the onset of a twenty-first-century imperialism that is openly avowed
by policy makers in the regime of Bush II (Daalder and Lindsay 2003; Ferguson 2003). In the past few years genocide and "ethnic cleansing" have
swept across East Timor, Central and West Africa, Colombia, and Gujarat
(to name only a few recent and current locales); indeed, there are many
survivors of genocide living among us: both victims and perpetrators. Peonage not too distinct from slavery persists on cocoa and rubber plantations,
in rug, shoe, and apparel factories, on electronic components assembly lines,
in urban informal economies around the world, and in the massive global
sex trade of women and girls.

Is it simply coincidental that the casualties of these practices are almost
universally racially distinct from their perpetrators? Are these patterns merely
aberrations? Local phenomena? To pick just one case: Is the murder of
approximately four million Congolese in the past decade linked to the mass
killing that occurred there under Belgium a century earlier (Hochschild
1998)? Does this killing spree have something to do with the contemporary
demand for natural resources—diamonds, copper, coltan[3]—found in that
country, a demand originating in New York, London, Frankfurt, and Tokyo?

Yes, we live in history. We live in continuity with a past that includes
not only conquest and slavery but also abolitionism, anticolonialism, and
unending efforts, large and small, to secure racial freedom, justice, and equality. So we live in the shadows not only of the predatory and degrading practices that were carried out against colonial subjects and coerced laborers—
past and present—by their putative "masters." We also live in the bright
sunlight of the rejection of these practices by those same subjects. Reassert-
ing freedom, refusing to surrender collective and individual autonomy, maintaining subjecthood by any means necessary—however imperfect or contradictory—have been the constant effort of the subordinated: this is the
work of workers, of women, of prisoners, as well as that of the colonized and
enslaved.

I have argued that the racial abyss that split the world at the origins of
the modern age, and that persists today, produced the political systems that
still shape our lives and world. The discovery and divulgation of the race
concept not only forged the chains of oppression but also gave underlying
form and structure to the concept of freedom. "Freedom," of course, remains
a utopian goal, yet all its varieties—the freedom of labor, of the body, of
sex and gender, and most centrally for my present purposes, the freedom of
political activity, of democracy—have their modern origins in the struggle

against racial domination. Abolitionism is perhaps the earliest "movement" example of this struggle, but the resistance to slavery obviously predates the appearance of organized movements. Anticolonial/anti-imperial movements are generally thought to have originated in the late eighteenth century, but the resistance to conquest also predates the appearance of organized movements.

The limited but real democracy of the present is thus a product of a vast labor: the herculean efforts of the enormous numbers of people who opposed and subverted slavery and empire, who organized labor and vindicated women's rights, who built and served and educated the communities and collectivities of the oppressed and exploited, who worked for reform, fomented rebellion, and made revolution. The achievement of labor rights, of the franchise, of popular sovereignty and freedom of expression, of national liberation from imperial rule, of reproductive rights and women's emancipation more generally, and of popular democracy in all its forms can be traced back to conflict over and about the racial divide, conflict fundamental to the modern world's gestation and development.

How has this heritage operated in our own time? How has it come down to us? For long periods in modern history, racial oppression has been entirely central to social organization on a world scale. For ages it was so indispensable to the accumulation of wealth and the extraction of labor, so intrinsic to elite rule in all its forms, so internalized as the bedrock of identity and culture, that it became normalized, "second nature." Of course, racial domination was never unopposed or unquestioned, but it was still taken for granted (by those in power at least) almost everywhere; it was seen as a "natural" and permanent human difference.

Racial rule therefore attained an enormous weight, one that bore down, shall we say, on both the individual psyche and the common weal. This great burden was composed of an immense amount of accrued indignity and injustice, of privilege and exclusion, of resentment and anger. It was akin to what Sartre (1982–90) called the "practico-inert"; he was referring there to Marx's concept of "dead labor": the embodiment in objects produced under capitalism of the labor that went into their creation. Notably capital itself—in the form of money, machinery, and the built environment (Harvey 1982)—is made out of this dead labor (think about it!); for Marx (via Sartre), capital is the key component of the "practico-inert."

Consider then—in light of this concept—the enormity of the bulk of accumulated racial injustice, the detritus of the exploitation and denial of humanity that fueled and continues to fuel the modern state and corporation. Much racial oppression has, so to speak, been burned off in the chimneys of sweated labor in factory, mine, and field. But much remains.

A great deal of racial injustice has also been "absorbed" through the forging of political barriers: through the denial of access to democracy.[4] But again, much remains. Because self-determination and self-rule have been proscribed, because the requirement that all rulers face to secure the legitimation of their authority has been flouted where race was concerned, because the social contract has been broken or repudiated so that the rulers of slave societies,[5] the conquerors of native lands, and the "lords of humankind" (Kiernan 1969) could do their business, the global social structure has been comprehensively racialized. These practices have curtailed the freedom of all humanity. The world has been filled with racial waste, with the shit of racism.[6]

How ingenuous and innocent we are (or are assumed by our rulers to be) when we think—or are told—that we have now entered a "color-blind" age, a "postracial" era! For so much racial waste remains all around us and inside us, polluting our political atmosphere and fouling our very souls. The waste takes both ideational and material form; it is composed both of beliefs and of material facts. Beliefs about race endure: these are significations and representations of its meaning. Material facts about race also endure: racialized social structures and institutions. As I have argued in previous work, racial formation is but the process that develops and links these materials. Through a virtual infinity of social practices in a thoroughly racialized world, these images and meanings are transmitted to us. We live our lives within these institutions and social structures. We work with these materials, carrying out racial "projects," both in our own personal experience and in collective action. We constantly produce and reproduce, and transform, and sometimes destroy racial meanings and racial institutions.

So much racial waste is left over from the practice of racial domination from the early days of the rise of Europe to the present! Indeed, it often seems that this enormous and odious waste pinions the social system under an immovable burden. How often have despair and hopelessness overcome those who bore this sorrow? How often have slave and native, peon and maquiladora, servant and ghetto dweller felt just plain worn out, encumbered by this deadening inertia composed of a racial injustice that could seemingly never be budged? And often, too, whites have felt weighed down by the waste, the guilt and self-destruction built into racism, and the "psychological wage."

Yet, politics is always unstable and contradictory. Racial rule is a tyranny that can never be fully stabilized or consolidated. Thus, at key historical moments, perhaps rare but also inevitable, the sheer weight of racial oppression—qua social structure—has become insupportable. The built-up rage and inequity, the irrationality and inutility, and the explosive force of dreams denied (Kelley 2002) are mobilized politically in ways that would have seemed almost unimaginable earlier.

When racially based challenges have occurred at this level, they have brought about "breaks" in the system: if not revolutions, at least serious social transformations. Such ruptural moments are rare and necessarily conjunctural. They arise only when large-scale social crises occur, crises that both enable such seismic political ruptures and are themselves produced by them. Racial breaks have occasionally involved revolutionary upsurges, as in Haiti at the turn of the nineteenth century. More often they have approached revolutionary levels of political upheaval, threatening to topple an already wobbling system of racial oppression, only to be defused by reform initiatives. At such times, more often than not the power elites have seen the need for reform, often after attempting and failing to contain movement opposition through domination and repression. When repression cannot succeed, when indeed it consolidates and enlarges opposition, ruling regimes have exercised hegemony: they have accommodated the radical potentialities of popular challenges to racial tyranny by employing reform initiatives.

In modern world history we can identify some moments of racial revolution: above all the Haitian revolution of 1791–1804, which combined anticolonialism and abolitionism. Other anticolonial and indigenous revolutions have included pivotal demands for abolition of slavery and for indigenous rights, notably for land rights: in this regard consider the Mexican revolutionary trajectory from Juarez through Zapata.[7] The Algerian revolution also was driven in part by opposition to colonial racism, as were the overthrow of Dutch rule in Indonesia, the extended Vietnamese revolution, and the revolutionary upheavals in post–World War II Portuguese Africa. Still other cases could be added to this list.

Because racial domination has been so fundamental in shaping social life and social structure in the modern epoch, successful challenges to it have always been radical upheavals. Although racial revolutions have occasionally occurred, most racial breaks have resulted in reforms, falling short of eliminating the system of racial domination tout court, even when they clearly included revolutionary currents. For example, the U.S. Civil War embodied a clear racial break not only in the country where it occurred but on a global scale, for it represented the most decisive, though by no means the last, defeat of racial slavery[8] and the first attempt at societywide racial reform: incorporation of emancipated slaves as citizens.[9] Du Bois (1935) argued that the Civil War and the Reconstruction period that followed it were in fact a revolutionary upsurge that was ultimately defeated or at least contained.

So racial breaks have not occurred very often. A lot of racial opposition has been defeated simply because it was very difficult to organize in politically effective ways. A great deal of resistance to racial domination occurs spontaneously, when people just get fed up with the "bukes and scorns" of everyday life, when they interrupt—not without risk—the routines of racial domination: the profiling, the surveillance in stores, the police and prison violence, the ubiquitous negative stereotyping. But this resistance, for all its vitality, originality, and necessity, is fundamentally defensive (Scott 1986). It does not generally result in political change.

In U.S. racial history we may discern two historical moments or periods when large-scale shifts were effected in the system of racial domination, two breaks, when the fabric of the veil was torn, if not dissolved: during and after the Civil War, and during and after World War II. These upheavals were primarily political events, phenomena of crisis. They occurred—*as have all other racial breaks, both locally and globally*—when the instability of the old racial system became too great and popular opposition had acquired too much disruptive power to be successfully ignored or repressed. They occurred when the dialectic of the racial oppression/resistance meant in practical terms that *the white supremacist system depended too comprehensively and openly on the racially oppressed*. In this situation, the logic of racial domination, the very fabric of what Du Bois called "the veil," threatens to burst apart.

After Hegemony

So now what? Is democracy still possible? Have race consciousness and racial injustice been driven off the political stage? Is the world regressing to a situation like that of a century ago, when white supremacy was taken for granted by those in power? Is the United States enacting a simulacrum of those times, living in a kind of racial Disneyland where race is a thing of the past, where the happy pirates can at last frolic again, undisturbed, on the Caribbean beach?

Today the bombs rain down once again on impoverished countries of the global South (and global East). A quarter century after we thought that the age of imperialism was finally over, dreams of empire have been revived.

Meanwhile the opposite dream, Dr. King's dream, of an inclusive and peaceful U.S. society (and world society) seems to have gone up in smoke. In the United States, state policy is being made by corporate predators, religious fanatics, and militarists. Society's vulnerable groups—the chief inheritors of the legacies of conquest, slavery, and imperialism—are being left to their own devices. The welfare state has been effectively ended, for the politically vulnerable anyway (for those with resources and influence, the state's largesse is unprecedented). The poor, racial and sexual minorities, women and children, the aged and infirm: let them eat cake! And since the United States wields the biggest stick in the neighborhood, these rules are being imposed far and wide, well beyond the country's frontiers. For most of the planet's population, which lacks adequate shelter, education, nutrition, and health care, the message is the same: get used to it! Don't dare to oppose the big brother from the North (or the West), don't assume your culture, your lands, your resources, or your media are truly yours. Empire rules.

And yet, and yet . . . , the horrors of the present are not the whole story. Social movements have emerged once again: different movements that strive to reinvent democratic politics. Opposition, noncompliance, critique, subversion, and, yes, service to those sacrificed on the altars of greed and the arrogance of power are flourishing as people in the United States and around the world explore new approaches to creating collectivity and cooperation, and as they experiment with new ideas about organizing. Where there is oppression, there is resistance. Empire falls.

But we are still a long way from that fall. The U.S. imperium retains a great deal of power, not only through its virtual monopolization of the means of destruction but also through its unending quest to reinforce and justify its own, uniquely American greed.

Much of that power and a great deal of that greed are framed in racial terms. This is the problem of the twenty-first-century racial rule: not the problem of the color-line, but the problem of how the color–line can be both affirmed and denied, simultaneously reinforced and undermined. This is also the problem of twenty-first-century movements for racial democracy: how to affirm racial identity/difference without reifying it; how to oppose racism without restricting racial autonomy.

Culturally, the principle of the "West against the rest" has been revived, sometimes only tacitly, and sometimes quite explicitly. Acknowledged or not, race still provides the line of demarcation that fractures the world: on one side there is "the land of freedom and free enterprise, the shining city on a hill"—more properly described as the U.S.-dominated global power structure, as frightened as ever despite all its weapons. On the other side are the impoverished and fractious multitude of "others" whose worldviews can never adequately approximate those of either the national security state or the Southern Baptist Convention.[10] Economically too, the North depends to an ever greater extent on its ability to exploit the South: to draw from it the cheap labor and resources it needs, to export its pollution there, and to thwart any efforts on the part of African, Asian, or Latin American nations to develop in a sovereign and democratic fashion, outside the discipline of the IMF, the WTO, and the other instruments of global economic power.

So the well-worn techniques of racialization, employed so often in the past to frame so many other political conflicts, are being pressed into service again to process North-South, and particularly West-East tensions. Especially for U.S. domestic consumption, racism is always useful. It helps us to recognize the players on the different teams if they are wearing uniforms of the right colors, so to speak. This is especially true on TV.

This racial polarization along North-South and West-East lines, however, conflicts with the postracial, postcolonial "common sense" that was generated by the wave of racial reform and democratization that swept across the world in the decades after World War II. What is to be done with race after the demise of the old empires and of the apartheid system, after the institution of civil rights reforms and extension of citizenship in various northern countries? Today the claims that racism has finally been transcended and that the "illusion" of race has finally been eliminated provide significant political "cover" for the new imperialism and the new racism of the twenty-first century. White supremacy cannot be revived without the worldwide (and domestic) delegitimation of "the world's only superpower."

So the post–World War II racial justice and anticolonial movements may have been incorporated by the national and global hegemonic systems they themselves helped create. The racial reforms they generated may have fallen short of producing the social justice and democracy they sought. But these movements have certainly not failed. They have created a new "common sense" that clashes with white supremacy, that deeply undermines the imperial logic of "the West against the rest," and that calls into question the division of the world along North-South or West-East lines. And that's not all. The post–World War II movements and reforms have been deeply nationalized and localized everywhere: they have pluralized the world, problematizing globalization from above and promoting globalism from below. The United States, for example, is today much more a global entrepôt than it is a Puritan "city on a hill"; Europe is assuming an independent role as an emergent power linking East and West; South Africa and Latin America are reencountering their cultural pluralism; and the Middle East, South and East Asia, and Africa have all been significantly westernized.

That is obviously not the whole story. But what is the whole story? As noted, the racial dimensions of the present crisis, both global and local, are not yet sufficiently recognized. We are in a transitional stage: not so distant from the insurgent racial politics of past decades that we have forgotten about the movements that redeemed (at least in part) the United States and the world it dominated, but not yet in possession of any movement resources of comparable potential either.

The movements of the post–World War II period advanced the cause of racial justice; they won significant victories, yet their accomplishments were incorporated in a new, and determinedly antidemocratic, global racial regime. How are we to interpret this? What does it mean for racial politics and for democratization more generally?

Winning Is Losing

Making gains under conditions of racial hegemony—winning reforms in state racial policy or concessions from dominant elites—involves moving from marginalized to incorporated status. As Omi and I suggested in our discussion of "trajectories" of racial politics (1994, 84–88), and as I have argued in various essays included here, movements challenging injustice (of all types, not only racial ones) seek to have their claims adopted by the state, embodied in policies of reform, and enforced throughout society.

This is what "winning" means under conditions of hegemony: that the state is pressured to adopt as many movement demands as possible. Of course, hegemonic states, seeking to subdue opposition, attempt to adopt as few reform measures as necessary, just enough to defuse their challengers' momentum and to reinforce their credibility with their supporters. This elaborate relationship, this complex political dance among states, elites, movements, and masses is what "hegemony" means. Racial hegemony/racial formation works by synthesizing the distinct elements of this conflict—at the macrolevel of institutions and social structures, and at the microlevel of experiences and identities. But hegemony is a process; no synthesis can be more than temporary. Gramsci describes hegemony as "the formation and overcoming of unstable equilibria" (1971, 182).

To understand movement politics under conditions of racial hegemony is to recognize that reforms won will usually be more "moderate" than what was demanded, that insurgent movements are generally split by their very achievements into accommodationist and radical fractions, and that gains thus achieved are purchased at the price of at least partial demobilization. The successful movement has undermined some of the conditions for its own existence. It falls back to a quiescent or marginalized phase of the political trajectory. Winning is losing.

But Losing Is Also Winning

If hegemony offers only temporary political equilibrium to the state and elites that achieve it, then it can only generate temporary quiescence for the movements that accept it. To achieve the incorporation of movement demands into state policies—winning the civil rights legislation, for example, that outlawed de jure segregation—is perforce to recognize the very limitations of any given set of movement demands. There is no dishonor in this, for the "horizon" of our demands is necessarily set by the terms of the injustices we face. Demanding desegregation was a logical thing to do when Jim Crow was the law of the land. Achieving it—however incompletely or imperfectly—was a great victory. Yet, after its achievement, the inadequacy of this moderate reform quickly became obvious. The "horizon" of racial democracy had moved. When no gains are possible and no movement exists (what I am describing as the phase of movement quiescence or marginalization), alternative possibilities become almost inconceivable. "That's just the way it is / Some things will never change" (Hornsby 1986): the "horizon" of possibility seems fixed. But as one advances toward the "horizon," it in turn recedes; the criticisms of the movement radicals who had previously resisted incorporation and denounced the reforms achieved as inadequate now appear vindicated. Indeed, entirely new demands begin to take shape as the new situation of racial hegemony is consolidated. There are new stirrings in the jug. The incorporation of movement demands ceases to be a solution and begins to look like a problem. New strategies, new tactics, are developed as those marginalized and afflicted by the power and greed of the racial state and dominant elites rouse their anger and discontent yet again. A new movement trajectory begins.

Acknowledgments

Almost every essay included here was first presented as a lecture or colloquium, usually more than once. I am grateful to the directors and organizers of the following departments, conferences, and lecture series for inviting me to share my ideas and analyses: the Socio-Economic Legacy of Slavery Series, Center for African-American Studies at the University of California, Los Angeles; the Graduate Students–Initiated Lecture Series, Department of Sociology, University of California, Los Angeles; the Color Lines Project, Harvard University; the Institute for Research in African-American Studies, Columbia University; the Department of Ethnic Studies and the Institute for the Study of Social Change, the University of California, Berkeley; the Department of African-American Studies, University of Wisconsin, Madison; the History of Women and Gender Program, New York University; the Center for Ethnicities, Communities, and Public Policy, Bryn Mawr College; the Alice Berline Kaplan Lecture in the Humanities Series, Northwestern University; and the Metropolitan Research and Policy Institute Lecture Series, University of Texas, San Antonio.

Special thanks for friendship, solidarity, and criticism to Doug Dowd, Mitch Duneier, Sherri Grasmuck, Michael Hanchard, Chester Hartman, David Kairys, Josie Negrete, Michael Omi, Lou Outlaw, Carrie Mullen, Bob Perelman, Arvind Rajagopal, Becky Thompson, Eddie Telles, Winddance Twine, and Tukufu Zuberi.

Notes

Introduction

1. Where does race come from, then? If racial classification is so arbitrary and racial categories so malleable, how can we account for their depth and sociohistorical persistence? These questions receive better answers later in this book than they do here. Still it is perhaps worthwhile to remark that the race concept has a clear genealogy. Race is a modern phenomenon. It owes its origins to European precursors such as the Inquisition and the anti-Semitism/anti-Islamism of the Middle Ages. Its generalization and intensification after the rise of Europe, the conquest of the Americas, and the onset of the Atlantic slave trade are best understood as a consequence of the practical requirements of colonial rule and mass labor extraction on the one hand, and of emancipatory aspirations and practices on the other. I have addressed these problems in greater depth in a recent book (Winant 2001).

2. Why only the modern world? The association of social difference and inequality with the body itself was quite uncommon before the onset of modernity. Some precursors can be found, but these were far from the rule. In the ancient and medieval worlds social difference certainly existed, taking many forms: class (and caste) and gender distinctions, of course, and also ethnic and national ones. The latter categories, however, were primarily cultural. They encompassed religious differences (which were of consummate importance), linguistic variance, and civilizational boundaries (the "civilized" vs. the "barbarians," etc.). They were generally not *corporealized*. Mobility across ethnic categories often existed. Where its possibility was foreclosed, this usually came from caste boundaries, which are primarily religious and occupational (as in the case of India). On these matters, see Hannaford 1996; Snowden 1983; Cox 1948.

3. "What constitutes social facts are the beliefs, tendencies and practices of the group taken collectively," Durkheim wrote in 1895. See his discussion, from which this sentence is taken, in Durkheim 1982, 5–59.

4. This is not to deprecate mainstream social scientific accounts, from which one learns a great deal. Some examples are, among many others, Rueter 1995; Swain 1993; and Nina Moore 2000. It is imperative, however, to recognize how much is taken for granted when theoretical questions are *not* posed. Alternative approaches that in my view are far more attuned to racial meaning—and thus converge on the territory I have called *racial formation*—include such works as Dawson 2001; Kelley 2002; Mills 1997; Gilroy 2000; Holt 2000; and Fredrickson 2002, again among many others.

5. Some of these topics have been addressed by students of "new social movements" and of the "cultural framing" of movements (Melucci 1989; Benford and Snow 2000; McAdam, McCarthy, and Zaid 1996). See below for more extensive discussion.

6. I mean by *racism* one or more of the following: (1) signifying practice that essentializes or naturalizes human identities based on racial categories or concepts; (2) social action that produces unjust allocation of socially valued resources, based on such significations; (3) social structure that reproduces such allocations.

7. The reference to Veblen's (1918) critical assessment could not be more timely. Note the full title of the work: *The Higher Learning in America: A Memorandum on the Conduct of Universities by Business Men.*

8. I draw the term *interpellation* from Althusser 1971.

9. "Our ability to interpret racial meanings depends on preconceived notions of a racialized social structure. Comments such as, 'Funny, you don't look black,' betray an underlying image of what black should be. We expect people to act out their apparent racial identities; indeed we become disoriented when they do not. The black banker harassed by police while walking in casual clothes through his own well-off neighborhood, the Latino or white kid rapping in perfect Afro patois, the unending faux pas committed by whites who assume that the nonwhites they encounter are servants or tradespeople, the belief that nonwhite colleagues are less qualified persons hired to fulfill affirmative action guidelines, indeed the whole gamut of racial stereotypes—that 'white men can't jump,' that Asians can't dance, etc. etc.—all testify to the way a racialized social structure shapes racial experience and conditions meaning" (Omi and Winant 1994, 62).

10. In *The World Is a Ghetto* (Winant 2001) I present this argument in much more detail.

11. A great variety of reform-oriented state racial policies were adopted in many countries from the 1960s to the 1990s as direct results of movement pressures of various types: civil rights, antiapartheid, and anticolonial movements in particular. The point here is obviously not to condemn these reforms as inadequate; they were unquestionably democratizing steps. But we should also grasp their limitations and the new configuration of racial they set in motion: what I have been calling here "racial hegemony." This is in fact a good definition of hegemony: the capacity of a political regime to incorporate its opposition (Gramsci 1971, 182).

One Hundred Years of Racial Politics

1. This cryptic claim smuggles into the present essay a particular "take" on a very large and contested philosophical discourse about human freedom. My intended reference is to Sartre's *Being and Nothingness* (1956).

2. Where political "voice" is not available, resistance takes the form of "war of maneuver" (Gramsci 1971). Under these conditions politics continues to exist but must find expression in subversion, noncooperation, and rebellion.

3. "The problem of the twentieth century is the problem of the color-line,— the relation of the darker to the lighter races of men in Asia and Africa, in America and the islands of the sea. It was a phase of this problem that caused the Civil War..." (Du Bois 1903b, 13).

4. Many Mexicans had roots in the state of Califas that predated its cession to the United States in 1848; they were thus not immigrants at all. See Pitt 1998.

5. McKinley explained his Philippine adventure as follows: "When I next realized that the Philippines had dropped into our laps I confess I did not know what to do with them. I sought counsel from all sides—Democrats as well as Republicans— but got little help. I thought first we would take only Manila; then Luzon; then other islands perhaps also. I walked the floor of the White House night after night until midnight; and I am not ashamed to tell you, gentlemen, that I went down on my knees and prayed Almighty God for light and guidance more than one night. And one night late it came to me this way—I don't know how it was, but it came: (1) That we could not give them back to Spain—that would be cowardly and dishonorable; (2) that we could not turn them over to France and Germany— our commercial rivals in the Orient—that would be bad business and discreditable; (3) that we could not leave them to themselves—*they were unfit for self-government*—and they would soon have anarchy and misrule over there worse than Spain's was; and (4) that there was nothing left for us to do but to take them all, and to educate the Filipinos, and uplift and civilize and Christianize them, and by God's grace do the very best we could by them, as our fellow-men for whom Christ also died. And then I went to bed, and went to sleep, and slept soundly, and the next morning I sent for the chief engineer of the War Department (our map-maker), and I told him to put the Philippines on the map of the United States (pointing to a large map on the wall of his office), and there they are, and there they will stay while I am President!" (Rusling 1987, 22–23; emphasis added).

6. General Smedley D. Butler: "I helped make Mexico, especially Tampico, safe for American oil interests in 1914. I helped make Haiti and Cuba a decent place for the National City Bank boys to collect revenues in. I helped in the raping of half a dozen Central American republics for the benefits of Wall Street. The record of racketeering is long. I helped purify Nicaragua for the international banking house of Brown Brothers in 1909–1912 (where have I heard that name before?). I brought light to the Dominican Republic for American sugar interests in 1916. In China I helped to see to it that Standard Oil went its way unmolested.

During those years, I had, as the boys in the back room would say, a swell racket. Looking back on it, I feel that I could have given Al Capone a few hints. The best he could do was to operate his racket in three districts. I operated on three continents" (Butler 1973).

7. Of course a great deal of labor could still be extracted by force: the corvée of Peter the Great and Louis XIV lived on in Africa well past the turn of the twentieth century.

8. Notably Germany came late to the banquet, but Belgium's bloodbath in the Congo was also the result of Leopold II's late-stage craving for an African empire. See Hochschild 1998.

9. On British colonial practices of indirect rule, see Laitin 1986.

10. I can only note in passing the significance of later writers and activists such as José Carlos Mariategui and José Maria Arguedas in Peru, José Vaconcelos in Mexico, and Gilberto Freyre in Brazil, and of the emergence of the indigenismo movement in the 1930s. The point here is a limited one: obviously not that the problematic of race was transcended, but that it became a far more central cultural and political issue in Latin America as the twentieth century advanced.

11. So brief a discussion cannot help but travesty the deep issues involved in Indian nationalism and anticolonialism. Still I must point out that from the standpoint I am advancing here, *satyagraha* represents an intermediate political strategy, appropriate in a situation where political "voice" (Hirschmann 1970) lacks official recognition, but where some access to the public sphere is still permitted. In other words, Gandhi's movement tactics, developed to some extent in South Africa, made sense in an anti-imperial setting located somewhere in the gray zone between political "war of maneuver" and "war of position," to employ the Gramscian framework yet again. Indians were denied their democratic rights, yet an insurgent movement existed that was possessed of the organizational resources and political knowledge to begin its challenge to the colonial/racial order. For a thought-provoking discussion of some of these themes, see Chatterjee 1993.

12. John Maynard Keynes was an exception. His *The Economic Consequences of the Peace* (1920) warned of the disastrous arrogance of the Versailles conferees, though his concerns were less about the presumptions of empire than about the emerging threats of "reaction" and "revolution" in Europe: "If we aim deliberately at the impoverishment of Central Europe, vengeance, I dare predict, will not limp. Nothing can then delay for long that final civil war between the forces of reaction and the despairing convulsions of revolution, before which the horrors of the late German war will fade into nothing, and which will destroy... the civilization and progress of our generation..." (quoted in Skidelsky 1983, 391).

13. The Leninist Third International in 1924 modified Marx and Engels's 1848 exhortation "Workers of the world, unite!" by adding an additional subject: "Workers *and oppressed peoples* of the world, unite!" Thenceforth the (anti)colonial conflict would be linked to the global class struggle in a far more explicit fashion.

14. The Palmer raids, initiated in the early 1920s under Attorney General A. Mitchell Palmer, were a series of constitutionally suspect roundups and deportations of immigrants (largely southern and eastern Europeans and Jews) whose left-wing politics were seen as particularly threatening in the aftermath of the Russian Revolution. The quasi-racist political rhetoric used to justify the raids greatly re-

sembled that employed earlier to stigmatize Asian immigrants, and that used a few years later to harass and expel various threatening black immigrants, notably those from the Caribbean: pan-Africanists, black communists, and Garveyites. See Feuerlicht 1971; W. James 1998.

15. The Immigration Act of 1924 was driven by much the same mentality as the Palmer raids of the same time. It set up a national quota system that cut southern and eastern European immigration in half. By a variety of devices and formulas the act revived nativist traditions in immigration policy. Compare the quotas applied to northern and western European countries to those implemented for southern and eastern Europe: in the former case immigration quotas were reduced by 29 percent; in the latter by 87 percent. The quota of Italians allowed to enter, for example, was reduced from 42,000 to 3,800. A newly instituted visa system forced would-be immigrants to submit to consular screening in their home countries. Though targeting southern Europeans and east Asians, the 1924 act largely exempted Latin America and dealt unevenly with the Caribbean, where Britain was still a colonial power and Puerto Rico, Cuba, and the Dominican Republic were U.S. semicolonies. Mexican workers were wanted on a temporary basis for agricultural labor in the Southwest. Migration from the African continent was very limited. Refugees and economic migrants were not distinguished under the new system, a practice that had disastrous consequences for Jews after fascism came to power in the 1930s. See Smith 1997; Jacobson 1998; Wyman 1998.

16. In the well-known case of *Buck v. Bell* the Court upheld the right of the state to involuntarily sterilize the "feeble-minded." The particular plaintiff in the case was a poor white woman, but the practices to which she was being subjected had been developed by the eugenics movement, which saw the fertility of nonwhites (and to some extent southern and eastern Europeans) as a threat to a superior white race. Supreme Court Justice Oliver Wendell Holmes Jr., perhaps the most distinguished jurist in U.S. history, wrote the decision: "We have seen more than once that the public welfare may call upon the best citizens for their lives. It would be strange if it could not call upon those who already sap the strength of the State for these lesser sacrifices, often not felt to be such by those concerned, in order to prevent our being swamped with incompetence. It is better for all the world, if instead of waiting to execute degenerate offspring for crime, or to let them starve for their imbecility, society can prevent those who are manifestly unfit from continuing their kind. The principle that sustains compulsory vaccination is broad enough to cover cutting the Fallopian tubes.... Three generations of imbeciles are enough" (*Buck v. Bell*, 274 U.S. 200 [1927]).

17. Neither in Korea nor in Vietnam—the two big wars of the period, did the armies of the superpowers ever confront one another, but the rivalry between what were variously labeled "East" and "West," communism and capitalism, the "Soviet bloc" and the "free world," was nevertheless an ongoing tension, what Kennedy called a "twilight struggle."

18. For a more extensive discussion of the complex dialectic of state-based incorporative reform, and civil society–based opposition movements, see Omi and Winant 1994, chap. 5.

19. To pick but one example, I have argued elsewhere that Duboisian racial dualism now applies in the U.S. context not only to blacks but to every racially categorized group (that is, to everyone), though obviously in quite different ways (Winant 1997; included here as "Racial Dualism at Century's End").

20. The Freiheitliche Partei Österreich (FPÖ) in Austria, led by Jörg Haider, is one of a number of European neofascist parties that have gained influence and legitimacy through racist means: nativism, anti-Semitism, and Islamophobia most particularly.

21. Marx's critique of the concept of equality still resonates powerfully with these themes more than 150 years after it was written. It is most clearly presented in his *On the Jewish Question*, a work that is marred, however, by some Jewish self-hatred that it also contains (Marx and Engels 1978, 26–52); see also Brown 1995, 100–121.

22. I refer to the traditions that spring from Pierce, James, Dewey, and Mead, and that were brought into the field of sociology not only by the Chicago School but very crucially by Du Bois. See West 1989; Joas 1993. See also Blumer and Duster 1980.

23. In acknowledging the central role that the concept of race played in the historical construction of modernity, we are returning to an old theme, visible in the explicit and reactionary racism of such authors as Gobineau and in the scientific racism of eugenics. See Mosse 1978; Horkheimer and Adorno 1972.

Dialectics of the Veil

1. This Freudian term is of course used anachronistically here, since Freud's work on "defense mechanisms" such as introjection was done after *Souls* appeared. Yet the substance of the concept is certainly visible in Du Bois's account of "double consciousness." Du Bois later lamented that he had not become acquainted with Freud's work sooner in his intellectual development. The Fanonian framework is also prefigured, of course, in the "double consciousness" idea.

2. The later pragmatist social psychology of George Herbert Mead, with its anatomizing of consciousness as simultaneously subjective and objective, constructed through the interaction of the "I" and the "me," can also be linked to the Hegelian dialectic.

3. The logic of this position may at first unsettle U.S. readers, who have been trained to see their country as "the land of the free and the home of the brave" since before they could question such rhetoric. I explore the claim of racism's centrality to the construction of the United States—and indeed of the modern world—more fully in *The World Is a Ghetto* (Winant 2001). That racial slavery (as well as racially organized conquest of native peoples) was fundamental to the founding of the "modern world system," the rise of Europe, and the organization of capitalism on a global scale are but some of the key elements of this analysis. Race and racism also shaped global experiences of political democracy, empire and national sovereignty, and cultural/individual identity in crucial ways. This argument is itself Duboisian and also owes a good deal to the work of C. L. R. James.

4. This account follows Althusser's (1969) analysis of revolution in the essay "Contradiction and Overdetermination."

5. Du Bois's account of the Civil War and Reconstruction (1935) emphasized (among many other important points) such matters as the precarious dependence of the rebellious South upon enslaved labor and the opportunities this presented for a "general strike" of black slaves. Politically the book stressed the incompleteness of the American Revolution and the vulnerability of democracy in a situation shaped by enslavement and disenfranchisement of millions solely on the grounds of race.

I have argued that the post–World War II racial break arose from rather similar factors: the legacy of an anti-fascist war whose enemy bore some uncomfortable resemblances to the system of rule in the South (and to some extent nationally), the onset of the cold war whose central arena of conflict was the vast and racially "other" colonial terrain, the dependence of the world's North on southern immigrant labor, and so on.

6. For a more expansive treatment of racial dualism among whites and other (non-black) "others," see Winant 1997.

7. *Race* can be defined as a concept that signifies and symbolizes sociopolitical conflicts and interests in reference to different types of human bodies. Although the concept of race appeals to biologically based human characteristics (so-called phenotypes), selection of these particular human features for purposes of racial signification is always and necessarily a social and historical process. There is no biological basis for distinguishing human groups along the lines of "race," and the sociohistorical categories employed to differentiate among these groups reveal themselves, upon serious examination, to be imprecise if not completely arbitrary. *Racism* can be defined as inhering in one or more of the following: (1) signifying practice that essentializes or naturalizes human identities based on racial categories or concepts; (2) social action that produces unjust allocation of socially valued resources, based on such significations; (3) social structure that reproduces such allocations.

8. But see my other work in which they are more seriously encountered: Omi and Winant 1994; Winant 2001.

9. A more comprehensive treatment of these issues—one more in line with Du Bois's lifework—would emphasize the global dimensions of the veil far more than has been possible here. Such matters as North-South conflict, global debt peonage and "sustainable development," environmental crisis and unequal distribution of natural as well as economic resources, HIV and other global health crises, and the injustices of the worldwide division of labor should all be considered as racial issues. They are all intelligible in terms of the veil. See Winant 2001.

10. Although race is a modern invention—appearing on the world historical stage only with the rise of Europe, the conquest of the Americas, the African slave trade, and so on—over subsequent centuries the concept has acquired such range and depth that it is now a permanent (although of course changeable) component of human and societal organization and consciousness.

11. A further consequence of this analysis extends the understanding of racism beyond whites—the dominant racially defined group—to all Americans. Duboisian double consciousness, as I have already noted, identified something like "internal-

ized racism" (or introjected racism) within the black self, and in the years since *Souls* appeared, a large literature has developed on this. But we can see today there is no reason to limit this dialectic to white or black racism, whether directed inward or outward. All Americans are socialized into the same racist system; all are subject to one variety or another of racial dualism. To recognize that racism is introjected by blacks is to recognize that black people can be racist, not only toward themselves but toward others; the same holds true of other racially defined minorities. This does not diminish, however, the veracity of the basic insight that racism in the United States is a system of white privilege. See Winant 1997.

Racism Today

1. Bob Blauner has argued that the central point distinguishing the two foregoing positions is the centrality afforded to race in one's worldview. For those to whom race is central, racism remains very present. And for those to whom race is less central, racism too is seen as "a peripheral, nonessential reality" (Blauner 1992).

2. By essentialism I mean a belief in unchanging human characteristics, impervious to social and historical context (Fuss 1989).

Behind Blue Eyes

1. In recent years, new right groups such as the Christian Coalition have mounted various initiatives to organize racially defined minorities. Numerous examples could be cited, from the campaign of Alan Keyes to the Promise Keepers.

2. More problematic is Gitlin's argument, in the book's concluding chapter, that the danger of identity politics is its alienation of white men. For them, "[T]here is no particular benefit in restraining their resentment. . . . Their fear and loathing is, in part, a panic against the relative gains of women and minorities . . . , [b]ut economic jitters are only one force behind the conspicuous loathing of Democrats of all factions. Symbols are fuel. The rage of dispossession has been at work . . ." (1995, 232–33). Since the rage of white men cannot be stemmed, according to Gitlin, racially defined minorities (and women and gays), should restrain *their* demands— which he admits are justified in terms of sustained social inequalities—so that white men may keep enough of their privileges to continue in coalition politics with their less fortunate class brothers and sisters.

3. Troy Duster has raised important questions about the idea that biologistic racism has been discredited, or at least relegated to a secondary status in contemporary debates about race. In his *Backdoor to Eugenics* (1990) he suggests that biologism is as susceptible to rearticulation as any other ideological dimension of racism. Additional evidence for this argument is provided by the appearance of Herrnstein and Murray's *The Bell Curve* (1994). I think that while scientific grounds for racism are no more dead than religious ones, the biologistic argument cannot regain the cachet it possessed in the nineteenth and early twentieth centuries; the political dimensions of race will persevere as its predominant determinants (Omi and Winant 1994).

Teaching Race and Racism in the Twenty-first Century

1. Of course, I do not mean this in the Arnoldian sense in which culture is seen as "the best that has been known and thought" (Arnold 1921), for what is best and even what is known are subject to continuous contention. But the point that what is taught and learned in university represents the general summa of intellectual life in a given society—including all the debates and controversies being explored—remains valid, it seems to me. It should also be noted that a great deal of knowledge is derived from experience rather than schooling (thanks to Gary Delgado for reminding me of this point).

2. A partial exception to this pattern was the belated but triumphant South African transition to racial democracy, but even this was fraught with difficulty.

Babylon System

1. Some portions of this section appeared previously in Howard Winant, "Durban, Globalization, and the World after 9/11: Toward a New Politics," *Poverty and Race* 11, 1 (Jan./Feb. 2002).

2. Note: CCA is going transnational, with prisons in the UK, Australia, and South Africa.

The Modern World Racial System

1. This essay is an effort to present in concise form some of the key arguments developed in part 2 of my *The World Is a Ghetto: Race and Democracy since World War II* (2001). Some text originally appearing there recurs here.

2. *Alexander v. Sandoval* (99–1908) 532 U.S. 275 (2001).

3. Though not a "national" case, strictly speaking, the European Union is becoming far more integrated in respect to racial policy, and thus can be practically considered as a single case. In the key areas of immigration, relaxation of border restrictions within the EU, and convergence of citizenship policies on jus soli principles, this "regional" entity is acting more like a nation-state as time goes by. The integration of the EU racial policy was greatly accelerated after the signing of the Schengen agreements in 1985; Schengen came into full implementation in 1995.

Reaching the Limits of Reform

1. For a detailed account of the August 2001 protests in the context of the WCAR, see Mann 2002. Conflicts over GEAR and the ANC's development policies more generally are examined in Hart 2002; Klug 2000; and Bond 2003.

2. For further material on racism and imprisonment, see Currie 1998; Beckett 1999; Gilmore 1998; and Robinson 2002.

3. A thorough consideration of these claims is beyond the scope of this essay, but in other work (Winant 2001) I have explored these ideas in much greater depth.

4. The "break" was full of "microlevel" dimensions as well. After being torn

from a rural province or urban slum, after being trained and armed, after having risked his/her life for freedom, the soldier from Senegal or Alabama, from Jamaica, West Indies, or Jamaica, Queens, was told to return to the back of the bus, to take off his hat when addressing a white, and not even to attempt exercising the franchise. The racial break was also linked to other, profound, democratic upsurges, such as labor struggles and the resurgent women's movement.

5. On absorption and insulation, see Omi and Winant 1994, 86–87.

6. Gramsci defines hegemony as an advanced system of rule that brings about "not only a unison of economic and political aims, but also intellectual and moral unity, posing all the questions around which the struggle rages not on a corporate but on a 'universal' plane . . . , thus creating the hegemony of a fundamental social group over a series of subordinate groups. It is true that the State is seen as the organ of one particular group, destined to create favourable conditions for the latter's maximum expansion. But the development and expansion of the particular group are conceived of, and presented, as being the motor force of a universal expansion, of a development of all the 'national' energies. In other words, the dominant group is coordinated concretely with the general interests of the subordinate groups, and *the life of the State is conceived of as a continuous process of formation and superseding of unstable equilibria* . . . between the interests of the fundamental groups and those of the subordinate groups—equilibria in which the interests of the dominant group prevail, but only up to a certain point, i.e. stopping short of narrowly corporate economic interest" (Gramsci 1971, 182; emphasis added).

7. For a far more systematic critique of civil rights–era reform policy formation than is possible here, see Steinberg 1995.

8. This all-too-brief section relies on Mamdani 1996; Seidman 1999; Adam, Moodley, and Van Zyl Slabbert 1998; Ebrahim 1998; and Toase and Yorke 1998.

9. On Latin American transitions, see O'Donnell and Schmitter 1986.

10. When die-hard Afrikaner nationalists led by General Constand Viljoen of the so-called Freedom Front and by militants in the neofascist Broderbond attempted to derail the transition through various armed interventions—notably a 1994 paramilitary assault at Mmabatho in the Bophuthatswana bantustan—they were quickly defeated by rank-and-file black soldiers who defied their officers and fired on the rebels.

11. The United States had a long history of covert opposition to the ANC. For example, during the apartheid years the CIA and BOSS—the South African secret police—cooperated closely.

12. Portions of this section appeared in Winant 2001.

13. The latter point is a particular scandal given the prevalence of HIV in the country and region, the exorbitant prices demanded by (largely U.S.) pharmaceuticals for AIDS medications, the prevalent practices of some southern countries like Brazil of producing these much needed drugs at far lower costs, and the scandalous refusal of the ANC government under Mbeki to adopt even rudimentary public health measures against HIV. See Gevisser 2001.

14. For a selection of critical documents on NEPAD, see Inter-Church Coalition on Africa, "Debt, Structural Adjustment, and Jubilee," http://www.web.net/~iccaf/debtsap/nepad.htm. See also Bond 2002.

15. As a side note: South African TV is still saturated with U.S. programming.
16. By 1999 Webster and Adler were arguing that South Africa was experiencing a "stalemate" between capital and labor. Only a strategy of "class compromise," they suggested, would allow the government to devise a new development strategy to balance growth with redistribution (1999).

The New Imperialism, Globalization, and Racism

1. "Islamophobia" (Halliday 1999) has a complex genealogy in Europe and the United States. Here I use the term in a narrow sense, as anti-Islamic (and by extension, anti-Muslim) prejudice.
2. Sign seen at 2003 anti–Iraq war protests in the United States: "What's OUR oil doing under YOUR sand?"
3. "There is no point in aspiring in vain for a proletariat or peasantry that will somehow detach itself from its insistence on the mundane objectives that will make for a tolerable material life and a modicum of dignity. There is, on the contrary, every point in seeing precisely these ends and their dogged pursuit through thick and thin as the central hope for a more humane social order—as the core of the critique, in symbol and in action, of any and all social orders erected above peasants and workers by those who claim to serve their interests" (Scott 1986, 350).
4. When one calls Luanda from New York, the link passes through Portugal. When one calls Luanda from Nairobi, the link passes through Portugal.
5. This is not to disparage the use of international peacekeepers where genocidal practices are being carried out.
6. Not to belabor the point, but at this writing Monsanto (headquartered in St. Louis) is pressuring Brazil over use of soy seeds it has patented. Shell Oil (headquartered in Houston) is demanding cordial U.S. relations with Angola (site of the Cabinda oil production complex) and simultaneously violating human rights through use of hired thugs in the Ogoni region of Nigeria (more oil production there—also massive contamination). Nike is fighting a lawsuit before the U.S. Supreme Court that charges it lied about use of sweatshop labor in Indonesia. This list can be extended indefinitely.
7. Extensive surveillance both by U.S. military forces and international agencies, constant "low-intensity conflict," and punitive economic sanctions were prescribed for Iraq in the aftermath of Gulf War I. But the country was not occupied; it was instead harried by the United States and its collaborators.
8. Theorists linked to the Bush II regime do not shrink from avowing an imperial agenda (L. Kaplan and Kristol 2003). Liberals and centrists got on board as well: for a small sample, see Berman 2003; Elshtain 2003; and Ignatieff 2003. And many Democrats, timid as ever, as well as prisoners of their long history of global interventionism, hesitated to criticize the emergent new imperialism.
9. At this writing U.S. forces are unable to find any WMDs in occupied Iraq. Predicated on the "preemption" doctrine and what now appears to have been manipulated intelligence and outright lying, the charge that such weapons were held by Iraq was the most forceful claim made by Bush and his myrmidons in support of the attack, and had the greatest effect on the U.S. public, which was still under the

influence of the Vietnam syndrome. Here, then, is another instance of classical imperialism: a chauvinistic manipulation of public opinion more redolent of 1898 ("Give
me the pictures and I'll give you the war...") than of any more recent precedent.

10. The Inquisition initially accepted conversion to Christianity (Roman, of
course). Later it renewed its persecutions against *conversos* or *novos cristaos*, whom it
now suspected (often correctly) of secretly practicing Judaism. So the problem was
no longer a Jew's beliefs but his or her essence, as depicted in the doctrine of *limpieza
de sangre*, that was seen as unredeemable. Thus, conversion would not insure the
homogeneity of the faithful: only expulsion or extirpation of the Jew would suffice
(Poliakov 1977; Mosse 1978; Arendt 1968; Netanyahu 1995).

11. It is worth noting the unreliability of such quotations, if only because their
translations are so susceptible to anachronistic readings. Nevertheless it is likely
that in their agitations for the Crusades, European leaders did employ this sort of
protoracist rhetoric, as frequently occurs in war fevers of various kinds.

12. I apologize for these abominable oversimplifications of long-standing macro-
historical conflicts. Let us simply stipulate that no ethnonational "boundaries" are
ever fully settled, that European expulsions of Muslims and Jews under the Inquisition were generally far more repressive than Muslim practices toward Jews and
Christians in the same era, and that ethnonational conflict and warfare have never
ceased in the Balkans. My point here is a relatively confined one: that contemporary
West-East conflicts have an extensive historical background that is inevitably being
exhumed by U.S. imperial activity in the Muslim/Arab world.

13. This is one of many dates that could be selected. On September 12, 1683,
Kara Mustapha, commander of a Turkish army of about 150,000 men, was defeated
in the Battle of Vienna by a combined Polish and Austrian army commanded by Jan
Sobieski. That struggle on the Danube represented the defeat of Islam in Europe. Or
did it?

14. A good example here is the Fome Zero (Zero Hunger) program now getting
under way in Brazil. Initially proposed by the late Herbert (Betinho) de Souza, Fome
Zero is an effort sponsored by the new president of Brazil, Luis Ignacio Lula da Silva,
to guarantee adequate nutrition to all Brazilians by the year 2004.

15. As Gramsci noted, incorporation of opposition plays a crucial role not only
in the achievement of reform but also in the maintenance of hegemony (Gramsci
1971, 182).

16. From the enormous literature on the demographics of immigration to the
United States, a useful overview, focused on historical data, is Gibson and Lennon
1999. Because they do not deal with successor generations, Gibson and Lennon have
a somewhat assimilationist assumption about immigrant communities.

17. As throughout modern history, terrorism achieves no positive political aims
for its practitioners and the causes they support. By what moral or political logic do
armed groups attack civilians in cafés, buses, or office buildings?

18. This figure is according to World Bank and IMF data (International Monetary Fund 2002; World Bank 2002). Data on remittances are notoriously underre-
ported and unreliable. On a related point, Middle Eastern countries have been
among the most substantial recipients of remittances from the United States; in
2001, for example, Egypt was the fourth largest national recipient of remittances,

receiving a total of $2.91 billion, of which a substantial amount came from the United States. Jordan was the seventh largest recipient, receiving a total of $2.01 billion, nearly 23 percent of annual GDP. Since 2001, however, these types of financial flows have come under heavy official surveillance and have been seriously curtailed. Data for 2002 were not available as of this writing.

19. How secular, as opposed to theocratic, is the Bush regime? What are the consequences in the United States—where constitutional "firewalls" supposedly protect both church and state from encroachment on the other's part—of the unparalleled rise of political Christianity? How much influence do our mullahs—Pat Robertson, Paige Patterson, Donald Wildmon, James Dobson, Paul Weyrich, Jerry Falwell, and others—exercise on the Bush regime? What would be the response to this question among reproductive rights advocates, gay rights organizers, and public education champions?

20. Grover Norquist, the right-wing ideologue who has become one of the most powerful men in Washington, once declared, "I don't want to abolish government. I simply want to reduce it to the size where I can drag it into the bathroom and drown it in the bathtub" (Krugman 2003).

21. The "Latino-Hispanic" category is defined by the U.S. census as an ethnic, not racial item. This reflects the continuing incapacity of the census to grasp the complexities of U.S. racial formation.

22. And if the past history of U.S. military adventurism is any guide, the termination of military occupations and closing of U.S. bases will bring new waves of compromised new imperial "allies" as immigrants to the United States. Like the *pieds noirs* who flooded into France after it withdrew from Algeria in 1962, like the Vietnamese allies who fled Vietnam after the U.S. defeat there in 1975, the United States may see substantial inflows of loyalists from the Middle East, the Horn of Africa, the Philippines, Afghanistan, the former Soviet Central Asian nations, and elsewhere after it decides to close its bases in all these sites.

23. As of this writing, the Supreme Court has not yet announced its decision on the most crucial test of affirmative action policy to have come before it in decades: the two University of Michigan cases, *Gratz et al. v. Bollinger* (No. 97–75231 [E.D. Mich.]) and *Grutter v. Bollinger* (No. 97–75928 [E.D. Mich.]).

One Hundred Years of Racial Theory

1. Religious, philosophical, literary/artistic, political, and scientific discourses all were directed in a never-ending flood of ink and image to the themes of "the Other," variations in human nature, and the corporeal, mental, spiritual, sexual, and "natural historical" differences among "men." To the extent that this discussion addressed itself to the problem of patterns of human difference/identity and human variability, it may be fairly characterized as about "race." To cite some valuable texts among a great many: Hannaford 1996; Gossett 1965; Todorov 1984, 1993; Kiernan 1969; Montagu 1997; Banton 1977.

2. Early treatments of the race concept in Europe and the United States combined a supposedly biologistic, or "natural history"–based, conception of race with a high degree of arbitrariness, if not outright incoherence, in their application. Numer-

ous groups qualified as "races": national origin (the Irish), religion (Jews), as well as the more familiar criteria of color were frequently invoked as signs of racial "otherness." Although this fungibility has been somewhat reduced and regularized over recent decades, it can never be fully supplanted by "objective" criteria or appeals to cultural/ethnic difference. See the discussion of "racial formation" later in the chapter.

3. "The discovery of gold and silver in America, the extirpation, enslavement, and entombment in mines of the aboriginal population, the beginning of the conquest and looting of the East Indies, the turning of Africa into a warren for the commercial hunting of blackskins, signalized the rosy dawn of the era of capitalist production. These idyllic proceedings are the chief momenta of primitive accumulation. On their heels treads the commercial war of the European nations with the globe for a theater. It begins with the revolt of the Netherlands from Spain, assumes giant dimensions in England's AntiJacobin War, and is still going on in the opium wars with China, etc." (Marx 1967, 351).

4. Instances of European chauvinism appeared in Weber's work especially during the World War I years, when Weber was somewhat afflicted with German nationalism.

5. In fairness, Weber also recognizes racism, notably anti-black racism in the United States. See his remarks on U.S. racial attitudes in Gerth and Mills 1958, 405–6. Weber's sensitivity to U.S. racial matters may be attributed, at least in part, to the orientation provided him by Du Bois. See Lewis 1993, 225, 277.

6. Racial categories are employed as "social types" in *Suicide*, for example. See Fenton 1980.

7. The Chicago theorists, particularly Park, proposed a deterministic version of this argument in the form of a "race relations cycle" through which macrosocial encounters between "peoples" were argued to pass. The four stages of the cycle were held to succeed each other more or less inevitably: first contact, then conflict, succeeded by accommodation, and finally assimilation. Residues of the "natural history" logic of race can be detected here, to be sure, but there is also something of a social constructionism at work. For example, Park suggests that alternative power dynamics among racially defined groups are possible at each of the cycle's phases.

8. One should cite much more of Du Bois's contributions to the foundations of U.S. sociology, and indeed to democratic theory and practice in respect to race: the Atlanta studies, the historical sociology (most notably *Black Reconstruction in America* [1935]), and an astounding wealth of other work (see Du Bois 1995 for a good selection of materials). While Du Bois was not entirely ignored by the "mainstream" of the field, he was hardly given his due recognition. As noted, Du Bois was associated with Weber, whom he had come to know in Berlin. The complex set of influences shaping Du Bois's intellectual and political development has been much explored in recent scholarship: he combined a "high German" philosophical, historical, and social scientific training with solid roots in American pragmatism (notably his work with William James), and a deep engagement with the popular African American traditions he first met as a college student in the South (see Du Bois 1903b, 1940; Lewis 1993; West 1989; Marable 1986).

9. Thomas and Znaniecki's *The Polish Peasant* (1923) prefigured the entire contemporary field of migration studies. Their book on what would now be considered a

"white ethnic group" could easily be seen as a "racial" work at the time of its original appearance.

10. For a good overview, see Bulmer 1984.

11. In this developing analysis, Chicago sociology not only led the field but established the beginning of an interdisciplinary social scientific consensus. The early contributions of Franz Boas in cultural anthropology—whom Du Bois invited to speak in Atlanta in 1911—were crucial here as well.

12. Myrdal's encounter with Du Bois was more problematic. There was little in *Dilemma* that did not touch upon research pioneered by Du Bois: in *The Philadelphia Negro*, the numerous empirical studies he had organized during his years at Atlanta University, his voluminous historical research, and his empyrean theoretical perspective. Yet Myrdal kept his distance from Du Bois, whom (prompted by his sponsors) he saw as a radical. Decades-long efforts by Du Bois to obtain support for the sort of comprehensive study that Myrdal carried out had been frustrated by the unavailability of research grants, as well as by southern antagonism to any black scholarly work.

13. Not exclusively, of course. Resistance to Nazism also bred important works, as did anticolonial struggle and cultural anthropology. A few examples: the Jewish and homosexual activist Magnus Hirschfeld first used (as far as I can tell) the term *racism* in a book he published with that title in 1935, whose topic was (logically) anti-Semitism. The pan-Africanist movement, which owed a lot to Du Bois, was well underway by this time, generating important works by such scholar-activists (and Marxists) as George Padmore, C. L. R. James, and others. Boas's students such as Gilberto Freyre and Ruth Benedict were producing important studies on race in Brazil, as was exiled anthropologist Claude Lévi-Strauss.

14. Notably the Garvey movement, the Harlem Renaissance, and the development of successful (though still effectively segregated) black media: music, film and theater, newspapers, etc.

15. A valuable survey of "mainstream" social approaches to race in the United States over the entire twentieth century is Pettigrew 1980. For a more critical perspective, see McKee 1993.

16. During the post–World War II years, UNESCO sponsored a range of studies and conferences on race and racism, producing collections of research on race and colonialism, for example, and deploying researchers in Brazil, the United States, the Caribbean, and Africa. For a sample of these writings, see UNESCO 1966; O'Callaghan 1980; and Bastide and Fernandes 1971. Studies of "internal colonialism" that systematically linked racial domination and "underdevelopment" in a variety of national settings—both "peripheral" and "core" in world-system theory parlance—proliferated during the same years. See Cotler 1970; Wolpe 1975; Hechter 1975; and Blauner 1972.

17. See, amid a vast literature, Geiss 1974; R. Allen 1970; Césaire 1972; Walters 1987; and Lemelle and Kelley 1994.

18. At a deeper level, governments often enacted racial reforms that were more symbolic than substantive, and enforced those they had managed to enact indifferently if at all. See Lipsitz 1998; and Massey and Denton 1993 for U.S. examples.

19. Perhaps the greatest effort to argue for a class-based contemporary racial

theory in sociology has been that of William Julius Wilson. For more than two decades, Wilson has sought to present racial progress as dependent on generalized full-employment policies and politics. In recent work he has striven to revive well-used "left" arguments about the indispensability of interracial solidarity (Wilson 1996). But for all that is valuable in this approach, its dismissal of the continuing effects of racism and of the experience of racial distinctions is crippling. The socio-cultural and organizational obstacles to interracial solidarity remain far more formidable than Wilson acknowledges.

20. "Cultural nationalism" as politics and racial theory in the United States, Brazil, and South Africa may have entered a cul-de-sac, but it is essentially benign. The same cannot be said of the devolutionist nationalisms of the Balkans, Rwanda, and parts of South Asia, which have reintroduced the quasi-racist program of "ethnic cleansing" in forlorn and bloody attempts to achieve the utopian congruence of state and nation. Quite apart from the resemblance of such policies to genocides ancient and recent, they testify once again to the near-total hybridity of the human population and the impossibility of achieving any societal homogeneity, especially in the present. Such policies also reveal the flexibility of racialization, which has time and again been applied to exacerbate human distinctions not easily recognized (at least from "outside") as corporeal or "phenotypic." Consider in this regard not only Hutu versus Tutsi and Bosnian Serb versus Bosnian Muslim, but also such cases of racialized conflict as German "Aryan" versus German Jew, Palestinian Arab versus Israeli Jew, and British versus Irish.

21. See Huber 1991; Giddens 1984; Collins 1987; Alexander et al. 1987.

22. In non-U.S. settings, the "new social movement" phenomenon has not always been so clearly recognized as racially structured. This is particularly notable in Europe where its study was prompted by the vicissitudes of the "new left," the resurgence of feminism, the rise of green politics, and the upsurge of terrorism in the 1970s (Melucci 1989). But in the "third world" the rethinking of political theory and political sociology in terms of issues of subjectivity and of "identity" often took on a racial dimension. Consider the legacy of Fanon, for example.

23. Numerous writers now employ racial formation perspectives, both within sociology and in other social scientific fields (as well as in cultural studies, legal studies, etc.). See, for example, Gilroy 1991; Crenshaw et al. 1995; A. Davis 1997; Almaguer 1994; and Espiritu 1992.

24. For example, the U.S. civil rights movement, antiapartheid struggles, SOS-Racisme in France, the Movimento Negro Unificado in Brazil.

What Can Racial Theory Tell Us about Social Theory?

1. Many examples of this sort of argument could be cited. Consider Kwame Anthony Appiah's view: "The truth is that there are no races. There is nothing in the world that can do all we ask race to do for us" (1992, 45).

2. For example, in their argument against affirmative action policies, Stephan and Abigail Thernstrom claim that "race-conscious policies make for more race-consciousness. They carry American society backward" (1997, 539).

3. But not before that. The concept of race is a distinctively modern notion, linked to the rise of Europe, the dawn of capitalism and the rise of seaborne empire, the Enlightenment, and the decay of absolutist rule. See Winant 2001.

4. At its most basic level, race can be defined as a *concept that signifies and symbolizes sociopolitical conflicts and interests in reference to different types of human bodies*. Although the concept of race appeals to biologically based human characteristics (so-called phenotypes), selection of these particular human features for purposes of racial signification is always and necessarily a social and historical process. There is no biological basis for distinguishing human groups along the lines of "race," and the sociohistorical categories employed to differentiate among these groups reveal themselves, upon serious examination, to be imprecise if not completely arbitrary.

5. See Tilly 1984 for a concise account of these theoretical currents.

6. For good contemporary collections of key pragmatist texts, see Menand 1997; Goodman 1995. For valuable debates about the contemporary revival of interest in pragmatist social and political theory, see Dickstein 1999.

7. In this regard consider the range of social scientific studies based in "rational choice" theory (e.g., Olson 1968; Elster 1989; Grafstein 1992; Chong 1991). For a non–rational choice account that attempts to follow the same macro-to-micro determinative sequence, see Giddens 1984. On "embeddedness," see Granovetter 1995.

8. Consider the problematic of "class consciousness" in Marx. Without succumbing to the "false consciousness" pitfall, the determinism of the class "in itself"/"for itself" formulation leaves little room for individual interpretation, much less agency.

9. To summarize the racial formation approach: (1) It views the meaning of race and the content of racial identities as unstable and politically contested; (2) it understands racial formation as the intersection/conflict of racial "projects" that combine representational/discursive elements with structural/institutional ones; (3) it sees these intersections as iterative sequences of interpretations ("articulations") of the meaning of race that are open to many types of agency, from the individual to the organizational, from the local to the global. See Omi and Winant 1994; Winant 1994a; Winant 2001.

Numerous writers now employ perspectives compatible with the racial formation approach, both within sociology and in other social scientific studies (as well as in cultural studies, legal studies, etc.). See, for example, Gilroy 1991; Crenshaw et al. 1995; Lowe and Lloyd 1997; Almaguer 1994; Espiritu 1992.

10. No early empire could attain truly global scope. None could exist without a central administrative nucleus, a politico-military authority that extended and disciplined the imperial domain, directing the empire's accumulative flow toward the center by various means (tributary, coercive, etc.), and accepting no rivalry within the boundaries of the system.

11. Does Wallerstein's formulation stand in the face of the current drive in Washington to enunciate a frankly imperial model for U.S. "preemption" of competing centers of power? While this question cannot be definitely answered, the Bush II regime's effort to revive imperial politics seems to be coming undone as of this writing (June 2003). For further discussion, see "The New Imperialism, Globalization, and Racism" in this volume.

12. Regarding the interaction of race and modernity, my argument is actually much deeper: not only parallels but (again invoking Myrdal) *causation* is involved. Race shaped modernity, made capitalism's rise possible, organized epochal struggles for democracy and popular sovereignty, and brought into being the concepts of identity and lineaments of culture that have long been our "common sense." These are positions that cannot be developed here, but that I have spelled out extensively elsewhere (Winant 2001).

13. Not only the pragmatist but also certain poststructuralist theoretical frameworks have stressed this point, notably the work of Michel Foucault.

14. I have made this argument elsewhere at greater length. See Winant 1997.

15. A good example is the work of Herbert Blumer on race. In his well-known article "Race Prejudice as a Sense of Group Position" (1958), the founder of symbolic interactionism (and pragmatist sociologist par excellence) convincingly shows that microlevel racist attitudes have macrolevel effects: they preserve exclusive forms of collectivity and also perpetuate racial divisions and conflicts. Yet the questions of *why* such exclusionism is desirable as a macrosocial organizing principle (in contrast, for example, to transracial class solidarity), and *why* racial divisions are selected as a primary line of macrosocial demarcation are not addressed in Blumer's account.

16. These last points are central to the comparative account of post–World War II racial politics presented in Winant 2001.

17. Mills probably came the closest but died too young to unify the disparate aspects of his thought.

Conclusion

1. "The problem of the twentieth century is the problem of the color-line,— the relation of the darker to the lighter races of men in Asia and Africa, in America and the islands of the sea." (Du Bois 1903b).

2. Probably the most acceptable of these relativist arguments was Bill Warren's *Imperialism, Pioneer of Capitalism* (1980), a work still open to serious criticism. For a good critique of Warren, see Ahmad 1996.

3. "From Columbia to Angola to Afghanistan people are dying every day because consumer societies import and use materials irrespective of where they originate.... If you purchase a cell phone, for example, you may very well be paying to keep the war going in the Democratic Republic of the Congo, where rival armies fight for control over deposits of coltan, a commodity that just over a decade ago had little commercial value, but is now vital for the one billion plus cell phones in use today" (Renner 2002).

4. On "absorption" of racial conflict, see Omi and Winant 1994, 87.

5. To argue that the "social contract" was broken where race was at play unfortunately does not do justice to the theme. Of course, slaves and conquered peoples were not considered worthy of consenting to any form of rule, slave or free. But more was involved in their subjection than their rulers' dismissal of their rights and humanity. As Charles Mills (1997) has argued, a "racial contract" was developed in parallel with the "social contract" we all learned about in school. This "racial contract" underwrote the "social" one by framing the social division between the

possessors of rights and those who lacked them. By claiming that this "contract" became implicit in all racialized systems of power, Mills is taking a position quite close to my argument about the foundational character of race in modernity.

6. Feagin and Vera (1995) also employ the concept of racism as "waste," drawing on Bataille to do so.

7. This legacy has been reasserted since 1994 by the Zapatistas, whose demands are particularly attuned to the rights of indigenous peoples. See Hayden 2001; Womack 1999.

8. Brazilian abolition in 1888 is usually seen as the final act of slavery's elimination, but in fact the practice has continued on a mass scale until today. See, among a large literature, Bales 1999. For more detailed information on the variety of contemporary slavery, see the Web site of Anti-Slavery International: http://www.antislavery.org/.

9. It is well known but still worth stating that the legal recognition offered by the U.S. state in the post–Civil War constitutional amendments thirteen through fifteen, in the ancillary civil rights and voting rights statutes enacted during the Reconstruction period (1865–77), and, in the administrative practices of the national army occupying the defeated South during those same years, fell far short of providing political equality to black people in the United States. These measures were reversed or ignored soon after Reconstruction was ended. From a vast literature, see Du Bois 1935; Foner 1988.

10. A new river of ink has been running in recent years on the topic of Western superiority and the ongoing barbarism of the "others," particularly the barbarians of Africa and Asia. See (among many others) the works of Robert Kaplan (1996, 2001, 2003). How different is this literary output—a combination of horrific travel writing and celebration of Western superiority—from the orientalism and condescension of nineteenth-century varieties of imperial discourse?

Works Cited

Adam, Heribert, and Kogila Moodley. 1993. *The Opening of the Apartheid Mind: Options for the New South Africa*. Berkeley: University of California Press.

Adam, Heribert, Kogila Moodley, and Frederik van Zyl Slabbert. 1998. *Comrades in Business: Post-Liberation Politics in South Africa*. Cape Town: Tafelberg.

Adorno, T. W., et al. 1950. *The Authoritarian Personality*. New York: Harper.

Agence France-Presse. 2002. "Civil Rights Groups Protest Detentions of Middle Eastern Men in US." December 20.

Ahmad, Aijaz. 1996. "Imperialism and Progress." In *Lineages of the Present: Political Essays*. New Delhi: Tulika.

Alba, Richard D. 1990. *Ethnic Identity: The Transformation of White America*. New Haven, CT: Yale University Press.

Alexander, Jeffrey, et al., eds. 1987. *The Micro-Macro Link*. Berkeley: University of California Press.

Allen, Mike, and Barton Gellman. 2002. "Preemptive Strikes Part of U.S. Strategic Doctrine: 'All Options' Open for Countering Unconventional Arms." *Washington Post*, December 11.

Allen, Robert. 1970. *Black Awakening in Capitalist America: An Analytic History*. New York: Anchor.

Allen, Theodore W. 1994. *The Invention of the White Race: Racial Oppression and Social Control*. Vol. 1. New York: Verso.

Allport, Gordon W. 1954. *The Nature of Prejudice*. Cambridge, MA: Addison-Wesley.

Almaguer, Tomás. 1994. *Racial Faultlines: The Historical Origins of White Supremacy in California*. Berkeley: University of California Press.

Althusser, Louis. 1969. "Contradiction and Overdetermination," in *For Marx*. New York: Pantheon.

———. 1971. "Ideology and Ideological State Apparatuses (Notes towards an Investigation)." In *Lenin and Philosophy and Other Essays*, trans. Ben Brewster. New York: Monthly Review Press.

Althusser, Louis, and Etienne Balibar. 1970. *Reading "Capital."* Trans. Ben Brewster. London: New Left Books.

Amin, Samir. *The Arab Nation*. 1978. Trans. Michael Pallis. London: Zed Press.

———. "Imperialism and Globalization." 2001. Paper delivered at the World Social Forum meeting, Porto Alegre, Brazil, January 2001. *Monthly Review* 53, 2 (June).

Anderson, Benedict. 1991. *Imagined Communities: Reflections on the Origins and Spread of Nationalism*. Rev. ed. New York: Verso.

Andrews, George Reid. 1991. *Blacks and Whites in São Paulo, Brazil, 1888–1988*. Madison: University of Wisconsin Press.

Anstey, Roger. 1975. *The Atlantic Slave Trade and British Abolition, 1760–1810*. Atlantic Highlands, NJ: Humanities Press.

Appadurai, Arjun. 1996. *Modernity at Large: Cultural Dimensions of Globalization*. Minneapolis: University of Minnesota Press.

Appiah, Kwame Anthony. 1992. *In My Father's House: Africa in the Philosophy of Culture*. New York: Oxford University Press.

Arendt, Hannah. *Antisemitism*. 1968. New York: Harcourt, Brace & World.

Aristotle. *Politics*. 1959. Trans. Harris Rackham. Cambridge, MA: Harvard University Press.

Armstrong, Nancy, and William Tennenhouse. 1989. *The Violence of Representation: Literature and the History of Violence*. New York: Routledge.

Arnold, Matthew. 1921. Preface to *Lives of the Poets*, by Samuel Johnson. London: Macmillan.

Baker, Houston A., Jr. 1986. "Caliban's Triple Play." In *"Race," Writing, and Difference*, ed. Henry Louis Gates Jr. Chicago: University of Chicago Press.

Baldwin, James. 1985. "White Man's Guilt." In *The Price of the Ticket*. New York: St. Martin's.

Bales, Kevin. 1999. *Disposable People: New Slavery in the Global Economy*. Berkeley: University of California Press.

Balibar, Etienne, and Immanuel Wallerstein. 1991. *Race, Nation, Class: Ambiguous Identities*. London: Verso.

Banton, Michael. 1977. *The Idea of Race*. London: Tavistock.

Barkan, Elazar. 1992. *The Retreat of Scientific Racism: Changing Concepts of Race in Britain and the United States between the World Wars*. New York: Cambridge University Press.

Bastide, Roger, and Florestan Fernandes. 1971. *Brancos e Negros em São Paulo; Ensaio Sociológico Sôbre Aspectos da Formação, Manifestações Atuais e Efeitos do Preconceito de Côr na Sociedade Paulistana*. 3rd ed. São Paulo: Companhia Editora Nacional.

Becker, Gary. 1957. *The Economics of Discrimination*. Chicago: University of Chicago Press.

Beckett, Katherine. 1999. *Making Crime Pay: Law and Order in Contemporary American Politics*. New York: Oxford University Press.

Bello, Walden. 2001. With Shea Cunningham and Bill Rau. *Dark Victory: The United States and Global Poverty*. Rev. ed. Oakland: Food First Books.

Benería, Lourdes. 1999. "Structural Adjustment Policies." In *The Elgar Companion to Feminist Economics*, ed. Janice Peterson and Margaret Lewis. Northampton, MA: Edward Elgar.

Benford, Robert D., and David A. Snow. 2000. "Framing Processes and Social Movements: An Overview and Assessment." *Annual Review of Sociology* 26.

Berger, Guy. 2001. "Seeing Past Race: The Politics of the Human Rights Commission Inquiry into Racial Representation in Post-Apartheid South Africa." Paper presented at Penn State University, March.

Berman, Paul. 2003. *Terror and Liberalism*. New York: Norton.

Bernasconi, Robert, and Tommy L. Lott, eds. 2000. *The Idea of Race*. Indianapolis: Hackett.

Bhabha, Homi K. 1994. *The Location of Culture*. New York: Routledge.

Blackburn, Robin. 1988. *The Overthrow of Colonial Slavery, 1776–1848*. London: Verso.

———. 1997. *The Making of New World Slavery: From the Baroque to the Modern, 1492–1800*. London, Verso.

Blauner, Bob. 1992. "Talking Past One Another: Black and White Languages of Race." *The American Prospect* 10.

Blauner, Robert A. 1972. *Racial Oppression in America*. New York: Harper.

Blumer, Herbert. 1958. "Race Prejudice as a Sense of Group Position." *Pacific Sociological Review* 1, 1 (Spring).

———. 1969. *Symbolic Interactionism: Perspective and Method*. Englewood Cliffs, NJ: Prentice-Hall.

Blumer, Herbert, and Troy Duster. 1980. "Theories of Race and Social Action." In *Sociological Theories: Race and Colonialism*, ed. Marion O'Callaghan. Paris: UNESCO.

Bonacich, Edna. 1972. "A Theory of Ethnic Antagonism: The Split Labor Market." *American Sociological Review* 37.

———. 1976. "Advanced Capitalism and Black/White Relations in the United States: A Split Labor Market Interpretation." *American Sociological Review* 41.

Bonacich, Edna, and Richard P. Appelbaum. 2000. *Behind the Label: Inequality in the Los Angeles Apparel Industry*. Berkeley: University of California Press.

Bond, Patrick, ed. 2002. *Fanon's Warning: A Civil Society Reader on the New Partnership for Africa's Development*. Trenton, NJ: Africa World Press.

———. 2003. *Against Global Apartheid: South Africa Meets the World Bank, IMF, and International Finance*. London: Zed.

Borstelmann, Thomas. 1993. *Apartheid's Reluctant Uncle: The United States and Southern Africa in the Early Cold War*. New York: Oxford University Press.

Branch, Taylor. 1988. *Parting the Waters: America in the King Years. 1954–1963*. New York: Simon and Schuster.

Brown, Wendy. 1995. *States of Injury: Power and Freedom in Late Modernity*. Princeton, NJ: Princeton University Press.

Brubaker, Rogers. 1992. *Citizenship and Nationhood in France and Germany*. Cambridge, MA: Harvard University Press.

Bullard, Robert. 1993. *Confronting Environmental Racism: Voices from the Grassroots*. Boston: South End.

Bulmer, Martin. 1984. *The Chicago School of Sociology: Institutionalization, Diversity, and the Rise of Sociological Research*. Chicago: University of Chicago Press.

Butler, Judith. 1997. *The Psychic Life of Power: Theories in Subjection*. Stanford, CA: Stanford University Press.

Butler, Smedley D. 1973. "War Is a Racket." In *Three Generals on War; Comprising Old Europe's Suicide, by Brig. General Christopher B. Thomson, War Is a Racket, by Major General Smedley D. Butler [and] The Men I Killed, by Brig. General Frank P. Crozier*. New York: Garland.

Cabral, Amílcar. 1974. *Return to the Source: Selected Speeches*. New York: Monthly Review Press.

———. 1976. *A Arma da Teoria: Unidade e Luta*. Vol. 1. Lisbon: Seara Nova.

Caraway, Nancie. 1991. *Segregated Sisterhood: Racism and the Politics of American Feminism*. Knoxville: University of Tennessee Press.

Carmichael, Stokely, and Charles V. Hamilton. 1967. *Black Power: The Politics of Liberation in America*. New York: Vintage.

Carnoy, Martin. 1994. *Faded Dreams: The Politics and Economics of Race in America*. New York: Cambridge University Press.

Carson, Clayborn. 1981. *In Struggle: SNCC and the Black Awakening of the 1960s*. Cambridge, MA: Harvard University Press.

Carter, Dan T. 1999. *From George Wallace to Newt Gingrich: Race in the Conservative Counterrevolution, 1963–1994*. Baton Rouge: Louisiana State University Press.

Centre for Contemporary Cultural Studies. 1982. *The Empire Strikes Back: Race and Racism in 70s Britain*. London: Hutchinson.

Césaire, Aimé. 1972. *Discourse on Colonialism*. Trans. Joan Pinkham. New York: Monthly Review Press.

Chatterjee, Partha. 1993. *The Nation and Its Fragments: Colonial and Postcolonial Histories*. Princeton, NJ: Princeton University Press.

Chayes, Antonia, and Martha Minow, eds. 2003. *Imagine Coexistence: Restoring Humanity after Violent Ethnic Conflict*. San Francisco: Jossey-Bass.

Chong, Dennis. 1991. *Collective Action and the Civil Rights Movement*. Chicago: University of Chicago Press.

Chua, Amy. 2002. *World on Fire: How Exporting Free Market Democracy Breeds Ethnic Hatred and Global Instability*. New York: Doubleday.

Cohen, Thomas M. 1998. *The Fire of Tongues: António Vieira and the Missionary Church in Brazil and Portugal*. Stanford, CA: Stanford University Press.

Cole, David. 2002. "Enemy Aliens and American Freedoms." *The Nation*, September 5.

Cole, Jeffrey A. 1985. *The Potosí Mita, 1573–1700: Compulsory Indian Labor in the Andes*. Stanford, CA: Stanford University Press.

Collins, Randall. 1987. "Iterated Interaction Ritual Chains, Power, and Property: The Micro-Macro Connection as an Empirically Based Sociological Problem." In *The Micro-Macro Link*, ed. Jeffrey Alexander et al. Berkeley: University of California Press.

Colvin, Mark. 1997. *Penitentiaries, Reformatories, and Chain Gangs: Social Theory and the History of Punishment in Nineteenth-Century America*. New York: St. Martin's Press.

Cooper, Frederick. 1987. *On the African Waterfront: Urban Disorder and the Transformation of Work in Colonial Mombasa*. New Haven, CT: Yale University Press.

Cornell, Stephen. 1988. *The Return of the Native: American Indian Political Resurgence*. New York: Oxford University Press.

Cose, Ellis. 1993. *The Rage of a Privileged Class*. New York: HarperCollins.

Costa, Emília Viotti da. 1982. *Da Senzala à Colônia*. 2nd ed. São Paulo: Livraria Editora Ciências Humanas.

Cotler, Julio. 1970. "The Mechanics of Internal Domination and Sociological Change in Peru." In *Masses in Latin America*, ed. I. L. Horowitz. New York: Oxford University Press.

Count, Earl W., ed. 1950. *This Is Race: An Anthology Selected from the International Literature on the Races of Man*. New York: Henry Schuman.

Cox, Oliver C. 1948. *Caste, Class, and Race: A Study in Social Dynamics*. New York: Monthly Review Press, 1970.

Crenshaw, Kimberlé, et al., eds. 1995. *Critical Race Theory: The Key Writings That Formed the Movement*. New York: The New Press.

Cunha, Euclides da. 1902. *Rebellion in the Backlands (Os Sertões)*. Trans. Samuel Putnam. London: Picador, 1995.

Currie, Elliot. 1998. *Crime and Punishment in America*. New York: Owl Books.

Daalder, Ivo H., and James M. Lindsay. 2003. "American Empire, Not 'If' but 'What Kind.'" *New York Times*, May 10.

Datafolha. 1995. *300 Anos de Zumbi: Os Brasileiros e o Preconceito de Côr*. São Paulo: Datafolha.

Davidson, Basil. 1992. *The Black Man's Burden: Africa and the Curse of the Nation-State*. New York: Random House.

Davis, Angela. 1997. With Lisa Lowe. "Reflections on Race, Class, and Gender in the U.S.A." In *The Politics of Culture in the Shadow of Capital*, ed. Lisa Lowe and David Lloyd. Durham, NC: Duke University Press.

———. 1998. *The Angela Y. Davis Reader*. Ed. Joy James. Malden, MA: Blackwell.

Davis, F. James. 1991. *Who Is Black? One Nation's Definition*. University Park: Pennsylvania State University Press.

Dawson, Michael C. 2001. *Black Visions: The Roots of Contemporary African-American Political Ideologies*. Chicago: University of Chicago Press.

Delgado, Richard, and Jean Stefancic. 2001. *Critical Race Theory: An Introduction*. New York: New York University Press.

Diamond, Sara. 1995. *Roads to Dominion: Right-Wing Movements and Political Power in the United States*. New York: Guilford.

Dickstein, Morris, ed. 1999. *The Revival of Pragmatism: New Essays on Social Thought, Law, and Culture*. Durham, NC: Duke University Press.

Drake, St. Clair, and Horace Cayton. 1945. *Black Metropolis: A Study of Negro Life in a Northern City*. Chicago: University of Chicago Press, 1993.

Drinnon, Richard. 1985. *Facing West: The Metaphysics of Indian Hating and Empire Building*. Minneapolis: University of Minnesota Press.

D'Souza, Dinesh. 1995. *The End of Racism*. New York: Free Press.

Du Bois, W. E. B. 1896. *The Suppression of the African Slave-Trade to the United States of America, 1638–1870*. New York: Longmans, Green.

————. 1897. "The Conservation of Races." In Du Bois 1995.

————. 1899. *The Philadelphia Negro: A Sociological Study.* Philadelphia: University of Pennsylvania Press, 1996.

————. 1903a. "Of Our Spiritual Strivings." In Du Bois 1995.

————. 1903b. *The Souls of Black Folk.* New York: Penguin, 1989.

————. 1915. "The African Roots of the War." In Du Bois 1995.

————. 1920. "The Souls of White Folk." In Du Bois 1995.

————. 1935. *Black Reconstruction: An Essay toward a History of the Part Which Black Folk Played in the Attempt to Reconstruct Democracy in America, 1860–1880.* New York: Atheneum, 1977.

————. 1940. *Dusk of Dawn: An Essay toward an Autobiography of a Race Concept.* New Brunswick, NJ: Transaction Publishers, 1991.

————. 1960. "Whither Now and Why." In *The Education of Black People: Ten Critiques 1906–1960,* ed. Herbert Aptheker. Amherst: University of Massachusetts Press, 1973.

————. 1995. *W. E. B. Du Bois: A Reader.* Ed. David Levering Lewis. New York: Henry Holt.

Dudziak, Mary L. 2000. *Cold War Civil Rights: Race and the Image of American Democracy.* Princeton, NJ: Princeton University Press.

Durkheim, Émile. 1947. *The Division of Labor in Society.* Trans. George Simpson. Glencoe, IL: Free Press.

————. 1982. *The Rules of Sociological Method.* Ed. Steven Lukes. Trans. W. D. Halls. New York: Free Press.

Duster, Troy. 1990. *Backdoor to Eugenics.* New York: Routledge.

Ebrahim, Hassen. 1998. *The Soul of a Nation: Constitution-Making in South Africa.* Capetown: Oxford University Press.

Edin, Kathryn, and Laura Lein. 1997. *Making Ends Meet: How Single Mothers Survive Welfare and Low-Wage Work.* New York: Russell Sage Foundation.

"Editorial: Abolish the White Race—By Any Means Necessary." 1993. *Race Traitor* 1 (Winter).

Edsall, Thomas Byrne. 1992. With Mary Edsall. *Chain Reaction: The Impact of Race, Rights, and Taxes on American Politics.* Rev. ed. New York: Norton.

Elshtain, Jean Bethke. 2003. *Just War against Terror: The Burden of American Power in a Violent World.* New York: Basic Books.

Elster, Jon. 1989. *The Cement of Society: A Study of Social Order.* New York: Cambridge University Press.

Engerman, Stanley L. 1999. *Terms of Labor: Slavery, Serfdom, and Free Labor.* Stanford, CA: Stanford University Press.

Espiritu, Yen Le. 1992. *Asian American Panethnicity: Bridging Institutions and Identities.* Philadelphia: Temple University Press.

Eze, Emmanuel Chukwudi, ed. 1997. *Race and the Enlightenment: A Reader.* Malden, MA: Blackwell.

Fanon, Frantz. 1967. "The Fact of Blackness." In *Black Skin, White Masks.* Trans. Charles Lam Markman. New York: Grove Press.

Feagin, Joe R. 2000. *Racist America: Roots, Current Realities, and Future Reparations.* New York: Routledge.

Feagin, Joe R., and Karyn D. McKinney. 2002. *The Many Costs of Racism*. Lanham, MD: Rowman & Littlefield.

Feagin, Joe R., and Hernán Vera. 1995. *White Racism: The Basics*. New York: Routledge.

———. 2002. *Liberation Sociology*. Boulder, CO: Westview Press.

Fenton, Stephen. 1980. "Race, Class, and Politics in the Work of Emile Durkheim." In *Sociological Theories: Race and Colonialism*, ed. Marion O'Callaghan. Paris: UNESCO.

Ferguson, Niall. 2003. "The Empire Slinks Back." *New York Times Magazine*, April 27.

Feuerlicht, Roberta Strauss. 1971. *America's Reign of Terror: World War I, the Red Scare, and the Palmer Raids*. New York: Random House.

Fields, Karen. 1985. *Revival and Rebellion in Colonial Central Africa*. Princeton, NJ: Princeton University Press.

Finley, M. I. 1983. *Politics in the Ancient World*. New York: Cambridge University Press.

Foner, Eric. 1988. *Reconstruction: America's Unfinished Revolution, 1863–1877*. New York: Harper & Row.

Forbes, Jack D. 1988. *Black Africans and Native Americans: Color, Race and Caste in the Evolution of Red-Black Peoples*. New York: Basil Blackwell.

Frank, Andre Gunder. 1969. "The Development of Underdevelopment." In *Capitalism and Underdevelopment in Latin America: Historical Studies of Chile and Brazil*. New York: Monthly Review.

Frankenburg, Ruth. 1993. *White Women, Race Matters: The Social Construction of Whiteness*. Minneapolis: University of Minnesota Press.

Fredrickson, George M. 1981. *White Supremacy: A Comparative Study of American and South African History*. New York: Oxford University Press.

———. 1995. *Black Liberation: A Comparative History of Black Ideologies in the United States and South Africa*. New York: Oxford University Press.

———. 2002. *Racism: A Short History*. Princeton, NJ: Princeton University Press.

Freyre, Gilberto. 1933. *The Masters and the Slaves: A Study in the Development of Brazilian Society*. Trans. Samuel Putnam. Berkeley: University of California Press, 1986.

Fuss, Diana. 1989. *Essentially Speaking: Feminism, Nature, and Difference*. New York: Routledge.

Gallagher, Charles. 1994. "White Reconstruction in the University." *Socialist Review* 94, 1–2.

Garrow, David J. 1988. *Bearing the Cross: Martin Luther King Jr. and the Southern Christian Leadership Conference*. New York: Vintage.

Geiss, Imanuel. 1974. *The Pan-African Movement: A History of Pan-Africanism in America, Europe, and Africa*. New York: Holmes and Meier.

Gerth, Hans, and C. Wright Mills, eds. 1958. *From Max Weber: Essays in Sociology*. New York: Oxford University Press.

Gevisser, Mark. 2001. "AIDS: The New Apartheid." *The Nation*, May 14.

Gibson, Campbell J., and Emily Lennon. 1999. "Historical Census Statistics on the Foreign-born Population of the United States: 1850–1990." Working Paper No. 29, Population Division, U.S. Bureau of the Census.

Giddens, Anthony. 1984. *The Constitution of Society: Outline of the Theory of Struc-turation*. Berkeley: University of California Press.

Gilmore, Ruth Wilson. 1998. "Globalisation and U.S. Prison Growth." *Race and Class* 40, 2–3.

Gilroy, Paul. 1991. *There Ain't No Black in the Union Jack: The Cultural Politics of Race and Nation*. Chicago: University of Chicago Press.

———. 2000. *Against Race: Imagining Political Culture beyond the Color Line*. Cam-bridge, MA: Harvard University Press.

Gitlin, Todd. 1993. "From Universality to Difference: Notes on the Fragmentation of the Idea of the Left." *Contention* 2, 2 (Winter).

———. 1995. *The Twilight of Common Dreams: Why America Is Wracked by Culture Wars*. New York: Henry Holt.

Glazer, Nathan. 1978. *Affirmative Discrimination: Ethnic Inequality and Public Policy*. 2nd ed. New York: Basic.

———. 1998. *We Are All Multiculturalists Now*. Cambridge, MA: Harvard Univer-sity Press.

Glazer, Nathan, and Daniel P. Moynihan. 1970. *Beyond the Melting Pot*. 2nd ed. Cambridge, MA: MIT Press.

Goldfield, Michael. 1997. *The Color of Politics: Race and the Mainsprings of American Politics*. New York: New Press.

Goodman, Paul. 1998. *Of One Blood: Abolitionism and the Origins of Racial Inequality*. Berkeley: University of California Press.

Goodman, Russell B., ed. 1995. *Pragmatism: A Contemporary Reader*. New York: Routledge.

Goodstein, Laurie. 2003. "Seeing Islam as 'Evil' Faith, Evangelicals Seek Converts." *New York Times*, May 27.

Gordon, David, Michael Reich, and Richard Edwards. 1982. *Segmented Work, Divided Workers: The Historical Transformations of Labor in the United States*. New York: Cambridge University Press.

Gordon, Linda. 1994. *Pitied but Not Entitled: Single Mothers and the History of Wel-fare*. New York: The Free Press.

Gordon, Milton M. 1964. *Assimilation in American Life: The Role of Race, Religion, and National Origins*. New York: Oxford University Press.

Gossett, Thomas F. 1965. *Race: The History of an Idea in America*. New York: Schocken.

Gotanda, Neil. 1995. "A Critique of 'Our Constitution Is Color-Blind.'" In *Critical Race Theory: The Key Writings That Formed the Movement*, ed. Kimberlé Cren-shaw et al. New York: The New Press.

Gould, Stephen J. 1981. *The Mismeasure of Man*. New York: W. W. Norton.

Grafstein, Robert. 1992. *Institutional Realism: The Social and Political Constraints on Rational Actors*. New Haven, CT: Yale University Press.

Graham, Lawrence Otis. 1995. *Member of the Club: Reflections on Life in a Racially Polarized World*. New York: HarperCollins.

Gramsci, Antonio. 1971. *Selections from the Prison Notebooks*. Ed. Quinton Hoare and Geoffrey Nowell-Smith. New York: International Publishers.

Granovetter, Mark S. 1995. *Getting a Job: A Study of Contacts and Careers*. 2nd ed. Chicago: University of Chicago Press.

Grant, Joanne, ed. 1968. *Black Protest: History, Documents, and Analyses, 1619 to the Present*. New York: Fawcett.

Grant, Madison. 1916. *The Passing of a Great Race: Or the Racial History of European History*. New York: Scribner's.

Grasmuck, Sherri, and Patricia R. Pessar. 1991. *Between Two Islands: Dominican International Migration*. Berkeley: University of California Press.

Greenberg, Stanley B. 1985. *Report on Democratic Defection*. Report Prepared for the Michigan House Democratic Campaign Committee. Washington, DC: The Analysis Group.

Greenhouse, Linda. 2003. "Supreme Court Hears Arguments in Affirmative Action Case." *New York Times*, April 1.

Hacker, Andrew. 1992. *Two Nations, Black and White, Separate, Hostile, Unequal*. New York: Charles Scribner's Sons.

Hadden, Sally E. 2001. *Slave Patrols: Law and Violence in Virginia and the Carolinas*. Cambridge, MA: Harvard University Press.

Hall, Stuart, et al. 1978. *Policing the Crisis: Mugging, the State, and Law and Order*. London: Macmillan.

Halliday, Fred. 1999. "Islamophobia Reconsidered." *Ethnic and Racial Studies* 22, 5 (September).

Hallow, Ralph Z. 2003. "GOP Leaders Warned to Shun Agenda of Gays." *Washington Times*, May 15.

Halperin, Jason. 2003. "Patriot Raid." *MoveOn Bulletin*, May 30.

Hanchard, Michael George. 1994. *Orpheus and Power: The Movimento Negro of Rio de Janeiro and Sao Paulo, Brazil. 1945–1988*. Princeton, NJ: Princeton University Press.

Hannaford, Ivan. 1996. *Race: The History of an Idea in the West*. Washington, DC: Woodrow Wilson Center Press/Baltimore: Johns Hopkins University Press.

Harris, Cheryl. 1993. "Whiteness as Property." 106 *Harvard Law Review* 1707.

Hart, Gillian Patricia. 2002. *Disabling Globalization: Places of Power in Post-Apartheid South Africa*. Berkeley: University of California Press.

Harvey, David. 1982. *The Limits to Capital*. Oxford: Blackwell.

Hasenbalg, Carlos A., and Nelson do Valle Silva. 1992. "Raça e Oportunididades Educacionais no Brasil." In *Relações Raciais no Brasil Contemporâneo*, by Nelson do Valle Silva and Carlos A. Hasenbalg. Rio de Janeiro: Rio Fundo/IUPERJ.

Hayden, Tom, ed. 2001. *The Zapatista Reader*. New York: Thunder's Mouth Press/Nation Books.

Hechter, Michael. 1975. *Internal Colonialism: The Celtic Fringe in British National Development*. Berkeley: University of California Press.

Hegel, G. W. F. 1807. *The Phenomenology of Mind*. Trans. J. B. Baillie. New York: Harper and Row, 1967.

Herrnstein, Richard, and Charles Murray. 1994. *The Bell Curve: Intelligence and Class Structure in American Life*. New York: Free Press.

Hirschman, Albert O. 1970. *Exit, Voice, and Loyalty: Responses to Decline in Firms, Organizations, and States*. Cambridge, MA: Harvard University Press.

Hochschild, Adam. 1998. *King Leopold's Ghost: A Story of Greed, Terror, and Heroism in Colonial Africa*. Boston: Houghton Mifflin.

Hodes, Martha, ed. 1999. *Sex, Love, Race: Crossing Boundaries in North American History*. New York: New York University Press.

Holt, Thomas C. 2000. *The Problem of Race in the Twenty-first Century*. Cambridge, MA: Harvard University Press.

Horkheimer, Max, and Theodor W. Adorno. 1972. *Dialectic of Enlightenment*. Trans. John Cumming. New York: Herder and Herder.

Hornsby, Bruce, and the Range. 1986. "The Way It Is." RCA.

Huber, Joan, ed. 1991. *Macro-Micro Linkages in Sociology*. Newbury Park, CA: Sage.

Huntington, Samuel P. 1996. *The Clash of Civilizations and the Remaking of World Order*. New York: Simon & Schuster.

Ignatieff, Michael. 2003. "American Empire (Get Used to It)." *New York Times Magazine*, January 5.

Ignatiev, Noel. 1995. *How the Irish Became White: Irish-Americans and African-Americans in 19th Century Philadelphia*. New York: Verso.

International Monetary Fund. 2002. *Balance of Payments Yearbook 2002*. Washington, DC: IMF.

Jackson, Walter. 1990. *Gunnar Myrdal and America's Conscience*. Chapel Hill: University of North Carolina Press.

Jacobson, Mathew Frye. 1998. *Whiteness of a Different Color: European Immigrants and the Alchemy of Race*. Cambridge, MA: Harvard University Press.

James, C. L. R. 1938. *The Black Jacobins: Toussaint L'Ouverture and the San Domingo Revolution*. New York: Vintage, 1989.

James, Lawrence. 1998. *Raj: The Making and Unmaking of British India*. New York: St. Martin's.

James, Winston. 1998. *Holding Aloft the Banner of Ethiopia: Caribbean Radicalism in Early Twentieth-Century America*. New York: Verso.

Jefferson, Thomas. "Notes on Virginia." 1787. In *Writings of Thomas Jefferson*, ed. Merrill D. Peterson. New York: The Library of America, 1984.

Joas, Hans. 1993. *Pragmatism and Social Theory*. Trans. Jeremy Gaines, Raymond Meyer, and Steven Minner. Chicago: University of Chicago Press.

———. 1996. *The Creativity of Action*. Trans. Jeremy Gaines and Paul Keast. Chicago: University of Chicago Press.

Johnson, Lyndon B. 1967. "To Secure These Rights." In *The Moynihan Report and the Politics of Controversy*, ed. Lee Rainwater and William Yancey. Cambridge, MA: MIT Press.

Kagan, Robert. 2003. *Of Paradise and Power: America and Europe in the New World Order*. New York: Knopf.

Kairys, David. 1993. *With Liberty and Justice for Some: A Critique of the Conservative Supreme Court*. New York: New Press.

———. 1994. "Race Trilogy." *Temple Law Review* 67.

Kaplan, Lawrence F., and William Kristol. 2003. *The War over Iraq: Saddam's Tyranny and America's Mission*. San Francisco: Encounter Books.

Kaplan, Robert D. 1996. *The Ends of the Earth: A Journey at the Dawn of the 21st Century*. New York: Random House.

————. 2001. *The Coming Anarchy: Shattering the Dreams of the Post Cold War*. New York: Vintage.

————. 2003. *Warrior Politics: Why Leadership Requires a Pagan Ethos*. New York: Vintage.

Kaus, Mickey. 1992. *The End of Equality*. New York: Basic.

Keck, Margaret E., and Kathryn Sikkink. 1998. *Activists beyond Borders: Advocacy Networks in International Politics*. Ithaca, NY: Cornell University Press.

Kelley, Robin D. G. 1994. *Race Rebels: Culture, Politics, and the Black Working Class*. New York: Free Press.

————. 2002. *Freedom Dreams: The Black Radical Imagination*. Boston: Beacon.

Kevles, Daniel J. 1985. *In the Name of Eugenics: Genetics and the Uses of Human Heredity*. New York: Knopf.

Keynes, John Maynard. 1920. *The Economic Consequences of the Peace*. New York: Penguin, 1988.

Kiernan, Victor G. 1969. *The Lords of Human Kind: Black Man, Yellow Man, and White Man in an Age of Empire*. Boston: Little, Brown.

Kilson, Martin A., and Robert I. Rotberg, eds. 1976. *The African Diaspora: Interpretive Essays*. Cambridge, MA: Harvard University Press.

Kim, Elaine. 1993. "Home Is Where the Han Is," In *Reading Rodney King, Reading Urban Uprising*, ed. Robert Gooding-Williams. New York: Routledge.

Kivel, Paul. 1996. *Uprooting Racism: How White People Can Work for Racial Justice*. Philadelphia: New Society Publishers.

Klug, Heinz. 2000. *Constituting Democracy: Law, Globalism and South Africa's Political Reconstruction*. New York: Cambridge University Press.

Kluger, Richard. 1977. *Simple Justice: The History of Brown v. Board of Education and Black America's Struggle for Equality*. New York: Vintage.

Krugman, Paul. 2003. "Duped and Betrayed." *New York Times*, June 6.

Kryder, Daniel. 2000. *Divided Arsenal: Race and the American State During World War II*. New York: Cambridge University Press.

Laclau, Ernesto. 1996. *Emancipations*. London: Verso.

Ladner, Joyce A., ed. 1973. *The Death of White Sociology*. New York: Random House.

Ladurie, Emmanuel Le Roy, Jean-Noël Barrandon, Bruno Collin, Maria Guerra, and Cécile Morrisson. 1990. "Sur les traces de l'argent du Potosi." *Annales: Économies, Sociétés, Civilisations* 45, 2 (March–April).

Laitin, David D. 1986. *Hegemony and Culture: Politics and Religious Change among the Yoruba*. Chicago: University of Chicago Press.

Lechner, Norbert. 1988. *Los Patios Interiores de la Democracia: Subjetividad y Política*. Santiago: FLACSO.

Lemelle, Sidney J., and Robin D. G. Kelley, eds. 1994. *Imagining Home: Class, Culture, and Nationalism in the African Diaspora*. New York: Verso.

Levine, Robert M. 1992. *The Vale of Tears: Revisiting the Canudos Massacre in Northeastern Brazil, 1893–1897*. Berkeley: University of California Press.

Lewis, David Levering. 1993. *W. E. B. Du Bois: Biography of a Race*. New York: Henry Holt.

Lichtenstein, Alex. 1996. *Twice the Work of Free Labor: The Political Economy of Convict Labor in the New South*. New York: Verso.

Lichtenstein, Nelson. 1989. "From Corporatism to Collective Bargaining: Organized Labor and the Eclipse of Social Democracy in the Postwar Era." In *The Rise and Fall of the New Deal Order. 1930–1980*, ed. Steve Fraser and Gary Gerstle. Princeton, NJ: Princeton University Press.

Lind, Michael. 1995a. "To Have and Have Not: Notes on the Progress of the American Class War." *Harper's*, June.

———. 1995b. *The Next American Nation: The New Nationalism and the Fourth American Revolution*. New York: Free Press.

Linn, Brian M. 2000. *The Philippine War, 1899–1902*. Lawrence: University Press of Kansas.

Lipsitz, George. 1995. "The Possessive Investment in Whiteness." *American Quarterly* 47, 3 (September).

———. 1998. *The Possessive Investment in Whiteness: How White People Profit from Identity Politics*. Philadelphia: Temple University Press.

Liptak, Adam. 2003. "Palmer Raids Redux: The Pursuit of Immigrants in America after Sept. 11." *New York Times*, June 8.

Litwack, Leon F. 1980. *Been in the Storm So Long: The Aftermath of Slavery*. New York: Random House.

Lott, Eric. 1993. *Love and Theft: Blackface Minstrelsy and the American Working Class*. New York: Oxford University Press.

Loury, Glenn C. 1995. *One by One from the Inside Out: Essays and Reviews on Race and Responsibility in America*. New York: Free Press.

Lovejoy, Paul E. 1983. *Transformations in Slavery: A History of Slavery in Africa*. New York: Cambridge University Press.

Lowe, Lisa, and David Lloyd, eds. 1997. *The Politics of Culture in the Shadow of Capital*. Durham, NC: Duke University Press.

Lynd, Staughton. 1998. "Black and White and Dead All Over: The Lucasville Insurrection." *Race Traitor* 8 (Winter).

Madigan, Tim. 2001. *The Burning: Massacre, Destruction, and the Tulsa Race Riot of 1921*. New York: St. Martin's Press.

Mailer, Norman. 1957. *The White Negro*. San Francisco: City Lights.

Mamdani, Mahmood. 1996. *Citizen and Subject: Contemporary Africa and the Legacy of Late Colonialism*. Princeton, NJ: Princeton University Press.

Mancini, Matthew. 1996. *One Dies, Get Another: Convict Leasing in the American South, 1866–1928*. Columbia: University of South Carolina Press.

Mann, Eric. 2002. *Dispatches from Durban: Firsthand Commentaries on the World Conference Against Racism and Post September 11 Movement Strategies*. Los Angeles: Frontlines Press.

Marable, Manning. 1986. *W. E. B. Du Bois: Black Radical Democrat*. Boston: G. K. Hall/Twayne.

Marcuse, Herbert. 1963. *Reason and Revolution: Hegel and the Rise of Social Theory*. New York: Humanities Press.

Marx, Karl. 1964. *Pre-Capitalist Economic Formations*. Ed. E. J. Hobsbawm. Trans. Jack Cohen. New York: International Publishers.

———. 1967. *Capital*. Vol. 1. New York: International Publishers.

————. 1978. "Theses on Feuerbach." In *The Marx-Engels Reader*, ed. Robert C. Tucker. New York: Norton.

Marx, Karl, and Friedrich Engels. 1978. *The Marx-Engels Reader*. Ed. Robert C. Tucker, New York: Norton.

Massey, Douglas, and Nancy Denton. 1993. *American Apartheid*. Cambridge, MA: Harvard University Press.

Mauer, Marc. 1999. *Race to Incarcerate*. New York: New Press.

McAdam, Doug. 1982. *Political Process and the Development of Black Insurgency. 1930–1970*. Chicago: University of Chicago Press.

McAdam, Doug, John D. McCarthy, and Mayer N. Zald, eds. 1996. *Comparative Perspectives on Social Movements: Political Opportunities, Mobilizing Structures, and Cultural Framings*. New York: Cambridge University Press.

McAdam, Doug, Sidney Tarrow, and Charles Tilly. 2001. *Dynamics of Contention*. New York: Cambridge University Press.

McKee, James B. 1993. *Sociology and the Race Problem: The Failure of a Perspective*. Urbana: University of Illinois Press.

McMillen, Neil R. 1989. *Dark Journey: Black Mississippians in the Age of Jim Crow*. Urbana: University of Illinois Press.

Mead, George Herbert. 1938. *Philosophy of the Act*. Chicago: University of Chicago Press.

————. 1962. *Mind, Self and Society from the Standpoint of a Social Behaviorist*. Ed. Charles W. Morris. Chicago: University of Chicago Press.

Melucci, Alberto. 1989. *Nomads of the Present: Social Movements and Individual Needs in Contemporary Society*. Philadelphia: Temple University Press.

Menand, Louis, ed. 1997. *Pragmatism: A Reader*. New York: Vintage Books.

Merton, Robert K. 1949. "Discrimination and the American Creed." In *Discrimination and the National Welfare*, ed. Robert W. MacIver. New York: Harper.

Michaels, Walter Benn. 1992. "Race into Culture: A Critical Genealogy of Cultural Identity." *Critical Inquiry* 18, 4 (Summer).

————. 1996. "Posthistoricism: The End of the End of History." *Transition* 70 (6, 20).

————. 1998. "Autobiography of an Ex-White Man: Why Race Is Not a Social Construction." *Transition* 73 (7, 1).

Miles, Jack. 1992. "Blacks vs. Browns," *Atlantic Monthly*, October.

Miles, Robert. 1989. *Racism*. New York: Routledge.

Mills, C. Wright. 1956. *The Power Elite*. New York: Oxford University Press.

————. 1964. *Sociology and Pragmatism: The Higher Learning in America*. Ed. Irving Louis Horowitz. New York: Paine-Whitman.

————. 1997. *The Racial Contract*. Ithaca, NY: Cornell University Press.

Mintz, Sidney W. 1985. *Sweetness and Power: The Place of Sugar in Modern History*. New York: Viking.

Montagu, Ashley. 1997. *Man's Most Dangerous Myth: The Fallacy of Race*. 6th ed. Walnut Creek, CA: AltaMira/Sage.

Montejano, David. 1987. *Anglos and Mexicans in the Making of Modern Texas, 1836–1986*. Austin: University of Texas Press.

Moore, Joan, and Harry Pachon. 1985. *Hispanics in the United States*. Englewood Cliffs, NJ: Prentice-Hall.

Moore, Joan, and Raquel Pinderhughes, eds. 1993. *In the Barrios: Latinos and the Underclass Debate*. New York: Russell Sage Foundation.

Moore, Nina M. 2000. *Governing Race: Policy, Process, and the Politics of Race*. Westport, CT: Praeger.

Moreno Fraginals, Manuel. 1976. *The Sugarmill: The Socioeconomic Complex of Sugar in Cuba, 1760–1860*. Trans. Cedric Belfrage. New York: Monthly Review Press.

Morgan, Edmund. 1975. *American Slavery, American Freedom: The Ordeal of Colonial Virginia*. New York: Norton.

Morris, Aldon D. 1984. *The Origins of the Civil Rights Movement: Black Communities Organizing for Change*. New York: The Free Press.

Morris, Aldon, and Carol McClurg Mueller, eds. 1992. *Frontiers in Sociological Movement Theory*. New Haven, CT: Yale University Press.

Morrison, Toni. 1992. *Playing in the Dark: Whiteness and the Literary Imagination*. Cambridge, MA: Harvard University Press.

Mosse, George L. 1978. *Toward the Final Solution: A History of European Racism*. New York: Howard Fertig.

Mouffe, Chantal, and Ernesto Laclau. 1985. *Hegemony and Socialist Strategy: Towards a Radical Democratic Politics*. London: Verso.

Murray, Charles. 1984. *Losing Ground: American Social Policy. 1950–1980*. New York: Basic Books.

———. 1993. "The Other Underclass" *Wall Street Journal*, October 29.

Myrdal, Gunnar. 1944. *An American Dilemma: The Negro Problem and Modern Democracy*. 20th Anniversary Ed. New York: Harper and Row, 1962.

———. 1963. *Economic Theory and Under-Developed Regions*. London: Duckworth.

Nagel, Joanne. 1995. *American Indian Ethnic Renewal: Red Power and the Resurgence of Identity and Culture*. New York: Oxford University Press.

Netanyahu, Benzion. 1995. *The Origins of the Inquisition in Fifteenth Century Spain*. New York: Random House.

Newfield, Christopher. 1993. "What Was Political Correctness? Race, the Right, and Managerial Democracy in the Humanities." *Critical Inquiry* 19, 2 (Winter).

Nkrumah, Kwame. 1965. *Neo-colonialism: The Last Stage of Imperialism*. New York: International Publishers.

Novick, Michael. 1995. *White Lies, White Power: The Fight against White Supremacy and Reactionary Violence*. Monroe, ME: Common Courage.

O'Callaghan, Marion, ed. 1980. *Sociological Theories: Race and Colonialism*. Paris: UNESCO.

O'Donnell, Guillermo A., and Philippe C. Schmitter. 1986. *Transitions from Authoritarian Rule: Tentative Conclusions about Uncertain Democracies*. Baltimore: Johns Hopkins University Press.

Okihiro, Gary. 1994. *Margins and Mainstreams: Asians in American History and Culture*. Seattle: University of Washington Press.

Olson, Mancur. 1968. *The Logic of Collective Action: Public Goods and the Theory of Groups*. New York: Schocken.

Omi, Michael, and Howard Winant. 1993. "The Los Angeles 'Race Riot' and Contemporary U.S. Politics." In *Reading Rodney King, Reading Urban Uprising*, ed. Robert Gooding-Williams. New York: Routledge.

———. 1994. *Racial Formation in the United States: From the 1960s to the 1990s*. 2nd ed. New York: Routledge.

Pagden, Anthony. 1995. *Lords of All the World: Ideologies of Empire in Spain, Britain and France, 1500–1800*. New Haven, CT: Yale University Press.

Parenti, Christian. 1999. *Lockdown America: Police and Prisons in the Age of Crisis*. New York: Verso.

———. 2001. "The 'New' Criminal Justice System: State Repression from 1968 to 2001." *Monthly Review* 53, 3 (July/August).

Park, Robert E. 1950. *Race and Culture*. Glencoe, IL: Free Press.

Parsons, Talcott. 1937. *The Structure of Social Action: A Study in Social Theory*. New York: Free Press, 1968.

Patterson, Orlando. 1982. *Slavery and Social Death*. Cambridge, MA: Harvard University Press.

———. 1998. *Rituals of Blood: Consequences of Slavery in Two American Centuries*. Washington, DC: Civitas/CounterPoint.

Peabody, Sue. 1996. *There Are No Slaves in France: The Political Culture of Race and Slavery in the Ancien Régime*. New York: Oxford University Press.

Peery, Nelson. 1995. *Black Fire: The Making of an American Revolutionary*. New York: The New Press.

Perinbanayagam, R. S. 1985. *Signifying Acts: Structure and Meaning in Everyday Life*. Carbondale: Southern Illinois University Press.

Perlman, Selig. 1950. *A History of Trade Unionism in the United States*. New York: Augustus M. Kelley.

Pettigrew, Thomas F., ed. 1980. *The Sociology of Race Relations: Reflection and Reform*. New York: Free Press.

Pitt, Leonard. 1998. *The Decline of the Californios: A Social History of the Spanish-Speaking Californians, 1846–1890*. Berkeley: University of California Press.

Plotke, David. "Democratic Breakup." Unpublished ms.

Podhoretz, Norman. 1997. "My Negro Problem—and Ours." In *The Essential Neoconservative Reader*, ed. Mark Gerson and James Q. Wilson. New York: Addison-Wesley.

Polanyi, Karl. 1944. *The Great Transformation: The Political and Economic Origins of Our Time*. Boston: Beacon Press, 2001.

———. 1968. *Primitive, Archaic, and Modern Economies: Essays of Karl Polanyi*. Ed. George Dalton. Garden City: Anchor Books.

Poliakov, Léon. 1977. *The Aryan Myth: A History of Racist and Nationalist Ideas in Europe*. Trans. Edmund Howard. New York: New American Library.

Portes, Alejandro, and Robert L. Bach. 1985. *Latin Journey: Cuban and Mexican Immigrants in the United States*. Berkeley: University of California Press.

Portes, Alejandro, Manuel Castells, and Lauren A. Benton. 1989. *The Informal Economy: Studies in Advanced and Less Developed Countries*. Baltimore: Johns Hopkins University Press.

Preston, Diana. 2001. *The Boxer Rebellion: The Dramatic Story of China's War on Foreigners That Shook the World in the Summer of 1900*. New York: Penguin/Berkley.

Przeworski, Adam. 1986. "Some Problems in the Study of the Transition to Democracy." In *Transitions from Authoritarian Rule: Comparative Perspectives*, ed. Guillermo O'Donnell, Philippe C. Schmitter, and Laurence Whitehead. Baltimore: Johns Hopkins University Press.

Ranger, Terence O. 1967. *Revolt in Southern Rhodesia, 1896–97: A Study in African Resistance*. Evanston, IL: Northwestern University Press.

Reed, Adolph. 2000. *Class Notes: Posing as Politics and Other Thoughts on the American Scene*. New York: New Press.

Reich, Michael. 1981. *Racial Inequality*. Princeton, NJ: Princeton University Press.

Renner, Michael. 2002. *The Anatomy of Resource Wars*. Washington, DC: Worldwatch Institute.

Ridgeway, James. 1990. *Blood in the Face: The Ku Klux Klan, Aryan Nations, Skinheads, and the Rise of a New White Culture*. New York: Thunder's Mouth.

Robinson, Randall. 2002. *The Reckoning: What Blacks Owe to Each Other*. New York: Dutton.

Rodney, Walter. 1981. *How Europe Underdeveloped Africa*. Washington, DC: Howard University Press.

Roediger, David R. 1991. *The Wages of Whiteness: Race and the Making of the American Working Class*. New York: Verso.

Roediger, David, and Philip S. Foner. 1989. *Our Own Time: A History of American Labor and the Working Day*. New York: Greenwood.

Rogin, Michael P. 1975. *Fathers and Children: Andrew Jackson and the Subjugation of the American Indian*. New York: Random House.

Rose, Arnold M. 1948. *The Negro in America*. New York: Harper.

Rueter, Theodore, ed. 1995. *The Politics of Race: African Americans and the Political System*. Armonk, NY: M. E. Sharpe.

Rusche, Georg, and Otto Kirchheimer. 1939. *Punishment and Social Structure*. New York: Columbia University Press.

Rusling, General James. 1987. "Interview with President William McKinley." In *The Philippines Reader*, ed. Daniel Schirmer and Stephen Rosskamm Shalom. Boston: South End Press.

Rustin, Bayard. 1964. "From Protest to Politics: The Future of the Civil Rights Movement." *Commentary* 39 (February).

Sacks, Karin Brodkin. 1994. "How Did Jews Become White Folks?" In *Race*, ed. Steven Gregory and Roger Sanjek. New Brunswick, NJ: Rutgers University Press.

Said, Edward W. 1978. *Orientalism*. New York: Pantheon.

Sartre, Jean-Paul. 1956. *Being and Nothingness: An Essay on Phenomenological Ontology*. Trans. Hazel E. Barnes. New York: Philosophical Library.

———. 1982–90. *Critique of Dialectical Reason*. Trans. Alan Sheridan-Smith. Ed. Jonathan Rée. London: Verso.

Sassen, Saskia. 2001. "Governance Hotspots: Challenges We Must Confront in the Post–September 11 World." Social Science Research Council, After September 11 Archive. http://www.ssrc.org/sept11/essays/sassen.htm.

Saxton, Alexander. 1990. *The Rise and Fall of the White Republic: Class Politics and Mass Culture in Nineteenth-Century America*. New York: Verso.

———. 1996. *The Indispensable Enemy: Labor and the Anti-Chinese Movement in California*. Berkeley: University of California Press.

Scott, James C. 1986. *Weapons of the Weak: Everyday Forms of Peasant Resistance*. New Haven, CT: Yale University Press.

———. 1990. *Domination and the Arts of Resistance: Hidden Transcripts*. New Haven, CT: Yale University Press.

Seidman, Gay W. 1999. "Is South Africa Different? Sociological Comparisons and Theoretical Contributions from the Land of Apartheid." *Annual Review of Sociology* 25.

Singh, Nikhil Pal. 1998. "Culture/Wars: Recoding Empire in an Age of Democracy." *American Quarterly* 50, 3 (September).

Skidelsky, Robert. 1983. *Hopes Betrayed, 1883–1920*. Vol. 1 of *John Maynard Keynes: A Biography*. London: Macmillan.

Skidmore. 1993. Thomas E. *Black into White: Race and Nationality in Brazilian Thought*. Durham, NC: Duke University Press.

Sleeper, Jim. 1990. *The Closest of Strangers: Liberalism and the Politics of Race in New York*. New York: Norton.

Smith, Rogers M. 1997. *Civic Ideals: Conflicting Visions of Citizenship in U.S. History*. New Haven, CT: Yale University Press.

Sniderman, Paul M., and Thomas Piazza. 1993. *The Scar of Race*. Cambridge, MA: Harvard University Press.

Snowden, Frank M. 1983. *Before Color Prejudice: The Ancient View of Blacks*. Cambridge, MA: Harvard University Press.

Solomon, Mark. 1998. *The Cry Was Unity: Communists and African Americans. 1917–36*. Jackson: University Press of Mississippi.

Solomos, John, and John Wrench, eds. 1993. *Racism and Migration in Western Europe*. Providence, RI: Berg.

Southern, David W. 1987. *Gunnar Myrdal and Black-White Relations: The Use and Abuse of An American Dilemma*. Baton Rouge: Louisiana State University Press.

Sowell, Thomas. 1983. *The Economics and Politics of Race: An International Perspective*. New York: Quill.

Stanley, Peter W. 1974. *A Nation in the Making: The Philippines and the United States, 1899–1921*. Cambridge: Harvard University Press.

Stannard, David E. 1992. *American Holocaust: The Conquest of the New World*. New York: Oxford University Press.

Steele, Shelby. 1990. *The Content of Our Character: A New Vision of Race in America*. New York: St. Martin's Press.

Steinberg, Stephen. 1995. *Turning Back: The Retreat from Racial Justice in American Thought and Policy*. Boston: Beacon.

Stepan, Nancy Leys. 1991. *"The Hour of Eugenics": Race, Gender, and Nation in Latin America*. Ithaca, NY: Cornell University Press.

Stiglitz, Joseph E. 2002. *Globalization and Its Discontents*. New York: Norton.

Stoler, Ann Laura. 1991. "Carnal Knowledge and Imperial Power: Gender, Race, and Morality in Colonial Asia." In *Gender at the Crossroads of Knowledge: Feminist Anthropology in a Postmodern Era*, ed. Michaela di Leonardo. Berkeley: University of California Press.

———. 2002. *Carnal Knowledge and Imperial Power: Race and the Intimate in Colonial Rule*. Berkeley: University of California Press.

Swain, Carol M. 1993. *Black Faces, Black Interests: The Representation of African Americans in Congress*. Cambridge, MA: Harvard University Press.

Taguieff, Pierre-André. 1990. "The New Cultural Racism in France." *Telos* 83 (Spring); also excerpted in *Racism*, ed. Martin Bulmer and John Solomos. London: Oxford University Press, 1999.

———. 2001. *The Force of Prejudice: On Racism and Its Doubles*. Trans. Hassan Melehy. Minneapolis: University of Minnesota Press.

Takagi, Dana Y. 1992. *The Retreat from Race: Asian American Admissions and Racial Politics*. New Brunswick, NJ: Rutgers University Press.

Takaki, Ronald. 1990. *Strangers from a Distant Shore: A History of Asian Americans*. New York: Penguin.

———. 1993. *A Different Mirror: A History of Multicultural America*. Boston: Little Brown.

Tarrow, Sidney G. 1998. *Power in Movement: Sociological Movements and Contentious Politics*. 2nd ed. New York: Cambridge University Press.

Telles, Edward. 1992. "Segregation by Skin Color in Brazil." *American Sociological Review* 57.

———. 1994. "Industrialization and Racial Inequality in Employment: The Brazilian Example." *American Sociological Review* 59.

Thatcher, Oliver J., and Edgar Holmes McNeal, eds. 1905. *A Source Book for Medieval History*. New York: Scribner's; viewed at http://people.westminstercollege.edu/faculty/mmarkowski/212/8/urban.html.

Thernstrom, Stephan, and Abigail Thernstrom. 1997. *America in Black and White: One Nation, Indivisible*. New York: Simon & Schuster.

Thomas, W. I., and Dorothy Swaine Thomas. 1928. *The Child in America*. New York: Alfred A. Knopf.

Thomas, W. I., and Florian Znaniecki. 1923. *The Polish Peasant in Europe and America*. Ed. Eli Zaretsky. Urbana: University of Illinois Press, 1994.

Thompson, Becky W. 2001. *A Promise and a Way of Life: White Antiracist Activism*. Minneapolis: University of Minnesota Press.

Thompson, Robert Farris. 1995. "The Kongo Atlantic Tradition," cited in Shelley Fisher Fishkin. "Interrogating 'Whiteness,' Complicating 'Blackness,' Remapping American Culture." *American Quarterly* 47, 3 (September).

Thornton, John. 1993. "'I Am the Subject of the King of Kongo': African Political Ideology and the Haitian Revolution." *Journal of World History* 4, 2.

———. 1998. *Africa and Africans in the Making of the Atlantic World, 1400–1680*. 2nd ed. New York: Cambridge University Press.

Thurow, Lester. 1969. *Poverty and Discrimination*. Washington, DC: Brookings Institution.

Tilly, Charles. 1984. *Big Structures, Large Processes, Huge Comparisons*. New York: Russell Sage Foundation.

Toase, F. H., and E. J. Yorke, eds. 1998. *The New South Africa: Prospects for Domestic and International Security*. New York: St. Martin's Press.

Todorov, Tzvetan. 1984. *The Conquest of America: The Question of the Other*. Trans. Richard Howard. New York: Harper and Row.

————. 1993. *On Human Diversity: Nationalism, Racism, and Exoticism in French Thought*. Cambridge, MA: Harvard University Press.

Toplin, Robert Brent. 1972. *The Abolition of Slavery in Brazil*. New York: Atheneum.

Toussaint, Eric. 1999. *Your Money or Your Life! The Tyranny of Global Finance*. Sterling, VA: Pluto Press.

Traub, James. 1998. "Nathan Glazer Changes His Mind, Again." *New York Times Magazine*, June 28.

Twine, France Winddance. 1997. *Racism in a Racial Democracy: The Maintenance of White Supremacy in Brazil*. New Brunswick, NJ: Rutgers University Press.

Uggen, Christopher, and Jeff Manza. 2002. "Democratic Contraction? The Political Consequences of Felon Disenfranchisement in the United States." *American Sociological Review* 67, 6 (December).

UNESCO. 1966. *Research on Racial Relations*. Paris: UNESCO.

Valdes, Francisco, Jerome McCristal Culp, and Angela P. Harris, eds. 2002. *Crossroads, Directions, and a New Critical Race Theory*. Philadelphia: Temple University Press.

Van den Berghe, Pierre. 1967. *Race and Racism: A Comparative Perspective*. New York: Wiley.

Van Zyl Slabbert, Frederik. 1992. *The Quest for Democracy: South Africa in Transition*. New York: Penguin.

Veblen, Thorstein. 1918. *The Higher Learning in America; A Memorandum on the Conduct of Universities by Business Men*. New Brunswick: Transaction, 1993.

Wallerstein, Immanuel M. 1974–89. *The Modern World-System*. 3 vols. New York: Academic Press.

————. 1976. "The Three Stages of African Involvement with the World Economy." In *The Political Economy of Contemporary Africa*, ed. Peter C. W. Gutkind and Immanuel Wallerstein. Beverly Hills, CA: Sage.

Walters, Ronald. 1987. "White Racial Nationalism in the United States." *Without Prejudice* 1, 1 (Fall).

————. 1993. *Pan-Africanism in the African Diaspora: An Analysis of Modern Afrocentric Political Movements*. Detroit: Wayne State University Press.

Warren, Bill. 1980. *Imperialism, Pioneer of Capitalism*. London: New Left Books.

Waters, Mary C. 1990. *Ethnic Options: Choosing Identities in America*. Berkeley: University of California Press.

Weber, Max. 1994. *Weber: Political Writings*. Ed. Peter Lassman and Ronald Speirs. New York: Cambridge University Press.

Webster, Edward, and Glenn Adler. 1999. "Toward a Class Compromise in South Africa's 'Double Transition': Bargained Liberalization and the Consolidation of Democracy." *Politics and Society* 27, 3 (September).

Weiss, Nancy J. 1983. *Farewell to the Party of Lincoln: Black Politics in the Age of FDR*. Princeton, NJ: Princeton University Press.

Weissman, Robert. 2000. "The IMF on the Run: The International Monetary Fund Tries to Outrun Its Critics." *Multinational Monitor* 21, 4 (April).

Welsing, Frances Cress. 1991. *The Isis Papers: The Keys to the Colors*. Chicago: Third World Press.

West, Cornel. 1989. *The American Evasion of Philosophy: A Genealogy of Pragmatism*. Madison: University of Wisconsin Press.

———. 1991. "Nihilism in Black America," *Dissent* Spring.

Wieviorka, Michel. 1995. *The Arena of Racism*. Trans. Chris Turner. Thousand Oaks, CA: Sage.

Williams, Eric. 1944. *Capitalism and Slavery*. Chapel Hill: University of North Carolina Press, 1994.

Williams, Lena. 1991. "When Blacks Shop, Bias Often Accompanies Sale." *New York Times*, April 30.

Williams, Walter. 1982. *The State against Blacks*. New York: McGraw-Hill.

Williamson, Joel. 1986. *A Rage for Order: Black-White Relations in the American South Since Emancipation*. New York: Oxford University Press.

Wilson, William Julius. 1980. *The Declining Significance of Race: Blacks and Changing American Institutions*. 2nd ed. Chicago: University of Chicago Press.

———. 1987. *The Truly Disadvantaged: The Inner City, The Underclass, and Public Policy*. Chicago: University of Chicago Press.

———. 1992. "The Right Message." *New York Times*, March 17.

———. 1996. *When Work Disappears: The World of the New Urban Poor*. New York: Knopf.

Winant, Howard. 1994a. *Racial Conditions: Politics, Theory, Comparisons*. Minneapolis: University of Minnesota Press.

———. 1994b. "On the Theoretical Concept of Race." In *Racial Conditions: Politics, Theory, Comparisons*. Minneapolis: University of Minnesota Press.

———. 1994c. "Where Culture Meets Structure: Race in the 1990s." In *Racial Conditions: Politics, Theory, Comparisons*. Minneapolis: University of Minnesota Press.

———. 1996. "Racial Dualism at Century's End." In *The House That Race Built*, ed. Wahneema Lubiano. New York: Random House.

———. 1997. "Behind Blue Eyes: Whiteness and Contemporary U.S. Racial Politics." *New Left Review* 225 (Sept.–Oct.).

———. 2001. *The World Is a Ghetto: Race and Democracy since World War II*. New York: Basic Books.

Wolpe, Harold. 1975. "The Theory of Internal Colonialism." In *Beyond the Sociology of Development: Economy and Society in Latin America and Africa*, ed. Ivar Oxaal, Tony Barnett, and David Booth. London: Routledge and Kegan Paul.

Womack, John, ed. 1999. *Rebellion in Chiapas*. New York: The New Press.

Woodward, C. Vann. 1973. *Tom Watson: Agrarian Rebel*. 2nd ed. Savannah, GA: Beehive Press.

World Bank. 2002. *World Development Indicators 2002*. Washington, DC: World Bank.

Wyman, David S. 1998. *The Abandonment of the Jews: America and the Holocaust 1941–1945*. New York: New Press.

Young, Iris Marion. 1990. *Justice and the Politics of Difference*. Princeton, NJ: Princeton University Press.

Zaman, Muhammad Qasim. 2002. *The Ulama in Contemporary Islam: Custodians of Change*. Princeton, NJ: Princeton University Press.

Zinn, Howard. 1985. *SNCC: The New Abolitionists*. Westport, CT: Greenwood.

Zolberg, Aristide. 1989. "The Next Waves: Migration Theory for a Changing World." *International Migration Review* 23, 3.

Publication History

"Racism Today: Continuity and Change in the Post–Civil Rights United States" previously appeared in *Ethnic and Racial Studies* 21, no. 4 (1998): 755–66. Reprinted courtesy of Taylor and Francis, http://www.tandf.co.uk/journals/routledge/01419870.html.

"Behind Blue Eyes: Contemporary White Racial Politics" previously appeared in slightly different forms in *New Left Review* 225 (September–October 1997) and in *Off White: Readings on Race, Power, and Society*, edited by M. Fine, L. Weis, L. Powell, and L. Wong (New York: Routledge, 1997). Reprinted by permission of Routledge/Taylor and Francis Books, Inc.

"The Modern World Racial System" previously appeared in *Rethinking Anti-Racisms: From Theory to Practice*, edited by Floya Anthias and Cathie Lloyd (New York: Routledge, 2002). Reprinted by permission of Routledge/Taylor and Francis Books, Inc. This essay was also published as "Race in the Twenty-first Century," *Tikkun* (January–February 2002).

"Durban, Globalization, and the World after 9/11: Toward a New Politics" originally appeared in *Poverty and Race* 11, no. 1 (January–February 2002): 19–22. Reprinted with permission of the Poverty and Race Research Action Council.

Index

263

and racial "break," 5, 32, 98, 113; and
racial dualism, 172; and state, 47; and
"the veil" (Du Bois), 32, 33; and white
antiracism, 182; and white racial
projects, 55–56, 64, 66
Civil War: and abolition, 96; Du Bois on, 7,
76, 86, 212, 221n3, 225n5; as racial
"break," 30, 211–12, 225n5, 237n9;
and social theory, 194
"clash of civilizations" thesis, 132, 140–41,
146–47
class: and liberalism, 60, 61, 62; and
militarism, 147; nonproblematic nature
of, 189; and racial dualism, 174, 175–
76, 177–78, 179; and racial theory,
160, 161–62, 233–34n19; and repressive racial policies, 138; and social
theory, 193; and transracial coalitions,
60–61, 173; and whiteness, 51–52, 67,
180, 184–85. See also resource distribution issues; wage labor
class consciousness, 199, 235n8
Clinton, Bill, 60–61, 122
coalition politics, 186. See also transracial
coalitions
"code word" phenomenon, 47, 56, 181
cold war: and armed conflict, 16, 223n17;
and Du Bois, 27, 28; and racial "break,"
5, 16, 18, 111; and South Africa, 116
Collins, Randall, 201
"color blindness" rhetoric. See postracialism
color consciousness, 44
"color-line." See racial dualism; "veil,"
dialectics of
coltan (columbite-tantalite), 208, 236n3
communism: and anti-imperialism/anti-
colonialism, 12, 13, 16, 222n13; China,
10; fall of, 20; and racial theory, 159;
South Africa, 117; and transracial
coalitions, 67; and white antiracism,
182; and World War I, 12. See also
anticommunism
"compassionate conservatism," 149
Compromise of 1877, 127
conflict theory, 196
Congo, 8–9, 208, 222n8, 236n3
Congress of Berlin (1885), 9
Congress of South African Trade Unions
(COSATU), 109, 120
"constitution" theories of society, 163

convict leasing, 91
corporations: and affirmative action, 73,
149; and Gulf War II, 137; power of,
174, 181; and racial dualism, 174; and
world economic order, 134, 229n6
corporeal difference. See biologistic theories
of race
Corrections Corporation of America
(CCA), 91, 227n2
corvée labor, 222n7
Cox, Oliver C., 203
criminal justice system, 149. See also prison-
industrial complex
critical race theory (CRT), 23, 127, 191,
197
Crummell, Alexander, 29
Crusades, 139, 140, 230n11
Cuba, 8, 10
cultural framing, 220n5
cultural nationalism, 42, 71, 162, 173, 174,
234n20

Darwin, Charles, 192
Davis, Angela, 82
death penalty, 149
debt peonage, 7. See also world economic
order
defense mechanisms, 224n1
de Klerk, F. W., 117
democracy: Brazil, 103–4; and fascism, 14;
and global democratic project, 142; and
new imperialism, 142; and pluralism,
127–28; and pragmatism, 194; and race,
94–95, 111; and racial pedagogy, 76;
resistance as source of, 76, 86–87, 95–
96, 111, 208–9; and slavery, 225n5;
South Africa, 102, 118, 119, 120; and
"the veil" (Du Bois), 37–38; and World
War I, 5; and World War II, 15, 17. See
also resistance movements
Democratic Party: and affirmative action,
149; interwar period, 31–32; and new
imperialism, 229n8; and racial "break,"
98; and UN World Conference Against
Racism, 122–23; and whiteness, 52
demographic heterogeneity, 97–98; European Union, 104–5; and racial
"break," 16–17; and racial theory, 162;
and U.S. politics, 148–49. See also
diaspora; immigration

Howard Winant is professor of sociology at the University of California, Santa Barbara. He is the author of *Racial Conditions: Politics, Theory, Comparisons* (Minnesota, 1994); *The World Is a Ghetto: Race and Democracy since World War II*; and, with coauthor Michael Omi, *Racial Formation in the United States: From the 1960s to the 1990s*.